Tiny Humans, Big Emotions

Tiny Humans, Big Emotions

How to Navigate Tantrums,
Meltdowns, and Defiance to Raise
Emotionally Intelligent Children

**Alyssa Blask Campbell, M.Ed.,
and Lauren Elizabeth Stauble, M.S.**

HARVEST

An Imprint of WILLIAM MORROW

Some names and identifying details have been changed.

HarperCollins books may be purchased for educational, business, or sales promotional use. For information, please email the Special Markets Department at SPsales@harpercollins.com.

FIRST EDITION

Designed by Tai Blanche
Part opener background texture © mikesj11/Shutterstock
CEP Wheel icon design and drawing by Lauren Stauble
CEP Deck created by Lauren Stauble and Alyssa Blask Campbell and illustrated by Viki Stathopoulos

Library of Congress Cataloging-in-Publication Data has been applied for.

ISBN 978-0-06-330626-4

23 24 25 26 27 LBC 5 4 3 2 1

LAUREN: *I dedicate this book to "Little Peggy Cassidy," who later became my grandmother. Her legacy of a love for books and people lives on through me.*

ALYSSA: *To Z & S for CEPing with me on a daily basis as we navigate imperfection, connection, and grace in relationship together.*

Contents

Introduction

*Relationships change us, reveal us, evoke more
from us. We do not live in a world that encourages
separateness. Only when we join with others do
our gifts become visible, even to ourselves.*
—Margaret J. Wheatley and
Myron Kellner-Rogers[1]

ALYSSA: "If you crawl under the pews to sit with Nora, you won't get a doughnut after church," my dad explained on our drive to church. "Okay, Daddy, got it," my three-year-old self confidently responded. Cue me, twenty minutes later, crawling under the pews to sit with Nora. No one stopped me. I was successful in my escape. Maybe they didn't even notice. After church, my mouth started to water, dreaming about that jelly-filled, powdered doughnut from our weekly trip to White Rose Bakery. When we went inside, my brothers all ordered, but as I went to order, my dad said, "No doughnut this week. You crawled under the pews." Devastated, I dropped to the floor in White Rose, sobbing and banging my fists and head on the ground. He silently carried me to the van, where my meltdown continued. The boys and Mom all came back into the van with sugar-, jelly-, and chocolate-covered faces, and my mom said, "Next week maybe you won't crawl under the pews if you want a doughnut."

From being that tiny human at White Rose Bakery to a twenty-something adult teaching tiny humans, I noticed familiar patterns of discipline and response to emotional outbursts. I was raised in a power-over culture from societal messaging to my master's degree classes on "classroom and behavior management," so by the time I was in charge of a classroom, it was deeply ingrained in me to try and stop big emotions from spiraling so that I didn't lose control of the situation—of the children. Sure, kids would have feelings, but it was my job to either remove them from other people (just the way my father pulled me out to the car on doughnut Sunday) or not feed attention into it and let it fizzle out.

This felt right to me until one day during a therapy session my therapist made the most ridiculous statement: "I wonder what that sadness is trying to tell you." "Sadness doesn't tell you anything; it's just a feeling. It's a bad feeling that you can cry out while binge-watching *Grey's Anatomy* and then it's gone, and you can go back to regular life," I responded. "Sadness doesn't feel like a part of regular life?" she asked. I got defensive in the moment, but that therapy session changed things for me. It sparked my curiosity. Did our emotions tell us things? What does that even mean? That was the start of my journey diving into all things emotions, and it would radically shift how I experience life.

LAUREN: I spent years avoiding shame, fear, and grief in my first marriage. I had all these ideas about what it meant to be a "good wife," and toward the end of seven years and thanks to therapy, I began to scratch the surface of this perfectionism, along with my unconscious, habitual roles. It became so unbearable that I chose to run, literally and figuratively. I left my marriage, and I also took up running, for exercise. I experienced shame for choosing to leave. Running became my one safe place. The more I ran, the more I began to wonder what I was running from. Then a friend reframed my question: "I wonder what you're running *to*?"

That simple shift in thinking caused me to slow down. I kept running but returned to therapy—mindfulness-based this time. The bulk of my work was learning to stay in challenging emotions rather than take action to avoid them. Allowing myself to feel them. I was able to cry—which says a lot, considering I'd cried all of three times in the seven years prior. I had never allowed myself to be vulnerable enough to feel tender emotions.

Now emotions felt vivid—whether painful or enjoyable, I didn't care—and I felt alive experiencing a range of them. I felt alive when I was happy. I felt alive when I was sad. I felt alive when I was calm. I started to experience what I'd read about in my meditation books—a kind of happiness that is all encompassing and includes hard feelings. It's not the kind of happiness we read about in fairy tales. This kind of happiness was rooted in my unconditional willingness to be present when I felt something. It wasn't easy, but the work of it felt good.

This is not to say I've reached a magical state of constant elation about life. It just means I'm a little more comfortable riding the waves—even when I get crashed under the surf. I'm willing to get back on the board. This process enabled me to show up for children in new ways.

We were at a brunch together in 2016, surrounded by tiny humans, when Lauren said, "I think we are doing something different and should write a book about it." We had met as new teachers at the same school—Alyssa was an infant teacher and Lauren a preschool teacher at the time. We observed each other teaching and recognized something familiar in one another—we weren't afraid of children's feelings or challenging behaviors. We both had assistant teachers requesting to be scheduled in our classrooms, because they had noticed we were doing something different—because we were confident when things got stressful (as they inevitably do). Our teammates were curious about our approach to the children's emotions and challenging behaviors, too, because it was innovative—nothing that they had studied in their child development or early childhood courses. Parents were intrigued, marveling at the ability of each of us to stay calm in a tense moment. We both arrived early and chatted regularly about our work with children and families.

Before working together, we'd experienced learning about a new teaching or parenting approach in a calm moment and then losing our cool in the thick of it with kids, not being able to put the new approach into practice. We needed a method that didn't simply consist of what to do *in the moment* with a child or even how to practice outside of the moment, but how to access that information as an adult. We needed something that was just as much, if not more, about *us* than it was about the *kids*. We wanted to be able to describe what we were doing.

We have master's degrees in child development and early childhood education and have worked for a combined thirty-one-plus years in the field of early childhood education, yet the method and framework we were seeking didn't exist. So we created it. Slowly and methodically, we started to unpack the steps involved in helping children understand and express their emotions. We shared stories of individual personal growth from our pasts that were related to emotions and had required reflection and vulnerability. We started to make connections between our personal work and our work with children and noted how we—and the children—processed emotions in these different contexts.

As we dove deeper into this work, we became even more passionate about our purpose—about the sheer importance of what we were doing. We connected over the fact that we'd both spent time and money in therapy and self-study learning how to feel stuff and develop coping strategies because we didn't get to learn those skills as children. Our experiences reflected those of our friends, too. Our parents' generation just didn't have access to the brain science and emotion science that we do today. Parenting in the '80s still meant teaching "resilience" by not making a big deal out of emotions. Phrases such as "turn it off" or "just ignore them" were meant with good intentions to strengthen us. Since the '90s, we've learned that emotional intelligence skills are connected to success in relationships and at work. We want children to learn these skills early on, while their brains are building a foundation. We share a vision of a future with emotionally intelligent communities—communities where people embrace dialogue and diversity because they are comfortable with their emotions and those of others. In this world, we are raising compassionate, confident, loving children who mature into adults who can count on one another to lead and to follow intelligently, respect personal boundaries and simultaneously reach out to those who are isolated, and acknowledge their mistakes and celebrate their strengths. This shared vision further ignited our drive to do this work.

It was a slow and tedious process to develop and articulate the method, but the name came early on: Collaborative Emotion Processing.

What Is Collaborative Emotion Processing (CEP)?

Collaborative Emotion Processing is a way to teach and learn how to feel stuff with other people that builds long-term skills for emotional intelligence. CEP is an opportunity for adults to become aware of their own emotion processing, which in turn allows and supports children to develop emotion processing experience and skills. It's designed for everyone who spends time caring for children: parents, grandparents, teachers, home-based providers, development specialists . . .

We've been practicing this method with children since 2016, and teaching it to early childhood educators and administrators since 2017. Alyssa has had the opportunity to practice it as a parent, as well.

Does It Work?

In short: yes!

Not only have we seen results firsthand in working with children and sharing this method with educators, but in 2018, we conducted action research with our colleague, Angela Garcia, and teacher participants. Our goal was to introduce Collaborative Emotion Processing. Our findings suggested that with training in CEP at the beginning of the study and reflection prompts throughout, teachers and parents became more aware of their emotions and/or there was an increase in the number of coping strategies that they knew to offer young children. Teachers and parents reported being less overwhelmed when they were using the CEP method.

And what about the kids? Recently, one of my early childhood education students, Marissa, wrote in a forum, "I would say my mom and dad's emotional goals for me as a child were to realize and recognize what you're feeling at all times. Whether I was upset or happy I was taught to always acknowledge how I was feeling to work through it. This taught me to be more vulnerable and open about my feelings instead of bottling them up, and I think this ultimately made me have a closer relationship with my parents because they always made it known that they were there for me no matter what I was feeling." Marissa's parents were practicing a key CEP concept—unconditional parenting when it comes to emotions. We imagine that the children who are growing up with CEP will also feel more connected to their parents as adults.

It's a Practice

We want to be clear that we do not intend for you merely to copy what we do, but hope you will integrate the philosophy, practical knowledge, and structure that we are offering into what you already know. Reflecting your cultural context in the way you implement CEP is of utmost importance. At times we offer you sample responses and phrases to use in the moment, but these are meant as samples, not text to memorize. You will choose specific words to explain and recognize emotions based on your own cultural understanding of them. Going through all the steps is important, but the *way* that you go through them is dependent on your personal style and social context. CEP is *not a script* you apply to make your problems disappear. It's *a practice* that will invite you deeper into your relationships with children (and most likely the adults in your life, too) so that what you choose to say is more meaningful to you and the children you care for. Staying connected to the community in which you are practicing is part of the process.

CEP isn't the absence of hard things; it's a method for being with and moving through the hard things.

There is no easy formula for this work. Relationships can't be planned. The very nature of human interactions is unpredictable and dependent on the developmental landscape of all participants. With that in mind, we have prepared a choose-your-own-adventure of sorts to enhance the quality of your experience in your interactions with your children.

How to Use This Book

Over the years of working with parents, teachers, and caregivers, we've received many questions. The majority of them are related to a desire to know *how* to handle big emotions with children, especially when those situations require decisions about holding a boundary versus reducing expectations, and when they relate to challenging behaviors. In response to requests, we've created this guidebook, which is intended for everyone who spends time caring for children. For simplicity's sake, though, we use the terms "parent" and "your child" throughout. Please know that when we use the term "parent," we are referring to the diverse set of roles that involve raising children, including teacher, caregiver, and grandparent. By "your child," we are referring to the child in front of you at any given moment in whichever role you play.

Maybe you're new to CEP, or maybe you've been working with us or following us online for a while. No matter where you're starting from, this book is designed to guide you through the CEP method so that you can navigate challenging behaviors and foster emotional intelligence in your little ones.

This book isn't a checklist item, as in "read the book—check." Instead, it's a practice of seeing ourselves and children through a different lens, one built from empathy that allows us to regulate and respond with compassion.

Since our generation was raised, there has been a pendulum swing in parenting and caregiving. There is a desire to save children from hardship, rescue them from the experiences we knew all too well and felt alone in. The notion that succeeding at raising them means stepping in to save them from feeling scared or disappointed or preventing them from feeling lonely or sad. CEP is a guide to noticing our habits and patterns and choosing our responses more thoughtfully. It is the key to allowing children to experience challenges or hard emotions and to building the tools for how to navigate them while knowing they aren't alone in the process.

Our goal with this book is to provide a comprehensive guide to understanding emotions, as well as an overview of how the CEP method works—and how to apply it in your own life. The book consists of three parts—Parts I and II are sequential and meant to be read in order, while Part III is a "choose what applies right now" section. Part I dives into us, the adults—recognizing what we learned in childhood, noticing our triggers, building skills for regulating ourselves as adults, and understanding what's happening inside our brains and bodies when the tiny humans have big emotions. Part II is a shift to the child. You'll learn how to respond to those big emotions, reduce the frequency of meltdowns, create and hold appropriate boundaries, and ultimately connect with and support each unique child. Part III is an opportunity to dive into specific circumstances and FAQs. It's a "check this chapter out when/if it applies" kind of section. From how to build empathy to supporting children through big transitions, such as a new school, a move, a new sibling, divorce, or death, we've got your back with ways to be emotionally supportive. We wrap this book up with a chapter on where to begin and how to use the tools you find here. The entire book is designed for circling back to over the long haul—we hope you return to relevant chapters time and time again. We've linked all the visuals from the book and bonus resources at www.seedandsew.org /more for you to dive deep into this work at your own pace.

We've included reflective questions throughout the book, and we recommend that you use a notepad, journal, art materials, or sticky notes to write down or draw your responses, and to make visual reminders for yourself about what you're learning. If you're listening to the audiobook, there's a complete compilation of the questions with room to write your reflections at www.seedandsew.org/more.

We want you to know that, in writing this book, we are not suggesting that we have achieved some idyllic state of emotional intelligence for ourselves. We are writing it from the perspective of two people engaged in our personal process of developing our own emotional intelligence skills, which are imperfect. The goal is not perfection but, rather, growth. Growth is vulnerable, it's messy, and it includes mistakes. Your mistakes are welcome here.

As two authors diving into this with you, we will tell personal stories throughout the book in the first-person format. You'll hear stories from Lauren's childhood and her experiences with kids, along with her training in yoga and how it's influenced her journey. As one of the oldest of twenty-three grandchildren on her mom's side, she was always looking after younger cousins when she was growing up. She loved to "play school" as a kid and still does today—this time as a college professor. Coaching teachers and families, especially with challenging behaviors, is a passion that she does through her business, Engage: feel.think.connect.

You'll hear stories from Alyssa about being a mom, a wife, a teacher, a sister, and a daughter. Alyssa has had a baby on her body since she was a tiny human. She was raised in a small, rural town in western New York as the only girl in a family with four brothers. Being in community is at her core and fills her cup. She started Seed & Sew, a movement to change the way adults experience children's emotions, and it has grown to include a global village of parents, teachers, and caregivers invested in raising emotionally intelligent humans. From the *Voices of Your Village* podcast, online courses, and a social media community, to the S.E.E.D. Certification for early childhood programs, this movement has spread like wildfire, and we can feel it already—the future is emotionally intelligent.

Part I

What Are Emotions and Why Do They Matter?

Chapter 1

What Is Emotional Intelligence?

What do you want for your child when they grow up?" I asked forty-two parents in a workshop. Thirty-eight of them replied with the same answer: they wanted their children to be happy. I get that. I, too, want to feel happiness. I want my child to be happy.

But is anyone happy all the time? What happens when someone takes their toy? Or knocks down the block castle they've been working so hard on? What will they do when someone tells them they don't want to play with them? Or they aren't invited to that birthday party? How will they get through the embarrassment of making a mistake at school in front of peers or the disappointment of not reaching their goals? What will they lean on when they feel scared to try out for the musical they've been practicing so hard for? What will come up for them when they're experiencing peer pressure to do something that isn't aligned with their values?

It's natural for parents to want their kids to be happy, but life isn't designed for us to feel happy *all the time.* Life is complicated, and the human experience comes part and parcel with a complex variety of emotions from a very young age. You can even argue that this rich tapestry of emotions—happiness, joy, anxiety, sorrow, fear, etc.—is what gives us such a rich life experience and is essential to what makes us human.

So when I really pause to consider what I want for my child, for your child, and for the children all around us, I want them to have the tools to navigate and process the inevitable hard stuff so they're able to live a life that feels connected, compassionate, and curious. I want them to understand their emotions and develop the skills and know-how to navigate their feelings in a healthy and secure way. In other words, I want them to be emotionally intelligent.

"Emotional intelligence" has become a buzzword, and for good reason. At Seed & Sew, the tag line is "The future is emotionally intelligent," but what does that mean? What is emotional intelligence?

The idea of emotional intelligence surfaced in the early '90s and has been studied by emotion and behavior researchers ever since. It's been applied to relationships at home, school, and work to understand the skills that help people thrive in those relationships. In 1998, it was defined by Daniel Goleman as "the capacity for recognizing our own feelings and those of others, for motivating ourselves, and for managing emotions well in ourselves and in our relationships."[1] There are five components to emotional intelligence: self-awareness, self-regulation, empathy, motivation, and social skills.

Self-Awareness

Jonah was hitting, kicking, and biting a lot. His body's reaction to many emotions and experiences was to go into fight mode—this could happen when someone came into the space he was playing in, when he was standing in line next to a friend, when he was trying to close the snack container and couldn't get it to seal, when his brother was playing with the white shovel that he was planning to play with—a plan no one else knew about. His internal experience of frustration matched his external reaction. There was no pause between "I'm feeling something" and "I'm doing something." His parents and teachers—even his classmates and siblings—wanted him to be able to find that pause, to have something happen and be able to make a choice about how he would respond.

This wasn't an issue of Jonah "not knowing better." Once Jonah was calm and regulated, he could tell you that hitting hurts or that he can take deep breaths or stomp his feet rather than kicking. But in the moment of anger or frustration, his access to those ideas vanished. Enter the CEP method.

Self-regulation begins with self-awareness. We started by helping Jonah notice what he was feeling in his body. Similarly to how we say "I have butterflies in my stomach" to identify excitement or nervousness, we helped him tune in to his insides by saying, "Your fists are so tight, your shoulders are up to your ears, and your voice is so loud, you sound frustrated!" We practiced this daily with him for months, working to catch instances before the volcanic eruption of emotion. "You're playing in the sandbox, and I noticed Kai coming over here, and I saw your eyes look up and your arms tighten together. Are you feeling nervous that she might have a different plan for the toys in here?" Within a couple of months, Jonah started to show self-awareness without our help. He would say, "My fists are tight, and my shoulders are at my ears, and my voice is loud! I'm frustrated!"

The key to self-regulation, empathy, and social skills is first developing self-awareness. When we are aware of what's happening in our bodies and minds, we can regulate and connect with the world around us. We have access to choosing our words and actions instead of operating from a place of threat and reactivity.

Self-Regulation

Once we are aware of what's happening inside—in other words, once we can allow and notice the feeling—then we can find the pause between our initial reaction and our response. Our initial thought and internal reaction to something is automatic. It occurs subconsciously. Instead of reacting on autopilot, choosing what to do next is self-regulation.

Once Jonah was aware of what was happening in his body, then he was able to choose what to do next. We started small by encouraging him to yell, "Help!" A parent or a teacher would respond and go over to help him regulate and calm his nervous system, so he didn't spiral. Then we built upon that. He went from "Help!" to eventually squeezing his fists and letting them go as he said the phrase that worked best for his body,

"Plan B." (We will dive into different ways to build your toolbox for self-regulation as well as a child's in the coming chapters.)

We want to emphasize that *self-regulation* and *emotion processing* are different. For example: The other day I was at a restaurant picking up food that I had ordered and paid for through an app. When I got there, the restaurant staff insisted that I press a confirm button on my phone before I could take the food. Since the button was nowhere to be found on my phone, they called the app customer service so that I could confirm over the phone. Forty-five minutes later I was still at the restaurant after being placed on hold twice and still not allowed to take the food. By the time I left, I had paid twice, and it was an hour after the original pickup time. I was boiling inside. The key here is *inside*. I did not raise my voice at any time during that hour . . . although I think I whined at some point. It wasn't the right place to process or the right people to process with. I stayed calm on the outside and self-regulated, but I didn't process any emotions. It's possible for someone to demonstrate self-regulation whether or not they have processed their emotions.

It is possible for someone to demonstrate self-regulation because they've *suppressed* feelings rather than *processed* feelings. Suppressed feelings don't go away on their own; sometimes they explode (or implode) when we least expect it. It's as if you've filed them away for later: you regulate to get through the situation and, later, process in an appropriate space. I definitely processed my emotions from the restaurant experience with my husband and friends when I got home!

Self-reg is important for succeeding in school and work for obvious reasons. Emotion processing is important to experiencing meaningful and intimate relationships, a personal sense of freedom, sustainability in human-centered professions, and endurance in achieving long-term goals. Self-reg and emotion processing are most valuable when we develop them in tandem, which is the goal with the CEP method.

Empathy

Simon, almost two years old, was building a castle out of blocks when his sister crawled in and excitedly knocked every last block down. My first thought was "That stinks, but you can build it again. That's the cool part of blocks." Then I had a flashback to the day before when I had just finished folding the mountain of laundry that seems ever-present. The piles lined the couch, waiting to head to the correct rooms, when the baby came whirling through and knocked them down. As I stared at those nursing tanks (which are like a Rubik's Cube to fold) strewn about, I filled with disappointment and frustration. I felt mad at an infant, frustrated that I had accomplished making it to the bottom of the laundry pile only to get to do it all again. Imagine if someone had said to me, "Don't worry. You can fold it again!" Nope. No, thank you. I already folded it. It was done. I don't want to fold it again.

All of a sudden, Simon's rage from his block castle being knocked down made perfect sense to me. It sucks to work hard at something and have it destroyed by someone else, regardless of the other person's intentions or skill set.

We don't empathize with *why* someone is feeling something; we empathize with *what* they're feeling. If you've ever felt disappointed before, you can empathize with someone else who is experiencing disappointment. Brené Brown says, "Empathy is feeling *with* people."[2] It's hard because it requires us to let go of trying to cheer someone up when they're suffering or trying to reason with them about why it's not so bad or how it could be worse.

My husband and I both have an undying urge to make it better for the other when they're feeling something hard. We met each other in yoga teacher training and often end up spouting out some pithy yoga concept to explain the way of the universe—which is inspiring during a yoga class but turns out to be extremely annoying for a person who is experiencing a big feeling. Over the last few years, we've been trying to let each other feel stuff without trying to make it better. It's clunky, but it feels so validating.

Motivation

Have you ever been so focused on something or with someone that the rest of the world melts away? In those moments we're on the top of our game because we're doing something that we want to be doing and/or that challenges us in a good way. We learn best when we're intrinsically motivated.

One year I was a resource team teacher, which means I would cover other teachers' absences as a substitute. When I took this role, I remembered that when I was a classroom teacher, every time my co-teacher was out and a substitute teacher was in, the children were more fragile, and it felt like I spent the day putting out fires instead of teaching. Curriculum plans took a back seat as I focused my attention on supporting the children who were most thrown off by a change in routine.

As a substitute teacher, I was determined to learn how to support those children, in this case when my own presence was the reason they were thrown off, so the classroom teacher could maintain the curriculum and classroom culture. I learned so much that year about how to build trusting relationships with the children who resisted and to be present with them when they felt most vulnerable. By midyear, these children expressed joy to see me when they found out I was teaching in their classroom that day. I was able to learn so much because I was doing something I wanted to be doing and it challenged me in a good way. In turn, I was modeling this for the children, and they learned that I was safe to take risks with. They were motivated to see what I had to offer.

It would be awesome if we could live from intrinsic motivation twenty-four seven, but it's not very practical when there are bills to pay, groceries to shop for, a home to clean, and the less inspiring aspects of our jobs to take care of. The good news is that we *can* support ourselves and children to cultivate motivation from within. One of the best ways to do this is to apply Daniel Goleman's work on motivation to our relationships with children. This has to do with how we talk to ourselves and children, how we celebrate our growth and theirs—no matter how small—by choosing encouragement and compassion over perfectionism, having a willingness to practice, and getting help when we need it.[3]

Social Skills

There are people in my life who identify as a "people person," others who saw the pandemic as a welcomed excuse to avoid socializing, and plenty of people in between. No matter your proclivity for being around other people, it's hard to deny that we need each other. Communication, including body language, and other behaviors are essential to playing, working, learning, loving, and being in proximity to other humans. How we communicate and learn to communicate is directly related to social skills.

Social skills require social knowledge, which "refers to the names and cultural conventions invented by people, like language and expectations for behavior."[4] In a very practical sense, we need these social rules and expectations in order to find each other in an otherwise chaotic world. And at the same time, it's meaningful to remember that they are *invented*, that they are social constructs. There are many correct ways to interact with other humans; what makes any given use of language or behavior "correct" is the context. That means what is appropriate to say and do at home is usually different from what is appropriate at school, synagogue, the grocery store, or your grandparents' house in the country where your dad was born.

One day in the middle of the school year, Patrick, one of my twenty preschoolers, dropped the f-bomb in our classroom. We thought that none of the other children heard it, so we refrained from acknowledging it. Preschoolers often have a strong urge to do whatever someone has asked them not to do, so we didn't want to draw attention to it unnecessarily. We were also working on emphasizing positive attention for Patrick, so when we could let something go, we would.

A little later that morning, Patrick used the f-word a few more times in an attempt to insult one of us: "You're a f-ing!" At that point one of us explained—just to him—that some families might feel comfortable with this word, but some feel uncomfortable with this word, so we don't use it in the classroom. The conversation included an attempt to validate the feeling that prompted a desire to insult a teacher, along with a suggestion of another phrase that would communicate those feelings. He could use the f-word at home *if* his family was comfortable with it, but at school we'd stick with words that everyone feels comfortable with. He nodded and went back to playing.

Within thirty minutes multiple children were dancing about, delighting in the communal use of this newly forbidden word—absolutely oblivious to its meaning. One of the children attempted to insult one of the other teachers at nap time: "You're f-ing!" While my entire teaching team found this kind of hilarious, we also knew that a big part of our work includes teaching social skills and that if all the children went home swearing, then their parents would surely be disappointed. Using the f-word, or any curse word, at school (and later in the professional environment) is, by social agreement, considered inappropriate. It's an expectation that the adults in our culture pass on to the children.

During this social skills emergency, we called a group meeting of the children to explain the social expectations associated with this word. We also explained that the word has a definition that we couldn't share with them because it's an adult definition. We also let them know that people have used it in a hurtful way at times. Then we revisited our classroom agreements about taking care of each other. We wrote a long message to families about what happened and how we handled it.

At pickup time that day, a parent of one of our most socially aware, rule-following students came to us quietly to ask if it was *her* daughter who had exposed the group to the new word. She said her daughter had overheard either her or her husband use it while driving and started saying it at home. We couldn't believe it! She had not been one of the children testing out the f-word that day, and we never would have guessed she would use it anywhere. But in the context of social skills development, it makes perfect sense that she would use it with her family and not at school. Since social learning came easily to her, she had picked up on when it was appropriate to use the word and when it was not. Naturally, most of the children needed some guidance to understand context, positive adult attention on more socially affirming use of language at school, and/or support in building the self-regulation skills to be able to refrain.

The range of skills and knowledge you need to interact effectively in each of the contexts you spend time in will be different, but for interacting within groups of humans, social skills and knowledge are required. This is not to say that these rules and expectations can't be changed, since they have over time—the nice thing about having invented them in the first place is that we can reinvent them. One example is the paradigm shift toward embracing the emotional nature of being human.

"The Future Is Emotionally Intelligent"

Our level of self-awareness, ability to empathize, self-regulation, motivation, and social skills affect the way we feel about ourselves, and they affect the feelings of the people around us. This popular statement found on wall decals, often attributed to Maya Angelou, resonates with me: "I've learned that people will forget what you've said, people will forget what you did, but they will never forget the way you made them *feel*."[5] There is something very powerful about the underlying sentiment that our behavior elicits emotions in others. While each of us can be empowered to own our emotions, we also have the power to make positive and negative social contributions to someone else's day.

Imagine a world where we can feel our feelings without drowning in them because we have the tools for regulation and processing.

This is why we're interested in how emotionally intelligent humans care for one another. How do emotionally intelligent people enter a debate or dialogue? How do emotionally intelligent people experience tumultuous times in life or at work? How do emotionally intelligent people respond to their own feelings, and the feelings of others? What tools do emotionally intelligent humans have for perseverance and resilience? How do emotionally intelligent humans treat rest and recharge? What boundaries do emotionally intelligent humans set in their work environments? How do emotionally intelligent people engage during triggering family dynamics?

Imagine having a balanced sense of self-awareness and exchanging that with your loved ones and colleagues. Imagine a world where we can feel our feelings without drowning in them because we have the tools for regulation and processing. What would it look like to live a life where you are safe to feel, and others won't try to stop your feelings out of fear or discomfort? Imagine a world where we collectively have the social skills to engage in a lively debate that leads to collaboration and shared vision for the growth of humanity, and the ability to recognize when we haven't fulfilled our intentions, without judgment.

This is emotional intelligence.

We envision communities where people embrace dialogue and diversity because they are comfortable with their emotions and those of others. In this world, we are raising compassionate, confident, loving children who mature into adults who can count on one another to lead and to follow intelligently, respect personal boundaries and simultaneously reach out to those who are isolated, and acknowledge their mistakes and celebrate their strengths.

This is emotional intelligence.

This vision of the future compels us to engage deeply—to labor together—in this work. And within the context of child development, emotional intelligence, parenting, early education and care, and mindfulness, we are not alone. There is a large and growing community of people invested in raising an emotionally intelligent world!

You know that saying "You can't teach an old dog new tricks"? It turns out that's just not true when it comes to humans. We've learned so much about the brain's ability to keep learning and changing throughout life. It is true that it's harder for adults to develop new skills than it is for children, but we can do it if we want to. Even genetics don't have as much power over who we become as we once thought. It turns out that what happens in our lives can influence whether our genes turn on or off.[6] Isn't that amazing? We've also learned that a little positive thinking, like taking a moment to recognize something or someone you feel gratitude for, goes a long way in terms of helping us embrace life's challenges. This means that we are capable of change, and that who we think we are today doesn't have to limit visions of our future selves.

All this is to say, when big emotions surface for the children in our lives, we have the power to *decide* how to respond, rather than react on autopilot. We can *choose* to respond in a way that leads to emotionally intelligent communities.

But what does that look like? How do we find clarity and a sense of agency when it comes to raising and teaching young children during the most crucial time in their development? And what does it look like when we are on autopilot, reacting instead of responding with intention? How can we reconnect and move forward, away from our desire for perfectionism?

In this book, we explore what it looks like to foster collective emotional intelligence that leads to empathetic, confident, trusting children who are able to interact with their environment, advocate for themselves, and respectfully engage in community. You'll be challenged to look at your relationships with children, families, and/or your classroom, and most importantly, at yourself. Buckle up for the messy, real conversations we will have about how to be in the hard stuff! Parts of this process may feel uncomfortable. Let's do this together, because we aren't meant to do it alone.

Chapter 2

Your Role in Your Child's Emotions

A few weeks ago, while visiting my parents, I was looking through photos from my childhood when I stumbled across one of tiny baby me in a container with some loose straps draped over my shoulders. "Was this my car seat?" I nerve-rackingly asked my mom. "Yeah, that was what they looked like then. Heck, when I was little, car seats weren't even a thing. My mom held us as babies and then we sat on the seat."

As generations have evolved, we've learned more about how to keep children safe in cars, and the car seat has evolved along with our knowledge. In years to come, I'm sure today's children will look back at photos of their rudimentary car seats (which seem absolutely cutting edge today) and feel just as flabbergasted as I did staring at that photo of mine.

At least, I hope they do. I hope we learn more. I hope we continue to evolve, grow, and change. Not just in the car seats we use, but in all areas of life. As we learn more, I hope our practices change in response to that knowledge.

The point of this story is twofold. First, it's that each generation does their best with the knowledge and resources they have. Second, it's that the way our loving, nurturing parents raised us—cutting edge as it may have been at the time—may be absolutely out of step with the latest science and research on child development.

Don't get me wrong—change can be hard, especially with something like parenting, where so much of the way we interact with children is hardwired from the way we were raised. There is comfort in what we know, in how we were brought up, and what we were exposed to. Those experiences will always be part of us. In our relationships with children, those memories surface to let us know when something feels uncomfortable or new, or when something leads us to feel nervous or anxious. Part of the CEP method is learning ways to recognize what triggers these experiences and memories and how to move forward with self-awareness in the present.

Sometimes I open my mouth and my mom comes out, and sometimes that's great. Sometimes it's something I really want to pass on to the kids. But sometimes it's something I've spent years trying to work through in therapy and really don't want to imprint on the child in front of me.

Our role in a child's life is crucial. We form the basis for how they will show up in relationships with others. One day, they will open their mouth and our voice will come out, and damn, that's a lot of pressure. In order to take a necessary dive deep into ourselves and our hardwired behaviors— into who we are and who we want to be—there's one key thing to note: perfection is *not* the goal. I have never once ended the day with kids and applauded myself with "Wow, I was a perfect parent or teacher today."

In her workshop for Seed & Sew's teacher professional development program, the S.E.E.D. Certification, psychologist Lynyetta Willis discusses this push-pull of past and present as a relay race of legacy blessings and legacy burdens. Legacy blessings are the experiences, phrases, and moments from our childhood that serve and support us in our lives. Legacy burdens are the challenges we are working through in order to write different stories. Our grandparents passed the baton to our parents, who passed on some blessings and healed some burdens. They passed the baton to us to heal more burdens, and we get to pass the baton to our children to continue to navigate their legacy blessings and burdens. One day, I hope our children grow up and tell us about the things they've learned and ways they are working to do things differently. You aren't failing if you aren't perfect. You're human. Your mess is welcome here.

Chronic Stress and Childhood ACEs

The brain is designed to handle a reasonable amount of stress, but chronically stressful environments can have a negative impact on the relationship between the survival brain and the rational thinking brain, and therefore on learning and development.

Professors of neuroscience Brian Kolb and Ian Whishaw explain, "Normally, stress responses are brief. The body mobilizes resources, deals with the challenge physiologically and behaviorally, then shuts down the stress response. The brain is responsible for turning on the stress reaction and for turning it off." This design allows us to be in a heightened state if there is a threat in order to react without thinking. If a child is in danger, the stress response helps us react instinctively to keep them safe and then turns off so that we can resume day-to-day life.

They go on to say, "If a stress response is not shut down, the body continues to mobilize energy at the cost of energy storage; proteins are used up, resulting in muscle wasting and fatigue; growth hormone is inhibited, and the body cannot grow; the gastrointestinal system remains shut down, reducing the intake of nutrients to replace the used resources; reproductive functions are inhibited; and the immune system is suppressed, increasing the possibility of infection or disease."[1] This is referred to as toxic stress.

A study beginning in 1994 looked at how toxic stress relates to adult health risk behaviors. The toxic stress factors that were researched are called Adverse Childhood Experiences, or ACEs. There are ten ACE categories:

1. Physical abuse
2. Physical neglect
3. Divorce
4. Sexual abuse
5. Emotional abuse
6. Emotional neglect
7. Living with a relative with a mental health illness
8. Having an incarcerated relative
9. Having a mother who's treated violently
10. Substance use in the home

How many of the ten have you experienced? That's your ACE score. You can find the ACE test at www.seedandsew.org/more. Sixty-seven percent of the US population has 1 ACE, and 1 in 8 have 4 or more ACEs. The study, and subsequent ACE studies, have shown that 4 or more ACEs can result in drastic physical and psychological health outcomes, which include being 12 times more likely to attempt suicide, 7 times more likely to have alcohol use disorder, and 2.4 times more likely to have a stroke.[2]

There is a vast difference between toxic stress and tolerable stress, as tolerable stress allows for the ebb and flow of stress hormones while toxic stress is an overflow of those hormones. Many ACEs are intergenerational, passed from one generation to the next. What's significant about this is that within this cycle, the primary caregiver has the power to heal their trauma and create a different narrative and outcome for the child. The CEP method has five components and only one is about adult-child interactions. The other four are centered on the adult. Our role in our own healing is incredibly powerful for the toolbox we pass on to children.

If you and/or your child is experiencing toxic stress, then there are things you can do to alleviate its long-term effects. Proactive self-care techniques such as therapy, accessing a food pantry, group meetings, or staying connected to your spiritual community are examples. The Center for Youth Wellness also has tools for supporting families living with toxic stress. Responsive self-care can include reaching out to someone to help you make a transition and set up the resources that you need to get through it. When you get to Chapter 13, we'll offer tips for building your village and how to get comfortable asking for help. We believe that every parent wants to be the best parent for their child, and no one is meant to navigate this journey alone. You are changing the game for your child as you take care of yourself. As *New York Times* bestselling author Britt Hawthorne would say, "We are rooting for you."

Attachment and Why It Matters

The cornerstone of emotional development lies in attachment. Let's get nerdy for a second.

The attachment theory, which includes four styles of attachment, is a result of John Bowlby's and later Mary Ainsworth's research. Attachment is specific to the relationship between a child and their primary caregiver(s).[3] This relationship is different from, but serves as the foundation for, other relationships, such as those with peers, siblings, and future partners. According to attachment theory, in order for a child to feel safe and secure so they can take risks, explore their environment, and separate from a caregiver, they must feel confident in the caregiver's ability to understand and meet their needs and keep them safe.

Part of me feels that I should be able to do it all and is afraid that if I keep asking for help, at some point I won't be lovable.

A major contributor to building this kind of trusting relationship is a reliable back-and-forth interaction between the baby and the caregiver, called serve-and-return. Do you know when a baby babbles, it's like they are *really* saying something? You may have noticed this with your own little one. They'll often pause after babbling, giving the adult an opportunity to respond. You may have found yourself doing this automatically.

Communication and connection are about so much more than the words we say to one another. Even before an infant can understand our words, they are learning to understand what we mean from our tone of voice, our body language, and our volume level. We communicate with children not just with the words we say, but how we say them, what our bodies say, and how we react in different scenarios. In this way, we start to form attachments with the child, attachments that let them know how to act and how not to act with us in order to feel safe, even before they are ready for language.

Attachment is rooted in safety—a human child is dependent on a caregiver for survival and that means being lovable so someone will be there to care for you. In each interaction, children are unknowingly asking, "Am I lovable? When? Am I safe? How do I stay/get safe?" They are constantly researching, through trial and error, noticing our reactions and adjusting their behavior accordingly. Over time, these patterns of interaction and adjustment form an attachment style:

1. **Secure attachment.** In a secure attachment, a child feels safe, seen, secure, and soothed. The caregiver is emotionally available for the child's experiences. Secure attachment relationships include rupture (mistakes, challenges, disconnections) and repair. (Remember, this does not require perfection on the part of the caregiver. More on this later.) In a secure attachment relationship, the adult takes responsibility for their own regulation.

2. **Anxious attachment.** In anxious attachment, a child feels responsible for regulating their own emotions in order to prevent their caregiver from being dysregulated. This can show up as codependence and a fear of conflict. The child learns that the adult is not comfortable with their hard emotions.

3. **Avoidant attachment.** In an avoidant attachment, a child feels disconnected or unseen. Their basic physiological needs are met, but their emotional needs are not. The caregiver may be dismissive of a child's emotions, using phrases such as "you're fine," "no need to cry about that," and "you don't need to be upset." The child learns that the adult is not comfortable with their hard emotions.

4. **Disorganized attachment.** This is often a result of abuse, trauma, or chaos. In disorganized attachment, a child may fear a caregiver and feel unsafe. The caregiver is sporadic and inconsistent, with unpredictable availability to meet the child's physical or emotional needs. The caregiver's responses may be hot and cold, leaving the child unsure of what reaction to expect at any given moment.

Facing Your Childhood Attachment Styles as an Adult

I grew up in a large family with parents who worked really hard to provide for our basic needs, so asking for help was not a way to show or receive love. There's a part of me that feels proud when I can go with the flow and don't have to rely on others to meet my needs. That part of me would rather suffer in silence than be "high-maintenance." As an adult, I've had to learn how to ask for help and know that when I do, I'm still lovable. My avoidant attachment style from childhood lives inside me and surfaces throughout adulthood, too. My basic needs were met, but as it was for so many of us, my parents didn't have the tools to meet my emotional needs. Inconveniencing others fills my body with such discomfort that it's a constant, often very sweaty and nervous, practice to say, "I need help."

This comes up in parenthood for me almost daily with the mental load—do we need more diapers, are his snacks and lunch ready for childcare, when did he wake up from nap, when was the last time his sheets were cleaned, do we need to order more sunscreen before our trip . . . ? The list goes on and on. At one time, I was nearing a breaking point. Every single time I thought of the myriad things it took to take care of our child and my partner didn't, I felt angry. I knew that for the sake of our relationship, I needed to do the deeply uncomfortable thing of inconveniencing him and asking for help rather than suffering in silence.

"I feel like I'm the one responsible for thinking of all the things for our child and then asking you when I need help with any of them and it feels overwhelming," I said with clammy hands and a fast heart rate one Saturday morning after breakfast. "I don't need a response right now if you want to take that in and we can chat about it during his nap."

(I've learned that it's important for me to pause in the midst of a conversation like this instead of filling the silence, because, boy, can I! The more I talk, the faster I talk, and the more overwhelmed my partner gets until we are snapping at each other or he shuts down. Since I hate being in that middle space where a conflict isn't resolved, it's taken me time to learn that we need to coexist for a while as we both self-regulate. Only then are we truly able to listen to each other.)

When we circled back during nap time, my partner said, "I feel like you notice the things before I do, and I don't know what to do about that." I had been taking these things on and delegating out the kid stuff I needed help with for so long that he was conditioned to not even know what to look for. We decided to form a more systematic approach to the workload so that we could share it easily. We made a spreadsheet of all the kid and household tasks we each do and divided them up. Now we have one shared master list that is forever growing and changing as our family does.

This wasn't easy for me to do, given the way I was raised. And a part of me surfaces full of discomfort when I have to ask for help with tasks that are typically my load to carry. Sometimes that part of me shows up with shame—part of me feels that I should be able to do it all and is afraid that if I keep asking for help, at some point I won't be lovable. That the people around me will realize I'm too needy and will leave me. I want to give that part of me a big hug and let her know she's allowed to have needs. That as a child, she was allowed to have needs, too.

When you think back on your childhood, what types of attachment resonate with you? These could be with parents, caregivers, teachers—anyone responsible for your care when you were young. As Tina Payne Bryson, author of *The Power of Showing Up: How Parental Presence Shapes Who Our Kids Become and How Their Brains Get Wired*, shares, "One of the reasons I love attachment science is that the research indicates that there is quite a bit of room for parents to be flawed and that we can make a lot of mistakes, but as long as we help our kids feel safe, seen, and soothed most of the time, their brains wire to securely know that if they have a need, we will see it and show up for them. And when we do that predictably (not perfectly), they learn how to find friends and mates who will show up for them (they come to expect it!), and they learn how to show up for themselves."[4]

Attachment relationships can change. If you are reading this after years of parenting or early care and education, know that it is never too early or too late to work toward a secure attachment. Wherever you are right now is a great place to start. The brain is flexible and can form new habits and patterns.

During one of our workshops, a dad raised a concern: "If I let my kid cry all the time, he's going to get bullied in school." If this dad experienced bullying during his childhood or knew someone who did, it makes sense for this part of him to try like hell to make sure his child doesn't experience that pain. We all have childhood experiences like his that live deep within us. They were formed and designed to work really hard to protect us in our early attachment relationships. The key to getting back in the driver's seat is in recognizing these parts of ourselves, getting to know the fears that provoke them, and building awareness of when they try to take charge. We tend to have common themes from childhood that surface in our roles as parents, teachers, or caregivers. Respect, obedience, kindness, accountability, and strength are a few examples. Do any of these resonate with you? Are there other themes that come to mind? Throughout this book, we will practice recognizing these themes without judgment.

Part of the work is about helping you tune in to your knowing, as Glennon Doyle calls it in her book *Untamed*, to make a conscious choice rather than acting out of habit.[5] Throughout this book, we are going to get to know the uncomfortable voices inside us that surface in different relationships and moments of conflict. Sometimes there are multiple voices—and some might be in conflict with one another. The goal is to help you tune in to them in order to choose how you want to respond. Regardless of what your childhood attachment styles were, as you build awareness of your habits and patterns, you can create and nurture a secure attachment with the child in front of you.

Being a Good Parent

The other day at dinner, a friend said, "I want my parents to be proud of who I am as a mom. I'm in my mid-thirties—why do I still need my parents' approval? I don't even want to do this the way they did it so why does it matter?" It makes complete sense for us to want to feel loved and cared for by our attachment figures. We don't age out of that, or how we use others' behavior to judge our own.

"She's such a good mom," I said in passing as we chatted about a friend. "What does that mean, 'good mom'?" my friend asked. It stopped me dead in my tracks. What *did* that mean? As parents today, it's easy to get caught in a comparison trap. It's not just while seeing other parents in real life at drop-off and activities, but also when scrolling through filtered social media posts of parents who seem to have "it" all together, or observing that parent in the grocery who is so patiently navigating her child's meltdown while we just lost it in the checkout line. It's so easy to see the Pinterest-perfect play space or the parent whose Instagram post about vacation is all blissful and magical and feel like we are failing. Like our messy insides don't match their curated outsides.

The truth is, my criteria for being a good parent might be different from my parents', sister-in-law's, friend's, or partner's. What would it look like to ask ourselves, "Am I proud of me?" or "Am I a good parent according to me?" Getting curious about these parts of ourselves is key to exploring how we want to show up with kids—how we want to interpret the child's behavior and how we want to respond. I realized that, to answer any of these questions, I had to dive into my goals and values as a parent. These are the three questions that guide me when I feel like I'm falling into the comparison rut:

1. What's my long-term goal for this child?
2. What's my goal for our relationship?
3. Am I modeling the values I want them to inherit?

Just the other day after scrolling through social media, a part of me surfaced saying, "Ugh, I never make cute shapes out of food for lunches." In the past, I would have immediately jumped to think that "good parents" do that. Now I pause and ask those three questions. Making a heart-shaped sandwich doesn't actually fit into *my* criteria of being a good parent. This allows me to find my way back to this work without being overwhelmed.

Biting Today, Bullying Tomorrow?

Birth preparation classes and pediatrics rarely discuss how to respond when a child screams at the top of their lungs every time they feel disappointed. Teacher preparation programs don't offer much in this category either. There is no course called "Tantrum in the Grocery Store 101."

But I do have a workshop for parents that I call "Biting, Flailing, and Other Behavior You Didn't Expect." The stories that parents share during this workshop are rich. In hindsight, and in the company of other parents with similar stories, it's easy to find humor in the unexpectedness of the behavior (except for when another child was hurt). Sometimes people laugh with relief that someone else understands. They feel validated that others know what it's like to think everyone's judging you because of your kid's behavior when it seems there's nothing you can do to stop what's happening.

When my husband was about four or five, he found some really cool "stickers" in the bathroom. They were white, long, oval, and squishy. They made an interesting crinkle sound. He decided to test out these new stickers on the window beside the front door. Later that evening, when his older sister's date was arriving, she realized her pads were there on the window for all the world—and her date—to see. She was extremely embarrassed. Of course, her reaction, which included shouting, gave my husband the impression at the time that he'd done something very "bad."

Whether you're with your own children or your students, when someone in your care behaves in such a way that is considered socially inappropriate, it can trigger feelings of shame and embarrassment. Those feelings have the potential to override logic, especially if these are painful feelings for you, and then other feelings can swoop in to "protect" you from the more painful ones. Anger and frustration are common protector feelings and unfortunately easy to dump on a child. When the adult doesn't know how to process their feelings, it can be scary for the child. They perceive it as being unlovable. If you're dependent on others and you think you're unlovable to them, it's a threat to your safety.

Of course, my husband, at five years old, had no idea the adult context of these fun, new stickers or that they were something very private. Often children have no idea about the context of their behaviors. (Understanding context is a social skill that children have to be taught.)

Sometimes children do understand that the behavior isn't socially appropriate, but they don't yet have the self-regulation skills to interrupt their impulse. One year in class, there were some chronic challenging behaviors that were concerning to us as teachers. One child's behavior—kicking, scratching, and pinching, which had physically hurt other children in the class—was also causing a lot of speculation and gossip among the parents. A couple of other preschool teachers and I invited the parents to a conversation about challenging behaviors. The parent whose child had hurt several other children came to tears as she identified herself and apologized for her child's behavior. It was a tender moment. The other parents came to see this mom as an engaged parent who was simply at a loss for how to support her child's development. She wasn't setting a bad example, in denial, or checked out as they had been suspecting. It became clear to the group that the teachers and parents were working together with specialists to figure out how best to support this child's development and curb the challenging behavior, but sometimes it's not as simple as we want it to be.

We may forget that some three-year-olds can learn to zip their jacket, so we do it for them, but we expect them to manage big emotions by themselves and efficiently. Kids need our help, our intentional response, to build the self-awareness, self-regulation, empathy, and social skills that will give them the ability and confidence to do something different next time. How can we teach social skills without transferring our embarrassment, our own shame, our own legacy burdens onto the child? How can we teach them that hurting other people is not okay without taking a blow at their self-esteem? How can we handle the behavior that's happening *in the moment* without jumping ahead and future-projecting, imagining what this behavior will mean in five, ten, fifteen, or twenty years. *Will they bully someone at school? Will they be abusive? Am I failing to teach them how to be kind?* We are so good at jumping into the future. Our brains are designed to do so, to try and prevent hard things from happening, to keep us safe. But what happens when this moment doesn't dictate how the rest of the day, week, month, year, or years will unfold? As we dive into how to respond in the moment when we are experiencing triggering behaviors, give yourself grace and know that you are not failing if your child is displaying a behavior that isn't socially acceptable. I've never met a single parent, teacher, or caregiver who escaped all the challenging behaviors.

Notice your reaction. Bring awareness to your fears. Keep an eye on who is in the driver's seat.

Chapter 3

What's Happening in the Brain and the Body When You Have Big Emotions?

When you hear the word "emotion," some images or memories may pop into your head: feeling angry after being cut off while driving, comforting your child while he cries, feeling nervous before a big presentation at work. But what exactly *are* emotions? Do *all* humans feel sad sometimes? Angry? Overwhelmed? Does everybody's brain light up in the same place when they feel a certain emotion?

Lisa Feldman Barrett, a behavioral scientist at Northeastern University, and her team have found that, surprisingly, emotions are *not* universal and recognized in certain facial expressions, as we once thought.[1] Instead emotions are concepts, learned through complex human experiences. Barrett's team has developed the Theory of Constructed Emotion, a theory we love because it fits perfectly with our understanding of attachment relationships.

Understanding Emotions

On a very basic level, emotions are concepts built on a person's experiences. For instance, while I was growing up, I might have heard the word "sad" when I saw someone crying and averting eye contact. Maybe I was also told an explanation of what caused this person to be "sad." From this experience, I get one data point to build the concept "sad" in my brain. The next time I hear the word "sad," it might be from a different person, who is not crying but looking down, shoulders falling forward, and I hear the correlating story for this particular situation. Now I have two data points to build my concept, and so on. Over time I have a more complex understanding of each emotion that gets built in my brain in a unique way according to my unique experiences.

Throughout life, we're taught which emotions are socially acceptable to have or not have, to express or suppress, and how much to pay attention to them or ignore them at any given moment.

These emotion concepts are built from a set of neural connections and pathways in the brain, like a web that gets more complex the more we learn. Emotion concepts can live in more than one region of the brain. Even if we claim to be experiencing the same emotion, our brains light up in different ways—across these connections and pathways—because no two people's experience is exactly the same.

One of my favorite inspiring, yet intriguing descriptions of the Theory of Constructed Emotion by Barrett is: "You are not at the mercy of emotions that arise unbidden to control your behavior. You are an architect of these experiences. Your river of feelings might feel like it's flowing over you, but actually you're the source of the river."[2] In other words, we construct our own emotions—but how?

Let's take a look at the emotion experience in super slow motion. First, something happens—a stimulus. Maybe the stimulus is that your friend walks into your apartment and the first thing she says is "Bad news." Her eyes are puffy and red. The stimulus could also be something internal, like a thought that pops into your head. But let's stick with the "Bad news" example. Your body starts reading signals from inside (hormones, sensations in your organs, etc.). This "sense of the physiological condition of the body" is called interoception.[3] Maybe your heart started beating a little faster before your friend uttered another word because you had already intuited that something is not good. You might not be aware of your interoceptive powers, but they are happening with or without your consent.

Interoception leads us to a very basic sense of feeling in two categories: arousal-calmness and pleasure-displeasure.[4] On the arousal-calmness spectrum, you could feel 100 percent aroused, or agitated, or you might feel 100 percent calm. You could also be anywhere in between. Similarly, on the pleasure-displeasure spectrum you might feel 100 percent pleasure, 100 percent displeasure, or anywhere in between. In our example with your friend, you would likely be at the arousal end of the spectrum rather than calm, and the displeasure rather than the pleasure end.

In order to make sense of what's going on, your brain will rely on clues from the world around you (sensory input) and your emotion concepts (past experience). You noticed puffy, red eyes (sensory input) and you're unconsciously mapping this experience with your previous emotion

Stimulus **+**	Interoception **+**	Past lived experiences **=**	Emotion
Information taken in from the senses.	The physiological sensations reacting to this stimulus. One may or may not have awareness of this.	The brain uses information drawn from previous experiences.	
Ex. Your friend enters with puffy, red eyes, saying, "Bad news . . ."	Ex. You feel your heart rate increase.	Ex. When someone cried previously, they were having a hard time.	Ex. I feel worried.

experiences. Your brain is creating a story about what is happening in an effort to understand the situation. These feelings could be visceral and/or abstract, but it's possible words have popped up in your thoughts, because humans use symbols—words, gestures, pictures—to communicate. Perhaps the word "worried" is popping up for you. You might even use this symbol to communicate with your friend: "I'm so worried! What happened? Are you okay?"

A stimulus, plus interoception and sensory input, plus emotion concepts built from past experience help us make sense of our experiences of emotion in the present.

Add our ability to take perspective and we're able to make an educated guess about what someone *else* might be feeling. Our perception of emotions turns out to be a meaning-making experience that engages many regions of the brain.[5] Throughout an emotion experience, the brain is communicating with the body through the nervous system, which includes both voluntary (running, lying down, etc.) and involuntary (blinking, sweating, releasing hormones, etc.) actions.

Since emotion concepts and symbols—just like other kinds of social knowledge—are defined by society and culture, cultural context matters, too. The way a specific emotion looks and feels for each of us and the stories that correlate are unique.

Emotions as Part of Social Constructs

One of my four-year-old students, Lu, had a pattern of screaming for a long time when she was picked up at the end of the day, and it took about forty-five minutes for her mom to get her out to the car after everyone else had left for the day. Big emotions are normal upon pickup after a long day at school, and we had been offering emotion cards and a social story in the interest of helping Lu process those feelings in a way that would help her feel more at peace when it was time to exit the building.

When we spoke with Lu's mom about how we were using the emotion cards, we learned that in their first language there were many words for anger, many for sadness, and many for other emotions, too. There were concepts that didn't have English translations. She was excited about the idea of pictures to explain emotions and volunteered to make a book of emotions in their first language so that her child would be able to gain information about the relationship of language to emotions in both cultures.

We tell this story to demonstrate how different regions of the world and different families have different words to describe their feelings. In other words, emotions are also governed by social conventions. Throughout life, we're taught which emotions are socially acceptable to have or not have, to express or suppress, and how much to pay attention to them or ignore them at any given moment.

As children we also learn about emotion concepts from our primary caregivers and the people around us. Just like with social knowledge and skills, there are many different ways to recognize and express emotion concepts. Learning the words their caregivers use for emotion concepts is how children learn to relate with their parents and other adults. Children can be best understood by their caregivers when they communicate using concepts that we've taught them, and in context.

Are your children co-parented by someone whose culture is noticeably different from yours when it comes to emotions? Do you teach children whose culture or cultures are vastly different from yours and/or each other's? See if you can notice which, if any, emotions carry value or carry shame in your own culture and then for those of your co-parents' or students' families. What kind of emotional expression is encouraged or discouraged, punished or rewarded? What else do you notice? You can even do a Google search on "emotions and culture" to see what else you can find out about how culture influences one's understanding of emotions. Allow the answers to these questions to guide your approach to partnering with the other adults in your child's life. When we approach differences with curiosity rather than judgment, we increase our ability to work and connect across cultures and nurture emotional development in a relevant way for each child and ourselves.

Emotional Code Switching

Just as humans can be multilingual, they can be multicultural. A friend of mine who grew up speaking English and Spanish, experiencing different cultures at home and at school, often refers to her two brains—toggling between two cultures is academically referred to as code switching. Pedro Noguera, a sociologist, commentator on educational issues, and coauthor of *The Crisis of Connection: Roots, Consequences, and Solutions*, emphasized the importance of teaching code switching over assimilation, at the 2022 Center for Equity & Cultural Wealth Institute at Bunker Hill Community College in Boston. Code switching allows someone to build social skills and language in more than one culture and then flow back and forth between them as needed. In contrast, assimilation teaches children that there is only one correct culture—typically the dominant culture—and to leave part of themselves behind in order to fit the mold.

Over the years, I've worked with many families where each parent was raised in a different culture. Studies show that kids who are bilingual and bicultural have more complex neural networks, and more advanced perspective-taking abilities and higher-level thinking skills than their monolingual, monocultural peers.[6]

No matter what our emotion concepts are, or the words that we use to describe them, we all feel stuff. In that way, we're the same. It's where we can truly see and be seen. It is from this place of sameness that we can begin to understand differentness and work together to help ourselves, children, and other loved ones feel whole when we're having big emotions.

Understanding the Nervous System

It's our nervous system's job to keep us safe, to notice everything around us all the time and ask, "Am I safe?" Right now if a car drives by, my nervous system says, "Not important, you're safe." I get to keep doing what I'm doing. If the fire alarm goes off, my nervous system screams,

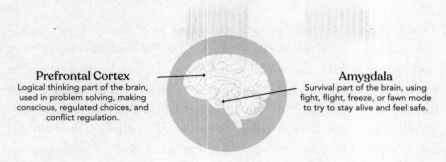

Prefrontal Cortex
Logical thinking part of the brain,
used in problem solving, making
conscious, regulated choices, and
conflict regulation.

Amygdala
Survival part of the brain, using
fight, flight, freeze, or fawn mode
to try to stay alive and feel safe.

"IMPORTANT! PAY ATTENTION!" My body gets a rush of adrenaline and cortisol that turns off my logical thinking brain, (prefrontal cortex) and turns on my reactive, survival brain (amygdala), where I enter fight, flight, freeze, or fawn mode.

This is a really important feature in our nervous system to keep us alive. If a child is running into a busy street, you don't want to pause and think, "Hm, should I stop them?" You want to react, without thinking, and scoop them up. The nervous system encompasses both the rational thinking brain and the reactive brain, as well as the sensory responses the body experiences, like the alert feelings when a fire alarm goes off.

All day long, your nervous system is doing something akin to running apps in the background of your phone. The more apps there are and the more you use them, the faster the battery drains. From the moment your phone is turned on, it starts to drain. Certain apps drain it faster than others. We can recharge it to avoid that red battery alert signal, or we can wait until it crashes, plug it in, and then wait until it's ready to restart.

The same is true for our nervous system. We can recharge it proactively to help it function, or we can wait until it crashes, recharge it, and give it time to restart. Let's dive into how to proactively recharge as well as what to do with the inevitable tantrum, meltdown, or reaction (read: nervous system dysregulation) that will occur.

Proactive Recharge

Our nervous system takes in information around us—the smell of food cooking in the kitchen, the way a shirt feels on our body, the pile of clothes on the stairs, the sounds of children playing, birds chirping, and cars driving by, the movement of someone as they walk into the room, and so on—and filters it. I think of it as a funnel, with all the information coming in at the top and the size of the opening at the bottom being different for each of us. Imagine you have a funnel with a small bottom opening and a funnel with a larger bottom opening and you pour sand into each of them from the top at the same rate. The one with the smaller opening will get backed up and start to overflow before the one with the larger opening. Folx with a smaller funnel opening are really good at noticing the details, allowing just a few specs of sand to pass through at a time. They can also get overwhelmed by stimuli and overflow with sand.

My husband's brain has a small funnel hole. He can hear the lawn mower from three houses down, notices the pile of clothes on the stairs, is observant of the way different clothes feel on his body, and is acutely aware if something changes in the environment, such as the nail clippers being on the other side of the medicine cabinet. He has a superpower in noticing details. It can feel overwhelming for him if there's clutter around the house, dishes in the sink, toys strewn about, and music or the TV running in the background.

I, on the other hand, operate much differently. The hole in the bottom of my funnel is bigger. For example, my husband and I had been together about ten years and had been living at my mother-in-law's house for a few months when I was walking down the stairs and noticed a new painting on the wall. "I love that artwork," I told my MIL. "Thanks," she replied. "It's been there for as long as we've known you." As information comes into the top of my funnel, it slides right through, allowing me to be surrounded by stimuli and not feel overwhelmed until it starts to back up. I can be in a room full of people with children running around yelling and piles of clothes lining the stairs and still feel able to filter it all and be present. However, I miss a lot of the details, such as the artwork on the wall for a decade or the piles of laundry that it would be helpful for me to notice in order to participate in household management.

Depending on how full our battery is, certain stimuli or experiences may be easier or harder to navigate. A change in routine or expectation in the morning right after a full night of sleep and breakfast may feel

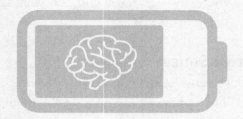

- Sleep
- Food
- Quiet
- Dark spaces
- Moving our bodies
- A long hug
- Connecting with
  someone we love
- Going upside down
- Spinning
- Swinging
- Dancing
- Deep breaths

- Hunger
- Tiredness
- Changes in routine
- Unknown expectations
- Things or people moving
  in our environment
- Sounds
- Clutter
- Screens
- How things feel or taste
- Experiencing emotions
- Experiencing other
  people's emotions

easier to accept than a change in expectation at dinnertime, when everyone is getting snoozy, feeling hungry, and has worked all day to process the world. The things that drain our battery are cumulative throughout the day, and that can affect our behavior. For example, in one study, judges were "significantly more likely to deny parole to a prisoner if the hearing was just before lunchtime. . . . Immediately after lunch, the judges began granting paroles with their customary frequency."[7] Stimuli add up, so as the day goes on, it's crucial that we are recharging in order to have some battery left; otherwise it can lead to sensory overwhelm.

As children we often learn about the five senses: taste, touch, smell, sight, and sound, but there are three other senses in our bodies that are vital for how we move through the world and what triggers us to lose control.

Proprioceptive Sense

The proprioceptive sense is body awareness—feeling where your body begins and ends. This is how we put on a shirt without actively thinking of each step—put my arm through the hole and push, put my other arm through the hole and push, and pull it up over my head. The body learns this pattern and can do it without even thinking about it. For long-term development and short-term recharging, it benefits from deep pressure (such as arm squeezes and hugs), or big muscle movement (such as jumping into a pile of couch cushions). Throughout this book, the proprioceptive sense will be referred to as the "big body play" sense because that is how we tend to see it show up.

Examples of Proprioceptive Input

- Going for a walk
- Running
- Jumping into a pile of pillows
- Participating in a relay race
- Doing frog jumps
- Having a hug
- Wearing a baby
- Rolling up a blanket or yoga mat
- Pushing something heavy
- Carrying something weighted
- Dancing
- Using resistance bands
- Massage
- Snuggling while reading a book

Vestibular Sense

The vestibular sense is awareness of movement and spatial orientation. It lets our body know where our head is in relation to the rest of us. This helps us navigate the world without bumping into everything and helps us understand how close we are getting to something. I can picture this two-year-old in my classroom one year who would go from one end of the room to the thing he wanted at the other end, plowing through anyone or anything in his way. Sometimes this kind of behavior is confused with aggression, but often—and especially in this case—he actually *couldn't feel* how close he was to others or the level of force he was crashing into them with. He always became wobbly as he got close to nap time, struggling to maintain his balance. We helped support his vestibular sense through activities such as swinging, going upside down in yoga, or dipping in our arms. He liked to spin in an office chair and bounce on a yoga ball to calm before his nap.

Recharging the Vestibular System

- Going upside down
- Swinging
- Spinning
- Doing dips with a young child in arms
- Somersaulting
- Bouncing on a yoga ball

Interoceptive Sense

The interoceptive sense is the perception of sensations inside the body. It lets us know when we are hungry, full, tired, or thirsty, and includes things such as butterflies in our stomach. As children are building self-awareness, they are tuning into their interoceptive sense to notice what is happening inside their bodies to give them clues to how they are feeling or what emotion they might be experiencing. Imagine if we had phrases like "butterflies in my stomach" to identify and communicate when we felt angry, sad, embarrassed, disappointed, scared, etc.

Supporting the Nervous System

Imagine that a child woke up in the morning and we waited until they were so hungry that they were sobbing (hangry, anyone?) and then we fed them. What if this was the cycle all day long? How exhausting would that be?

Instead, we stay ahead of the hangries. We feed kids breakfast, snack, lunch, snack, and dinner when they start to get hungry to prevent them from melting down out of hunger. We can do this for the nervous system as a whole. There are five ways to proactively recharge the nervous system before the red battery light comes on:

1. Predictable, consistent eating times

When our nervous system knows what to expect, it feels at ease and safe. Because food is a part of our ability to stay alive, knowing when we will have access to it is a primal desire. A predictable, consistent schedule for food lets children know that they will have opportunities to eat throughout the day. We particularly love Ellyn Satter's work on the Division of Responsibility,[8] which explains that adults are responsible for the structure of a meal (what is served, where, and when) and that children are always responsible for their bodies (if and how much they will eat). A meal schedule for children with food *offered* every two to three hours helps them learn to develop internal cues for being hungry and full.[9]

2. Access to sleep as needed (varies by age)

My child is currently cutting a tooth, so he went from sleeping mostly through the night to waking up two to three times crying, wanting to nurse back to sleep. The last couple of days I've woken up under-resourced, starting my day tired. We had a pretty standard morning with typical behaviors, but every little thing felt like a big thing. I was snappy and impatient. I didn't have the energy to cope with his humanness because I was already treading water, trying to stay afloat through my exhaustion. When we don't have access to the sleep our bodies need, accessing regulation is *really* hard. We can proactively support our regulation by getting as much sleep as possible in a given season. Pro tip: If you're in a season with minimal sleep—such as pregnancy insomnia, newborn care, or professional and educational obligations that drain your resting time—reduce your expectations of the day-to-day as much as you can. It won't always be like this; it's an exhausting season that is temporary.

3. Brain break

We've all been there—a draining morning with big emotions from all the tiny humans, a domino effect of meltdowns going from one human to another, or an extraordinarily stressful start to the workday.

When this happens, it helps to take a brain break. Brain breaks are when we reduce the stimuli around us—decreasing light, sound, and touch. This gives our nervous system a break from scanning the environment to try and keep us safe. This could be lying in a dark room, looking up at the sky, taking a bath, closing your eyes and breathing, turning down the lights and turning off background noise such as music or a TV, playing a whisper game with kids, or humming as you rock a child to sleep.

What would it look like to schedule two five-minute brain breaks in a day? Maybe at the start of nap time or in the transition from work to parenting? As a teacher, I once had a parent who would drive up, park, and sit in her car for five minutes before coming in to pick up her little one. She would sit phone-free, close her eyes, and take a brain break. Pause and think about your day—where can you build in two brain breaks?

4. Big body play

You know when you start to feel stir crazy? Whether it's during that long car ride or a meeting that's lasting forever and you just need to move your body. Or you see it in the child who cannot stop climbing your body or jumping off the things around them. There's actually a scientific explanation for that: Our bodies need proprioceptive input (aka big body play; see page 46 for a list of examples) every ninety minutes to two hours. Sometimes it's a short sensory "snack," such as a twenty-second hug, and other times it's a longer activity, such as going for a run. We think of these longer play sessions as sensory "meals" rather than "snacks"—just like we stay ahead of the hangries, we stay ahead of the body going stir crazy.

You don't have to carve out time for proprioceptive input, but instead you can build those moments with a child into your day. "I wonder how many frog jumps it will take to get from here to the door to go outside." "Oh no! The floor is hot lava. How can we get to the kitchen?" "Let's put on your favorite song. I wonder if we can clean up the toys before it ends. Ready, set, go!" What are two big body play activities you can incorporate into your day? What are two big body play activities a child can do?

5. Movement and balance practice

"When Khalil comes home from school, he's hanging upside down off the couch during his screen time. Is there something I should do to help him?" a parent messaged. Khalil is doing exactly what his body needs at that moment, recharging his vestibular system (see page 47 for a list of examples). This is the system responsible for movement and balance. As my toddler gets sleepy, he gets clumsy. We tracked his bumps and falls to find out that he's six times more likely to fall within an hour of nap or bed time. *Six times*. Isn't that bonkers? As his battery gets closer to empty, his vestibular system needs support. Vestibular input can last awhile in the body, generally four to eight hours, but every human is unique. Some will need more and some less. What are two activities you can incorporate into your day? What are two activities a child can do?

You can visit www.seedandsew.org/more for more ways to recharge the brain. All five of these ways are unique to the individual. I have a low vestibular sense, so I used to trip often. Going upside down in yoga was my favorite thing for about ten years. I didn't know it at the time, but I probably loved it because I was getting a lot of information about where my head was in relation to the rest of my body. These days, I still trip sometimes but a lot less than I used to. One person can spin on a merry-go-round for ten minutes and feel great, while another person feels nauseous after one minute. One person can wear a baby all day and have their cup filled, while another person will feel touched out after twenty minutes. And, likewise, one baby will feel good being worn all day and another will squirm to get down after a few minutes. The amount of food, rest, and length of brain breaks that one body needs is different than that of another. It takes trial and error to learn what works best for you or your child. My occupational therapist (OT) friend Lori Goodrich introduced me to a saying from OT Regi Boehme: "If you try, it's assessment, and if it works, it's intervention." We are detectives working to figure out how to best recharge our battery as well as our children's throughout the day, and we all have a slightly different plug.

We are meant to cycle through different experiences, and it's natural to cycle through different states of regulation. Being regulated means your nervous system is at ease; it feels safe and is thus able to control how calm and/or alert you are. Dysregulation can show up in many forms, which we will explore in more depth in Part II. You can proactively give yourself and your children a chance to recharge your batteries all day long. This will help you have greater success at accessing tools in moments of dysregulation when your nervous system is overwhelmed—your battery is depleted—but it will not prevent dysregulation altogether. There is not one human on the planet who is regulated and uses their problem-solving, rational thinking brain (prefrontal cortex) all the time. That isn't the goal. When a child screams in my face or throws something across the room, my insides aren't chill. I'm not completely regulated, like "Oh, this is totally fine. I feel calm and serene." I'm not supposed to be. Also, it's normal for a child to get frustrated as they're trying to figure out something tricky, such as how in the world to get those two Legos to stick together. Since we can't expect them to calmly navigate the process, what do we do in the moment? How do we help keep them from spiraling out of control?

Triangle of Growth

This morning at childcare drop-off, my little guy was sad to say goodbye. He was sobbing and was pulled off my body by the provider he adores as he reached and cried for me. She acknowledged his experience by saying,

"It's sad to say goodbye to Mama." And then she went right into supporting his body with regulation. She started squeezing his arms gently from the shoulder down to the hand and then repeating it again and again as she softly hummed a tune. He stayed in that exact place as she went through this process. After about five minutes, he stopped crying, and she asked if he wanted a hug. He grabbed his beloved slothy stuffed animal and snuggled into her. She continued to hum as she held him. When he sat up, she validated his experience again and let him know it makes sense to feel sad.

Just because he stopped expressing doesn't mean he stopped feeling. She was working her way up the Triangle of Growth.

Triangle of Growth

Language

Emotional Regulation

Sensory Regulation

Imagine you are angry at your partner, your heart is pumping fast, fists tight, shoulders are up to your ears, voice shaky and snappy. My friend calls this her vortex, where she doesn't feel in control of the words coming out of her mouth, but her body takes over and tries to suck the other person down with her. When she is able to take space and calm the physical reaction, it allows her to acknowledge the emotion, put words to her feelings, and navigate conversation with the other party involved. It doesn't take away the anger, but it brings her brain back in control when her body had previously been in the driver's seat.

Sensory (nervous system) regulation and emotional regulation are different. That out-of-control, my-body-is-calling-the-shots feeling stems from the nervous system. In those moments, when children are reacting and spiraling, not able to access emotional regulation, we have two choices: we can dig in our heels and oppose them as they further spiral out of control, or we can connect, help them calm down (co-regulate), and help them feel safe so they can access emotional regulation and communication skills. In his book *Self-Reg: How to Help Your Child (and You) Break the Stress Cycle and Successfully Engage with Life*, Stuart Shanker says, "We are designed to draw energy from one another and restore energy through one another."[10]

At drop-off, my little guy knew he was safe and would have fun at school. He knew that I would be back at the end of the day. But he couldn't talk about his emotions yet. He wasn't able to move through the feelings yet. His body was in the driver's seat of his brain. The teacher helped his logical thinking brain come back online by giving him those squeezes, humming, and snuggling. As his body exhaled that big dose of adrenaline, he could engage in conversation with her and navigate the next steps of being in the emotion without being overwhelmed by it.

Mara, twenty-two months old, was building with Magna-Tiles when someone bumped into the table and her creation crashed. She let out a loud cry and was melting down. I noticed this happen, paused to take a deep breath, and was ready to have the perfect, most supportive response. I knelt down beside her to support her when she slapped me across the face. *Whoa.* My body filled with cortisol, and I went into my amygdala (survival or reactive brain) and was in full-on fight mode. I looked at her, and while I wanted to say and do so many things in that moment, I regulated enough to say the kindest thing I could: "I'm going to the bathroom. I will be right back." I knew that I needed to regulate my nervous system before I could support her regulation and processing. Since she was physically safe, I walked away to take deep breaths, repeating to myself, "Her body is out of control. She needs support." I returned to her a couple of minutes later and focused on the Triangle of Growth. Sensory systems first. "I won't let you hit me." I held her hands as I continued, "Oh man, you were working so hard on that castle, and it crashed. That's so frustrating." [*Pause.*] "Let's do ten big jumps!" She grabbed my hands and we jumped together, counting each one as we went. By the end of jumping, she was no longer crying. She was moving from her body to her brain. "It's so frustrating when you're working hard on something, and it gets ruined. You can take your time to feel frustrated. I'm here if you want to snuggle or read a book." [*Pause.*] She looked at me, went and grabbed a book, and came back to my lap. We read together and I felt her physically exhale as her body was curled up in mine. "Would you like to try building again or are you feeling all done with Magna-Tiles for now?" She signed "All done" and went off to the play kitchen.

After she'd been playing in the kitchen for about fifteen minutes, I popped over to play with her. While playing, I pretended to get frustrated as I was trying to open a container. "Ugh, I'm soooo frustrated! I want to open it and it's stuck!" [*Pause.*] "My voice is loud, and my face is scrunched. *Ugh!* I really want to hit. I'm going to jump!" Then I jumped like a frog five times. "Phew, that feels better. Now I can ask for help. Mara, can you help me open this? It's stuck!" She leaned over and patted my back with her hand. Then she grabbed the container and opened it with a proud smile.

Emotional regulation and processing were possible for Mara only after first regulating her nervous system. The big jumps were a tool for sensory regulation. We can often learn during proactive sensory meals and snacks what types of activities can be helpful for kiddos in the moment of dysregulation. Once Mara had emotionally regulated and processed, then, and only then, was she able to tell me she was all done, accessing her whole brain for communication and problem solving. Then, and only then, was she ready to learn about her reactive behavior versus what she could do next time. She knows she isn't supposed to hit me. She doesn't want to hit me. Just like I don't want to yell at people, and sometimes I do. Sometimes our bodies override our brains because learning how to find the pause between initial reaction and secondary response is a skill to hone. It doesn't just develop. We are helping Mara build a new skill through our response to her reaction and reinforcing it through shame-free role play thereafter.

Have you ever felt out of control and said or done something you regret? Welcome to the human experience! What's your tendency in these situations? Maybe you can hear the words shouting out of your mouth and it feels like there is nothing you can do to stop them. Or perhaps you pack your bags and leave? Maybe you shut down, closing yourself off from connection. Or maybe you backtrack, suppress your needs, and go into super people-pleaser mode? As you get to know the ways your nervous system reacts, we can dive deeper together into what to do next. Remember, our initial reaction is often unconscious. We can hone the skill of noticing the initial reaction and then finding the pause for our secondary response to be intentional.

Chapter 4

The Collaborative Emotion Processing Method

After reading Chapter 1, you became 100 percent emotionally intelligent, right? And if you read it to the kids, they will be, too? Not so much.

Simply telling people information, no matter their age, usually doesn't change their behavior. When I was struggling in my first marriage, I thought that doing some reading on mindfulness and meditation would solve the problem. I would finish a chapter or a book and feel ready to be the partner she needed, the partner I wanted to be. But as soon as I started interacting with my partner, I was right back in my familiar, old patterns.

Reading alone didn't work because I wasn't *practicing* anything. It was only after lots of therapy, two yoga teacher trainings, and a robust self-care routine that I even *started* to feel my behavior lining up with my values in the context of an intimate relationship. For better or worse, this was years after my first marriage ended. All the work that I did, and continue to do, in community and in therapy to transform my thought processes, my actions and reactions, has been crucial to my emotional intelligence (EI) development.

Memorization is not enough to change human behavior, to align our actions with our vision of who we want to be, who we envision our children will become. Getting information is one part of learning, but there's a lot more to it. If we want to develop emotional intelligence skills—our own and children's—we need a method that honors how humans learn. This method is Collaborative Emotion Processing, and we designed it for humans to learn *with each other* and *through experience*.

What Is Teaching?

Before you dive in, let's take a moment to explore how humans learn, and how to effectively teach new skills. There are four things we do to teach, according to Melvin Konner in *The Evolution of Childhood: Relationships, Emotion, Mind.*[1]

1. Provide intentional modeling

Children learn a lot by watching and listening. David was a preschooler in my class one year whose parents were in the field of psychology. My teaching team noticed that David was affectionately squeezing his friends all the time, but it was too tight for them, and they pushed him away. We brought this up to David's parents so that we could figure out how to handle it together. A couple of days later as David's dad was saying goodbye to him at drop-off, he squeezed David so tight that David squirmed and pushed his dad away. As if a light bulb had turned on, David's dad remarked, "I guess that's why he does that!"

Has your child or student ever "used" your own phrases against you? Have you ever yelled, "Stop yelling!" to a child who is yelling? It is rare for a child to learn to "do what I say, not what I do." Children learn to do what we do. When adults and other children teach this way, intentionally or unconsciously, it's called modeling.

The first year I had a childcare program in my home, I was the only adult with the children all day. I quickly started to hear my own words and phrases bounced back at me—and they didn't always sound good! All of a sudden, I was able to hear myself saying, "I'm not going to . . . until you . . ." because the children were using this phrase, this tactic, with me. I realized I needed to change my phrasing, and my tactics, to reflect the way I wanted to be spoken to if I wanted the children to change how they were speaking to me. I made some changes, and within a few weeks, I was pleased with the way we were talking to each other.

When you talk to children, or to the adults in your life in the presence of children, it's way more likely you'll get the language and behavior you're looking for if you intentionally model it. Even when you think they're too young to understand, they are always paying attention!

Is there a phrase you hear falling out of your mouth often that you'd like to let go of? Can you remember a time when you really liked the way someone spoke to you when you were feeling something, or they needed to make a request? If answers to these questions are flowing freely right now, then write them down so that you can refer to them later. If nothing is coming to you right now, that's okay, too. Make an intention to listen to yourself in the coming weeks. Later on, we'll walk you through making the changes you want to make.

It's worth noting that some children and adults don't learn much through modeling. They need more explicit teaching strategies, strategies that actually benefit everyone. We'll be talking about both in Part II.

2. Give active encouragement

My mom taught me how to drive a car with a manual transmission. Her tone of voice was calm and positive, and her body language—looking to make sure my feet were on the pedals and hand on the shifter—suggested she was paying attention to what I was doing. This behavior gave me the impression she thought I could do it. When I made an awful sound with the gears, cringing, she kept encouraging me by letting me know it was okay, that that happens when anyone is learning to drive with a standard shift, and to try again.

3. Exaggerate to make the qualities of the task more obvious

I have a very distinct memory from first grade of the teacher demonstrating how to carry scissors safely. She would hold up the scissors and point to the sharp parts. Then she would close the scissors, and slowly wrap one hand around the closed blades. Next she would dramatically lower her arm, so the scissor handles were pointing down, emphasizing the downwardness by bouncing her hand up and down a couple times. Then she would walk slowly and pretend to trip, to further demonstrate why this was the safest way to carry scissors.

4. Break down the task to clarify the steps to completion

When I teach three-year-olds how to turn their jacket sleeves right side out, I use a story to break down the steps. It goes, "Pretend your arm is a snake—here is the mouth [*I open and close my hand like a mouth*]. The snake is hungry, so here it goes down the garden hole [*holding up the entrance to the sleeve and sticking my arm through . . . maybe even hissing if they're into the story*]. Now the snake opens its mouth [*on the other end of the sleeve my hand is out, and I open my hand wide*] and takes a bite [*quickly closing my hand around the end of the sleeve*]! Then holding on tight, the snake comes back out of the garden hole! Ta-da!" The sleeve is now right side out and I walk them through the steps to do the second sleeve themselves.

Teaching works only when someone is *ready* to learn the new skill; in other words, they have the foundational skills, and they feel emotionally safe. You can't teach someone to draw if they don't yet know how to hold a pencil. However, if they already know how to use a pencil to make scribbles, with teaching they will be ready to learn how to make a purposeful mark.

Learning happens when someone is emotionally engaged in a safe way and/or when they are calm.[2] This is when they can best activate their rational thinking brain (prefrontal cortex). Learning does not happen while their survival brain (amygdala) is in the driver's seat and they are experiencing a fight/flight/freeze/fawn response.

When Teddy is flailing on the floor of the grocery store, it isn't a teaching moment. He isn't ready to learn and cannot take in our words and concepts. His body is driving, and our goal is to get his brain back online, by helping him feel physically and emotionally safe first.

Sometimes our reaction in moments like these has less to do with effectively teaching our child and more to do with our insecurities around what the other children or adults are thinking about us. But saying "It's not okay to hit" to the flailing child—just so that the other kids or the other parents won't think we condone hitting—doesn't actually teach Teddy not to hit. Teddy likely knows you don't want him to hit. In fact, it's not the knowledge that "hitting is not okay" that helps a child stop hitting.

So what should you do when Teddy is melting down? When children do not feel safe, their amygdala is activated, and they instinctually prioritize protecting themselves over learning or using their rational thinking to motivate their behavior. In these moments we need to soothe. We can teach later. When people feel safe, their rational thinking brain (prefrontal cortex) is accessible, and they are ready to learn. They can take in new ideas, hear feedback, reflect, and problem-solve. This is a great time to teach.

It's not the knowledge that "hitting is not okay" that helps a child stop hitting.

In Chapter 5, we'll explore what it looks like when a child's amygdala is in the driver's seat and when the prefrontal cortex is online—in other words, how to know whether it's time to soothe or time to teach—and provide strategies that *do* help a child learn to stop challenging behaviors.

If someone is *not ready* to learn, they will lose interest and/or get frustrated. It's possible to get a child's attention with lights or prizes before they're truly ready to learn, but this comes with a risk of rote memorization rather than true comprehension, without the ability to apply what's learned out of context. Additionally, this may result in a child who is constantly looking for a prize instead of hanging on to the intrinsic motivation for learning that children enter the world with.

What's Going On in the Brain?

When your brain notices something through your senses (a stimulus), neurons in the brain send messages to other neurons, making a series of connections as a response. A repeated series of connections in the brain creates neural pathways. A neural pathway gets stronger each time the stimulus-response pattern repeats.

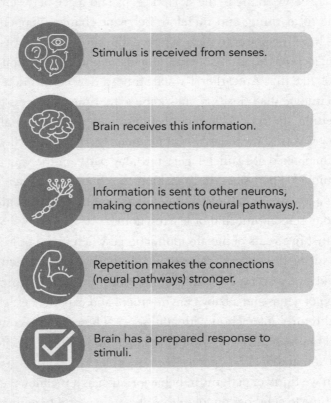

Stimulus is received from senses.

Brain receives this information.

Information is sent to other neurons, making connections (neural pathways).

Repetition makes the connections (neural pathways) stronger.

Brain has a prepared response to stimuli.

For example, let's say your little one has a meltdown when it's time to get ready for school every day. The stimulus could be the phrase you use to signal it's time, such as: "Time to go to school. Turn off the TV and get your shoes on!" Maybe it's been a few weeks and the child has learned that if they don't turn off the TV, you'll ask two more times before you come in to turn the TV off yourself. Then they scream and flail and you pay all kinds of attention to them by telling them what to do and then eventually you get the shoes, pick up the child, and dump everyone and everything into the car. The pathways for both of you are pretty strong since it's been a few weeks of the same situation on repeat.

When learning, we make neural pathways with these connections. When the neurons connect, there's a little electrical burst called a synapse in the space between them, the synaptic gap. The space between is where the magic of learning, and therefore behavior change, happens—that's where we have the power to make a new pathway.

When it comes to getting out the door for school, a new neural pathway might look like this: An earlier TV start time, a new connection-oriented phrase to initiate the transition, and some extra time to process emotions before getting shoes on. The connection-oriented phrase might sound like: "How is your show today? [*Wait for an answer.*] I wonder if you'll tell me what happened at Daniel Tiger's birthday party on the way to school this morning?" Then start the transition to school *at least* ten minutes earlier for a few weeks so there is time to process emotions that are related to the end of screen time and/or leaving home.

The first five years of life are foundational when it comes to learning because, during this period, "more than 1 million new neural connections are formed every second. Neural connections are formed through the interaction of genes and a baby's environment and experiences, especially 'serve and return' interaction with adults. . . . These are the connections that build brain architecture—the foundation upon which all later learning, behavior, and health depends."[3]

When we think of patterns in behavior, such as a meltdown every day when it's time to get shoes on for school, it can be useful to remember that neural pathways are at the root. The good news is that you can change patterns. Keep in mind that it's actually harder for you to change patterns in *your* behavior with children than it is for the children to change their patterns *in response* to your behavior. "The brain's capacity for change decreases with age. The brain is most flexible, or 'plastic,' early in life to accommodate a wide range of environments and interactions, but as the maturing brain becomes more specialized to assume more complex functions, it is less capable of reorganizing and adapting to new or unexpected challenges." The brain's ability to change peaks in the first year of life and goes down notably after age five.[4] In my experience, when adults are consistent with their new behaviors, children's start to change in about two weeks—sometimes after a period of resistance. When they don't, there might be something else going on developmentally. Connect with your child's pediatrician to assemble your village of support.

Why Is It Called Collaborative Emotion Processing (CEP)?

The Collaborative Emotion Processing method is based on how humans learn. Its name makes the connection between the what and the how.

The word "collaborative" leads us to the *way* that we learn self-awareness, self-regulation, empathy, motivation, and social skills. Etymologically, "collaborate" comes from the Latin meaning "to labor together."[5] This method is "collaborative" because of our innate desire to connect with other humans, and because no one ever developed emotional intelligence sitting alone on a mountaintop. Working together benefits our bodies and minds. For example, in the documentary *Happy*, neuroscientist Read Montague explains that humans release the motivation/reward hormone (dopamine) when they put their individual desires aside in the interest of cooperation that serves the group.[6]

The second word, "emotion," refers to what we're paying attention to and what we all have in common—we all feel stuff. The last word, "processing," is what we're *doing*. Our definition of emotion processing is one's ability to experience and fully integrate emotions.

Why the CEP Wheel?

Prior to Collaborative Emotion Processing (CEP) there wasn't a method that encompassed both the adult's experience and the child's. After combing through research, approaches, and methods in social-emotional learning, we identified the gaps and created the CEP method. We broke it down into five components in order to highlight its comprehensiveness. Remember that one of the ways we teach is to "break it down so the steps to completion are clearer"? That was our intention when we created the CEP Wheel:

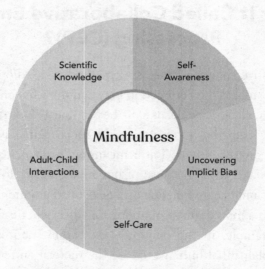

Collaborative Emotion Processing and this chart developed by Lauren Stauble and Alyssa Blask Campbell (original 2017, updated 2018).

Notice that "adult-child interactions" is just one of the five components. That's because there is a lot we can do as adults for our own development that positively impacts our interactions with children. It's one thing to scroll through social media or tune in to a podcast about how to interact with a child, and a whole other ball game to be able to recall those tools and language in the moment. Focusing solely on the child neglects the incredible importance of the adults who are raising the child.

Are you wondering about "mindfulness" in the hub? Mindfulness guides our exploration and practice of the five components.

The visual design, a wheel, is a nod to modern interpretations of yoga and the roots of mindfulness. It's not a ladder because when we metaphorically climb the rungs of a ladder, it takes us away from living fully—up and out of our humanness and away from our loved ones. When we climb the spokes of a wheel, it helps us learn to live fully here on the ground—to be comfortable staying in our human bodies and minds, and with each other.

Five Phases of Emotion Processing

Another way we break CEP down into meaningful steps is through the Phases of Emotion Processing. These are the five steps we navigate to process emotions. We will dive deep into them in Part II to learn how to help children process emotions, but as with all things CEP, it starts with us adults. So let's dive in.

The phases function as steps to guide us through big emotions. They also provide an overview of where we are in our emotion processing development over time, and give us a map of the skills we can help ourselves and our children develop in order to process emotions with a greater sense of agency. They help the supportive adult answer the question "What can I teach right now that the child might be ready for?" You'll know you've processed emotions when you feel better afterward, you have more clarity about what happened, and you have more clarity about yourself.

Phase 1: Allowing one's emotions to exist

This first step—**allowing one's emotions to exist** and to be seen—is also the first phase of emotion processing. It is easy to mistake a self-regulated or emotionally regulated person for someone who has processed emotions. Likewise, someone who has suppressed their emotions can be easily

Five Phases of Emotion Processing

1. **Allowing one's emotions to exist**
   Do I resist the urge to distract or suppress?
2. **Recognizing the perceived emotion: associating symbols with feelings**
   Do I associate words (happy, sad, disappointed, etc.) with my feelings or physiological responses to situations, and use them (spoken or in sign language)?
3. **Feeling secure in experiencing a range of emotions over time**
   Do I experience a full range of emotions? Do I recognize each emotion as temporary and one of many possible emotions that I will feel over time?
4. **Seeking support through coping strategies**
   Where do I land on the spectrum of mechanisms versus strategies?
5. **Moving on: solving the problem or letting it go**
   Do I go back to try again? Do I engage in a new experience?

Phases identified by Lauren Stauble and Alyssa Blask Campbell for Collaborative Emotion Processing (original 2017, updated 2019).

mistaken as self-regulated or emotionally regulated. Just because you're regulated doesn't mean you've processed emotions. Emotion processing is one's ability to experience and integrate emotions.

Phase 2: Recognizing the perceived emotion

Once you've allowed your emotions to exist, you can match them up with a symbol: a word, a gesture, or a picture.

Remember the story in Chapter 3 about a friend showing up with puffy, red eyes? In order to make sense of what was going on, your brain relied on clues from the world around you (sensory input) and your emotion concepts (past experience). You noticed puffy, red eyes (sensory input) and unconsciously mapped this experience with your previous emotion experiences. Your brain created a story about what was happening in an effort to understand the situation. These feelings could be visceral and/or abstract, but it's possible words popped up in your thoughts, because humans use symbols—words, gestures, pictures—to communicate. Perhaps the word "worried" popped up for you. You might even use this symbol to communicate with your friend: "I'm so worried! What happened? Are you okay?"

This is the second phase: **recognizing the perceived emotion: associating symbols with feelings**. In Phase 2, we have an opportunity for connection, to feel seen and understood. Whether it's recognizing our emotion for ourselves (or those parts of us driving the bus at the time), or someone else seeing us in that moment and asking how we are feeling, this recognition helps the nervous system feel safe.

Phase 3: Feeling secure in experiencing a range of emotions over time

Once we're comfortable in Phases 1 and 2, we start to explore emotions as they arise, and we make sense of them in the context of our lives.

A couple of years ago, I became aware that I had a pattern of experiencing big feelings seemingly out of nowhere. I just didn't detect them until they were impossible to ignore. In situations like this, think of self-awareness as a volcano. We want to notice the bubbling *before* the explosion. It's about noticing and tuning into what's happening inside our bodies and minds. Because I was paying attention, and withholding judgment as often as possible, I started to notice when I "turned off" warning signs, such as my jaw getting tight, an urge to look at my phone, racing thoughts, or even my husband asking me thoughtfully, "Are you okay?" Therapy was a helpful tool for me in learning to notice these "bubbling up" signs and responding to them with coping strategies, preventing eruption. (We'll cover coping strategies in Phase 4.)

When you get that call from childcare. When your mom makes that comment about your parenting. When that car cuts you off in traffic. When your child dumps the water outside of the tub. When your boss hands you a deadline that falls right after your vacation. What is happening inside your body in response? Where do you feel it? What is the quality of your thoughts?

Once we have a toolbox for recognizing what's happening inside and what we are feeling, then we can observe the habits and patterns we have in place and decide if they are serving us. When we know how to do this for ourselves, we can teach children to notice these signs, too.

Jaxson was hitting and kicking a lot at school. To support Jaxson in developing new tools for expressing his emotions, we began by helping him notice what was happening in his body before the explosion. "Your shoulders are up to your ears! Your fists are so tight! Your voice is loud! You sound frustrated!" Then we would pop in and help his body feel safe in order to calm before diving into next steps (we will explain these steps in greater detail in Part II).

After a couple months of focusing on building his body awareness, Jaxson started to yell, "MY SHOULDERS ARE UP TO MY EARS! MY FISTS ARE TIGHT! MY VOICE IS LOUD! I FEEL FRUSTRATED!" We cannot regulate what we are not aware of. The first step in helping Jaxson make a choice outside of hitting or kicking was to help him notice what things felt like in his body when emotions were building.

This is an example of interoception, which is one of the body's eight sensory systems. It's a key one for emotions in that it helps us build self-awareness. When I say, "I have butterflies in my stomach," you might know that feeling and understand that I'm feeling nervous or excited. What if we could identify what's happening inside our bodies for more emotions? What if we knew what disappointment or embarrassment felt like? How rad would it be to notice sadness or anger before it became all-consuming?

When we pause and pay attention to emotional expression—in ourselves or others—resistance stops and seeing happens. At the core of every person, there is an intrinsic desire to see and be seen, and these moments of expression are an opportunity to offer that gift. So why is it so hard for us to do that? Why is it that at times we feel inconvenienced by someone else's emotions? Why do we sometimes feel angry, or anxious, or sad when others express emotions? Implicit bias and attachment style influence how our emotions get tangled up with others', so we'll cover those next. In Chapter 6, we'll talk about how our expectations can play a role, too.

Our brains are designed to reflect others' emotions, but it doesn't mean we stop there. In fact, we need this function in order to feel empathy, "to feel *with* people," as Brené Brown says. We have the power to "change the brain," which means that we get to choose how to proceed when faced with someone else's emotions. Just because we have a pattern or habit now doesn't mean that we're stuck with it. Over time, and with practice, we will begin to feel secure in feeling stuff. We will begin to soften our resistance to tricky emotions as we understand that emotions are temporary. What you're feeling at any given moment is one of many emotions that you will feel over time. We begin to understand the words of Lisa Feldman Barrett, which we shared in Chapter 3: "You are not at the mercy of emotions that arise unbidden to control your behavior. You are an architect of these experiences. Your river of feelings might feel like it's flowing over you, but actually you're the source of the river."

This is the third phase of emotion processing: **feeling secure in experiencing a range of emotions over time**. Emotions are temporary, so with practice, we can grow more comfortable, or at least less uncomfortable, for long enough to explore the moments that bring them up, the way we construct them, and what we do with them.

Phase 4: Seeking support through coping strategies

No matter where you're starting from—learning to notice when you feel stuff, learning to navigate your reactions to other people feeling stuff—it can be comforting to remember that emotion processing concepts are relatively new to the general public in the United States. It's rare to meet an adult whose primary caregivers named and validated emotions and then helped them move on. For most of us, learning to feel comfortable with emotions, to name and validate them, plus moving on, takes time. Tara Brach teaches, "There is only one way to free ourselves from limiting beliefs and that is bringing full presence to the raw feelings that drive them. Yet contacting these feelings—the shame, the fear, the grief—can be painfully difficult, even intolerable. That is why we can spend years or decades reacting to the world out of our beliefs rather than investigating their emotional roots."[7]

Many people may seek a therapist or counselor for support through the mindfulness and self-awareness process. Others prefer to grow in the company of a few very close friends, and still others may desire a social context, such as a regular meeting group. This is a personal process. We believe in the power of processing collaboratively because shame breeds in secrecy and silence. Healing and growth flourish with vulnerability and safety. Self-care is a powerful tool to support your self-awareness development, and a key part of phase four of emotion processing: **Seeking support through coping strategies**.

Coping *strategies* are actions or nonactions you can take that support you as you process your emotions, and they make up the contents of your Coping Strategies Toolbox. They are essential for the fourth phase of emotion processing. Children have a Coping Strategies Toolbox, too, which we'll dive into in Part II. Coping strategies can and should be utilized in a variety of scenarios.

Phase 5: Moving on: solving the problem or letting it go

With a sturdy self-care practice and an openness to the first four emotion processing phases, you'll be able to move through the last phase—**moving on: solving the problem or letting it go**. It's surprisingly simple to move through this phase if you've done the work that comes before it. When we are regulated and have returned to having a safe, calm nervous system, we can see a clearer picture. We can get our brain back into the driver's seat, and navigate conflict resolution, problem solving, and repair.

This is the phase where owning our mistakes happens and where we are truly ready to listen to someone else, take in their perspective, experience empathy, and figure out what the next steps are. In Phase 5, we are in our rational thinking, problem-solving brain. If you find yourself getting defensive or escalating inside, those are signs that you may need more time in the other phases; you might not be ready for Phase 5 yet, and that's okay.

Now that we've covered all the phases, where do you think you are in your development? In these phases? Are you in a different phase when you're with your child than you are when you're with your best friend, or at work, or with your family of origin? Maybe you experience the phases differently with different emotions. It might be easier to move through the phases in sadness than in fear or with embarrassment than with disappointment. Wherever you are today in any of these contexts is the right place to *start*.

Mindfulness and the Five Components of CEP

"The ocean doesn't say, 'If only I could get rid of all this messy seaweed and all these fish, I could get down to being the ocean.'"[8] This metaphor, explained by my yoga teacher, Patty Townsend, distinctly captures what I've learned about mindfulness over the last twenty-four years. Sometimes people, including myself at the beginning, confuse mindfulness with a feeling of peacefulness. It's easier to feel peaceful when you're doing something that nourishes you. For me, looking out from the peak of a mountain is nourishing and I usually feel peaceful when I'm up there. But mindfulness includes a lot more than peacefulness. When you feel calm, serene, or peaceful, please pay attention to these feelings.

But also pay attention to the "messy seaweed and all these fish." Some feelings are less comfortable. Disappointment, confusion, anger are the seaweed and fish in my otherwise clear waters. What feelings are you more likely to pay attention to? Which ones do you avoid? Another way to explore that second question would be to ask, "Which feelings do I never feel?" because sometimes we are so expert at avoiding challenging feelings that we push them away before we're conscious they were ever there. It's worth mentioning that some people's *un*comfortable feelings are the ones we're "supposed" to enjoy, such as happiness and excitement.

No matter which feelings are your seaweed and fish, many of us unconsciously try to escape uncomfortable feelings and avoid paying attention to them. For better or worse, when we avoid them, it doesn't make them go away; it just makes them go unaddressed. Susan David teaches the value of paying attention to a range of emotions: "Our contract with life is a contract that is brokered with fragility, and with sadness, and with anxiety. And if we're going to authentically and meaningfully be in this world, we cannot focus on one dimension of life and expect that focusing on that dimension is going to then give us a well-rounded life."[9] With mindfulness we learn to see, and then tolerate *all* feelings. This helps us show up for ourselves and children in more fulfilling ways.

The roots of mindfulness are thought to have originated during or before ancient times in many places and cultures around the world. Perhaps the most commonly associated place and time is East Asia as far back as 3000 to 1900 BCE, where it was developed as a spiritual practice in Buddhism as a way to seek enlightenment and liberation from human suffering.[10] Over the last four thousand years or so, we've learned that practicing mindfulness is versatile, leading to benefits in mental and physical health across cultures, religions, and ages. A quick online search for "mindfulness" will produce a plethora of definitions and explanations, which reflect a range of perspectives. One of my favorites is from global spiritual leader, poet, and peace activist Thích Nhất Hạnh: "keeping one's consciousness alive to the present reality."[11]

Mindfulness can be practiced while you are doing something or nothing. It's awareness that you can experience as often as you choose to. You can practice mindfulness while you are folding laundry, on your way to work, caring for children, eating lunch, etc. Ultimately you can practice mindfulness anytime you remember to.

One of the hardest parts of mindfulness can be nonjudgment. Especially when your values come into play. Do you find yourself triggered when your child or a child in your care hurts someone else in a seemingly intentional way? It seems safe to say that if you are reading this book, you believe that hurting others on purpose is not aligned with your values. We certainly want to teach children our values. But how do we untangle our judgment when someone doesn't live up to our values? Becoming aware of, or paying attention to, our feelings of anger, sadness, shame, or disappointment when a child hurts someone else is mindfulness. Changing those feelings is not.

Choosing to become aware of your own emotions and allowing yourself to feel them without judgment means you refrain from deciding that this situation and these feelings are good or bad, supposed to be happening or not. Instead we recognize that they just *are*. The goal is to practice mindfulness *before* you respond to the child. But that doesn't mean it's reasonable to expect this from yourself every time or even half the time.

Mindfulness is . . .	Mindfulness is not . . .
Noticing your feelings when they come up.	Expressing your feelings to the child as they come up.
Noticing if you judge the feeling as good or bad.	Trying to not have the feeling because you don't think you should be having it.
Allowing yourself to have the feeling even if you judged it.	Blaming someone else for "making" you feel this way.
Noticing any physiological manifestation of the feeling (increased heart rate, tension or tightening, impulse to hide or leave).	Feeling serene.
Focusing your attention on your breath.	Holding your breath.
Noticing when/if the feeling dissipates.	Holding on to the feeling in order to justify an action.

Lauren's teacher, Patty, offers compassionate guidance on this complex process: "We all feel these things. It can be a trap to feel one *shouldn't* be judgmental. So often one can't help it. The judgment isn't inherently the problem; the problem is believing it." This awareness allows you to acknowledge the presence of judgment and then choose something else. With practice we can learn to validate our own feelings and reduce the chances that we will suppress or reject them, inadvertently taking them out on the child. An adult-child interaction will be more productive and empathetic when it is mindful. Check out the "Mindfulness Is" table on page 73 to see some indicators that you are or are not exercising mindfulness when you're with children.

All this is true, and at the same time please keep in mind Patty's wisdom: "We are safe to feel our own judgment. We have a profound responsibility not to project it onto others. You could even go so far as to say that true compassion and love arise out of nonresistance to our own judgment. Freedom. A great place to relate from!"

In order to teach emotional intelligence skills to children, you'll need to be open to whatever you find within yourself—even when it's messy. Acceptance of *what is* is the only true place to begin. Self-awareness, from where we cultivate self-compassion, is a sturdy partner for your mindfulness practice and it's one of the five components of CEP. Daniel Goleman is credited with saying this about self-awareness: "Mindfulness is one method for enhancing this essential capacity—it trains our attention to notice subtle, but important signals, and to see thoughts as they arise rather than just being swept away by them."[12]

Surface acting is when we judge our emotions or an event as bad and as a result push aside, shove down, or suppress our own feelings and act as if everything's great. Researchers are studying the effects of surface acting on job dissatisfaction and burnout among people who work in human-services-related fields.[13] We know that teacher burnout is a real thing, and it seems probable that surface acting could be a contributing factor. When your profession is related to human services, pressure to prioritize other people's feelings or comfort over your own can be self-destructive when judgment is a thought pattern and part of the routine.

Mindfulness Resources

Want to take a deeper dive into mindfulness? The following are some additional resources for further exploration:

Exercises and/or Routines to Practice Mindfulness

- Therapy styles that explicitly support mindfulness development in the context of emotions: mindfulness-based, somatic, and dialectical behavior therapy
- Mindful eating: https://kripalu.org/
- Life drawing: community courses, or at home
- Yoga—make sure the style is alignment-based and right for your body
- Martial arts: Tai Chi, Chi Gong, etc.
- Journaling
- Meditation group
- Prayer

Websites

- Podcast with Patty Townsend: https://podcasts.apple.com /us/podcast/clarification-patience-and-the-ocean-with-patty -townsend/id1115392724?i=1000434171766
- Mark Bunn, Simple Wisdom for Conscious Living: https://markbunn.com.au/

Recommended Reading

- Anything by Thích Nhất Hạnh or Pema Chödrön
- *The Goodness of Rain*, by Ann Pelo
- *The Power of Now*, by Eckhart Tolle
- Poetry by Alice Walker, Mary Oliver, or Danna Faulds

Have you ever felt ashamed, confused, or mad in the presence of a parent, student, supervisor, or team member? Did you judge the feeling as good or bad? Did you judge the other person for *causing* you to feel that way? Did you judge yourself for having the feeling? When that happened, did you push it down and try to pretend that you were not having that feeling? Wish that you were not having the feeling? Maybe you outwardly dismissed your feelings with a positive statement or something neutralizing, such as "Oh, it's fine, don't worry!" Or did you pause and notice how you felt without making any judgments? This last approach is responding to your emotions with mindfulness.

Not surprisingly, initial studies suggest that mindfulness could be associated with less surface acting and more job satisfaction! This is not to suggest that you should share your emotional landscape with everyone at your workplace. It is a delicate process to be aware of your emotions and also to regulate and communicate with intention. A sturdy self-care routine will help you determine when and how to process those emotions so that you can maintain professionalism at work.

Self-Awareness

Daniel Goleman defines self-awareness as "the ability to monitor our inner world—our thoughts and feelings."[14] The "monitor" is in charge of deciding when to let go, what to work on, and what to celebrate, using thoughts and feelings as guides and tools. Think of the hall monitor in school. They see a student coming down the hallway, and their job is to pause the student, inquire about their destination, and then allow the student to continue on or make any adjustments to the student's path. They support the functioning of the whole system. In order to monitor your thoughts and feelings, you need to be paying attention to them. As you become aware of these thoughts and feelings, you first have to pause them, like the hall monitor does with the student, find out more about them, and then choose the most appropriate action or decide that nonaction is best.

What does self-awareness look like when it comes to emotions and children? In Chapter 2, we explained that our job is to demonstrate that we aren't afraid of children's feelings; we can handle them, instilling the self-confidence that they can, too. But what if you feel like you can't handle them? What if you *are* afraid of their feelings? What if you are afraid of your own? In your own childhood, you may have learned that emotions are scary. This is very common—many of us were raised in households and/or communities where big feelings weren't welcomed.

One year I had a teammate who felt I was "coddling" the children by acknowledging their emotions, setting them up for failure in kindergarten. As a child, she had been in an underfunded and under-resourced school system for kindergarten, not dissimilar from the system our students were bound to enter. Her priority was to teach the children to be ready for kindergarten in a way I had never considered because of my own more validating experience in school as a child. Her goal for the children was to help them stay out of the principal's office because it wouldn't be a safe place for them. She prioritized teaching them to sit quietly and be obedient. So when the children expressed sadness or disappointment with tears streaming down their faces, she would sternly tell them, "Stop crying." If they visibly expressed frustration or anger, they were expected to sit down next to her without playing for a long time. She predicted they would be most likely to succeed in this school system if they refrained from expressing emotions or needs, and by being able to look like they were paying attention.

In hindsight, it seems like our students were being taught the skill of surface acting. They were learning that expressing emotions and needs wasn't safe. The idea was that kids who learned to surface-act could survive the system because they wouldn't "need" anything from their future teachers and could steer clear of disciplinarians.

Do you identify with my teammate? If so, that is a fine place to start. Protecting our children is something we can all get behind. Then practice self-awareness: What would it be like to validate the urge to teach obedience? What would it be like to validate your childhood obedience as a way you protected yourself? Or maybe you were the kid who just couldn't figure out how to be obedient. What would it be like to validate your childhood effort or resistance to meeting the adults' expectations of you? Whew! Take a breath. Cultivating self-awareness about old patterns can be a tender process. It might be why self-awareness can be one of the most fertile places for transforming these hardwired patterns, especially coupled with mindfulness. It's okay if starting out, you're afraid of feelings. Becoming aware of this is an important step toward growing comfortable with feelings. Remember—we can change our brains and the goal is not perfection.

With the help of the monitor, self-awareness includes the ability to reflect and decide what to do differently next time. It is the process of recognizing when we've made a mistake and owning up to it and/or feeling motivated to make a change. Noticing what went well and celebrating personal strengths and accomplishments are also part of self-awareness.

We want to make the clear distinction between self-awareness, which includes the element of monitoring, and self-consciousness, which can be associated with anxiety and/or depression and the absence of monitoring. Self-consciousness will likely leave you fixated on your mistakes long after an event is over, and it adds to continued suffering. The "monitor" has gone to sleep, and your thoughts and feelings are running amuck in the hallways without guidance. One of our favorite social science researchers, Brené Brown, cautions us against neglecting this practice: "Without self-awareness and the ability to manage our emotions, we often unknowingly lead from hurt, not heart. Not only is this a huge energy suck for us and the people around us, it creates distrust, disengagement, and an eggshell culture."[15] True self-awareness is coupled with self-compassion and acceptance. Self-awareness requires us to accept that we will make mistakes, and that they are part of learning.

Years ago, I had agreed to do a reading for an event, and completely forgot that I'd made that commitment until the person who'd organized the event called to find out where I was and if I was okay. I was mortified that I had made that mistake, and I started to apologize profusely, expressing shame. The person interrupted me to say, "Beating yourself up does not serve either of us. It's okay!" Hearing those words changed my life. That moment was a catalyst for the shift in my own heart from self-consciousness to self-awareness. Often when I make a mistake, I still feel shame and resist accepting it, but I've given up the habit of holding on to it. Mindfulness allows me to notice the shame and resistance without judgment. Then, with self-awareness, I can work to accept that I made the mistake and learn from it. In the case of the calendar mishap, it took me years to develop reliable strategies for consistently remembering my commitments, but it was self-awareness that invited me to keep trying.

Do you allow yourself to feel emotions? How do you talk to yourself when emotions come up for you personally? Do you notice patterns in when you allow yourself to feel and what you allow yourself to feel in different circumstances or with different people? "Your feelings aren't a problem you're supposed to ignore. Or fix. They're feedback from your body and nervous system about how you're doing and what you need in life!" author of *Notes from Your Therapist*, Allyson Dinneen, reminds us.[16]

When we make the effort to be self-aware and mindful, we gain a sense of agency about how we engage with life. You'll start to feel the power to *decide* how to proceed rather than handing over the keys to your amygdala.

Self-awareness includes social skills awareness. The pause to notice our emotions in relationship to other adults' emotions, especially patterns, gives us an opportunity to make a choice about how to proceed. The key component that allows us to respond instead of react is that pause for self-awareness. Organizational psychologist Adam Grant tweeted, "What others say doesn't directly affect your emotions. Between their words and your feelings is your interpretation of their intention. Agency lies in the space between stimulus and response. A sign of emotional intelligence is recognizing your power to change your assumptions."[17] The ability to find the pause between initial reaction and secondary response is an incredible skill to hone and one built on self-awareness. We cannot find that pause, regulate, and respond with intention until we are aware of our reaction first.

This is especially true in the context of our adult relationships, specifically relationships with adults that we co-parent or co-teach with. Children learn how to be in relationships from the ones they observe. (Remember modeling?) We must develop self-awareness of our social skills in order to model behaviors and relationships with intention. Check out the resource box below to dive into tools for developing self-awareness, including addressing vulnerability, releasing what is no longer serving you, and finding ways to identify, name, and communicate emotions, needs, and behavior change requests in a productive, receivable way.

Self-Awareness Resources

Websites

- Atlas of Emotions: http://atlasofemotions.org/
- Center for Nonviolent Communication: https://www.cnvc.org/
- Find a Therapist: https://www.psychologytoday.com/us /therapists (use the filters for location, insurance, style)

Recommended Reading

- *The Four Agreements: A Practical Guide to Personal Freedom*, by Don Miguel Ruiz
- Anything by Brené Brown
- Anything by Pema Chödrön
- *Parenting from the Inside Out: How a Deeper Understanding Can Help You Raise Children Who Thrive*, by Daniel J. Siegel and Mary Hatzell

Self-Care

What is self-care? *Hint: It isn't necessarily a massage or a weekend getaway, but it can be.*

"Self-care" is pretty buzzwordy these days and it can often feel unattainable. Where are people finding the time for a thirty-minute run, or how did they find their village to call on to be able to tap out? In the first fifteen months of parenthood, I went out to dinner with a friend *once* and had *one* overnight away from my child (thanks, Nana). Both were stressful, as I'd planned all the logistics ahead of time and, ultimately, woke up at 3 a.m. engorged and leaking because, oh right, I'd completely forgotten I needed to pump. Neither of those big outings were practices of self-care for me.

One morning, after going to pee with a toddler playing around me in the bathroom and trying to poke my belly button, I watched my husband simply walk into the bathroom and close the door while my child sat on the other side of it saying "Dada" on repeat. "I'll be out in a minute when I'm all done," he replied. I wondered what it would be like to go to the bathroom without getting my belly button poked. And what my battery reserves might look like if I had little moments of recharging throughout the day.

Personal growth is often the result of our authentic commitment to self-care and coping strategies. As we move from coping mechanisms to coping strategies, it can be hard to tell them apart. Any strategy can quickly turn into a mechanism if it goes out of balance. And some mechanisms are so enjoyable that they can be confused with a strategy. For example, enjoying a glass of wine with your friend might be a coping strategy as you connect and recharge your battery. But reaching for the glass after an emotionally draining or emotionally charged day is a coping mechanism. Going to the gym for some cardio, yoga, or a lifting routine is a coping strategy. Going to the gym twice a day and working out until you feel sick or overexhausted after an emotionally draining or charged day is a coping mechanism.

If you're reading this book, then part or most of your work is caretaking. This means that in order to sustain the flow of care that you need and presumably want to provide, you'll have to make time to care for yourself. There are three types of strategies to do so:

Proactive: Life is emotionally demanding, so planning ahead to address your self-care needs on a weekly and/or daily basis is crucial to preventing burnout or overwhelm. In Chapter 3, we listed five ways to proactively recharge the nervous system before the red battery light comes on—these were examples of proactive self-care!

Responsive: What helps to calm you down when your amygdala is activated? The most accessible responsive strategy is breathing intentionally. It is physiologically impossible for your sympathetic nervous system to be active at the same time that you are belly breathing (directing your breath into your belly so your belly, rather than your chest, moves in and out with your inhale and exhale).

Supplemental: These are special occasions that fill your emotional cup, such as a retreat or vacation. They can also be something simple, such as cleaning out your closets and drawers or turning off your device for a certain amount of time. They need to fit your annual rather than weekly budget because they happen much less frequently than proactive and responsive strategies.

Proactive Self-Care

After the bathroom observation, I started really paying attention to my day. What was draining my battery from the minute I woke up? What was in my control? What wasn't? I started committing to one small act of self-care a day for a week. Just one recharge of the battery at a time that I would focus on. Mine began with breakfast. I promised myself that I would make my breakfast as I made my child's and would sit and eat with him rather than eat his leftovers and grab whatever was easiest to supplement that.

Next, I added pausing for five minutes of screen-free time after his nap started. I always had a to-do list and time felt too limited to pause, sit, and drink my coffee, but I made a promise to myself and kept it. Also, let's get real, have you ever reached the end of the to-do list? If so, please email me notes because mine feels endless—that to-do list will always exist, right? Learning to pause and recharge our batteries is key to being able to access everything in this book. Bonus: When we are intentional about taking care of ourselves throughout the day, we are showing kids how to proactively recharge their batteries, too.

This might be hard at first. It might go against how you were raised or the values you were taught in school. Many of us were conditioned to "power through" even when sick, resist showing neediness or asking for help, and put everyone else's needs above our own for fear of being rude or disliked. If you grew up this way, you may feel guilt, shame, abandonment, or embarrassment when you practice self-care as an adult. You can respond with compassion and create a new narrative. "It makes sense to feel scared of taking care of myself right now. I learned not to do so in childhood. It is safe for me to get my needs met now."

What follows is a list of some coping strategies that can help you recharge your batteries. This isn't meant to be exhaustive—experiment to see what works best for you.

Coping Strategies Toolbox

- Movement arts*
  (practicing, not performing:
  yoga, dance, hooping)
- Meditative exercise*
  (walking, long-distance
  running, swimming)
- Muscular exercise*
  (lifting, group classes)
- Therapy
- Counseling
- Walking or hiking in the
  woods*
- Meditation/prayer
- Writing arts expression
- Visual arts expression
- Musical expression
- Reading
- Cooking
- Sewing
- Breath work
- Belly breathing
- Looking at the sky
- Stepping outside
- Spiritual practice
- Alone time
- Screen-free time
- Talking to a friend or loved
  one
- Organizing your desk or
  closet
- Soothing music
- Spending quality time with
  your family

*Consult with your physician or primary care practitioner before starting a new exercise or physical activity routine.

Just as we want to lean on coping strategies, we want to be mindful that we aren't reaching for coping mechanisms instead of strategies. Below is a list of coping *mechanisms*. Mechanisms are unconscious habits. They are things that you use to pacify yourself during big emotions or to avoid them altogether. Caution: It is possible to overuse toolbox *strategies* so that they become *mechanisms*.

Coping Mechanisms

- Shopping
- Texting mindlessly
- Having a drink or using a substance
- Working extra
- Exercising excessively
- Planning excessively
- Cleaning or organizing compulsively
- Playing video games
- Scrolling social media
- Avoiding a discussion

Did you recognize any of your habits on that list of mechanisms? If so, congratulations—you're human! Be careful not to confuse the goal here—we are not recommending that you try to eliminate your coping mechanisms. There is likely a self-protective reason that you developed those mechanisms in the first place, and you need to exercise self-compassion as you notice yourself using them. The goal is to be aware of them and to choose a coping strategy instead of a coping mechanism as often as you can. It should feel like a gentle stretch, a little uncomfortable.

Responsive Self-Care

Okay, great, you're taking care of yourself throughout the day, recharging that battery, and now you'll always show up regulated and ready for what the world brings your way, right? The reality is that no one is regulated all the time. That's not how life works and that isn't our goal. Practicing self-care proactively throughout the day supports our bandwidth for the hard moments. But how do you take care of yourself *in the moment*? We call this responsive self-care.

When you feel your blood starting to boil and that volcano is nearing explosion, you can tap into responsive self-care strategies—aka coping strategies—to help regulate your nervous system. There are two things we can tap into in the moment: movement/grounding and brain engagement.

As an example, I was working with a hot glue gun and scissors when my toddler spotted them and started to climb up onto the table. "That's hot, buddy! I'm going to move your body to keep you safe," I said as I scooped him up. He immediately started flailing and sobbing. As I carried him to the living room, he inadvertently slapped me across the face. *Woosh!* A rush of cortisol and adrenaline flowed through my veins, and I went into fight mode. My jaw tightened, my arm muscles clenched, and my heart was racing. I laid him on the carpet and sat on the ground nearby, but safely away.

I started with *grounding*. "My butt is on the floor. I'm dropping my shoulders down from my ears. I'm relaxing my jaw," I said in a low whisper to myself. Then I moved into *brain engagement*. "You are safe. His body is out of control. Your energy can calm him," I repeated to myself internally. I felt my body start to calm as I tapped into these coping strategies. Bonus: By sitting on the ground and relaxing my body, rather than towering over him, I sent *his* nervous system signals that I was not there to attack him. This can help children who are out of control begin the process of feeling safe enough to calm down.

I have had to work really hard to learn how to pause, breathe, and tap into coping strategies during moments like this. In addition to reciting mantras, I find it also helps to take space, sometimes for just two minutes while my kids are in a safe place (even if they are screaming), so I can just breathe. It isn't like a trip to the spa, where you enter into a Zen space. The goal is to get calm enough to be able to return and support the kids. You can say, "I'm going to go to the bathroom to calm my body for one minute. I'll be back to help you." As long as everyone is safe, I put in earplugs or headphones for two minutes so I can hear a different sound. I step outside or open a window and let the air hit my face, often forcing me to breathe. I hum a familiar tune softly. This calms my nervous system, helps my body feel safe, and allows my brain to reenter the driver's seat. (Check out the Coping Strategies Toolbox on page 83 for more responsive self-care ideas.)

What tools do you have in your daily practice to help keep you balanced? What do you turn to in those heated times, when your blood pressure is rising and you want to explode? The goal is not that this will happen with perfection 100 percent of the time. We are practicing each day. We will dive into how to repair with children when we lose our cool in Chapter 7.

The Importance of Taking Care of Yourself

For so long, I told myself this lie that it was selfish to take care of myself. The truth is it may be the best gift we can give our children, our partner, our family, our colleagues, our friends, *and* yes, ourselves. There's no right way to do this. The best approach is the one that works best for your family unit. Need a monthly date night to connect with your partner? Do it! Maybe you can swap childcare with a friend to make it happen. Love snuggling your little one to sleep every night (instead of date nights out)? Do it! Need a getaway weekend with your pals? Do it! Taking time for yourself may come with feelings of shame or guilt at first. It's okay to welcome them in, respond with compassion, and choose a different narrative. In cultures where folx are praised for giving selflessly, it can be hard to prioritize taking care of yourself. It's okay to be uncomfortable as you learn to do so. Start with one thing. Commit to one change, until it's routine. Don't think of this like a New Year's resolution that's overly ambitious and bound to be short lived. Sustainable change is implemented slowly. Take it a step at a time and give yourself grace along the way.

Here's the other thing you need to know about self-care and coping strategies: you don't need to overhaul your life or your budget to feel better. On a daily basis we get societal messages about what we deserve or what should make us feel better. Usually this comes in the form of some kind of "treat yourself" advertisement that requires us to spend money, such as a massage, an expensive gym membership, a new outfit or pair of shoes, an expensive vacation, or an overpriced coffee. You might actually feel better after doing one of those things, but remember that sometimes self-care looks like putting aside the to-do list to sit and finish your coffee, or spending ten minutes reading a good book, or taking the time to make yourself a nourishing breakfast during a hectic morning. Practicing self-care and learning to use these coping strategies won't always come naturally or

Self-Care Resources

Websites

- Self-Compassion Scale: https://self-compassion.org/test-how-self-compassionate-you-are/
- Kripalu retreats: https://kripalu.org/ (there are financial aid options)
- Find a Therapist: https://www.psychologytoday.com/us/therapists
- Fireweed Collective: https://fireweedcollective.org/
- Find a local meditation group or prayer group
- NA Find a Meeting: https://www.na.org/meetingsearch/
- AA Find a Meeting: https://www.aa.org/pages/en_US/meeting-guide

Recommended Reading

- *The Gifts of Imperfection* or anything by Brené Brown
- *The Places That Scare You*, by Pema Chödrön

feel easy. It is much easier to reach for a glass than it is to investigate the emotional roots of our beliefs, as Tara Brach points out. Yet she suggests that this is the only way to liberate ourselves from limiting beliefs.

What is one self-care practice you start today? Just one way you can proactively take care of yourself. Remember, sometimes self-care is peeing without a kid on your body. If that's your starting point today, that's enough right now.

Uncovering Implicit Bias

When's the last time you felt sad? If you were going to describe or illustrate your concept of *sad*, what would it look/sound like? What is your relationship with sadness? How would you answer these same questions about anger? Exploring *how you feel about feelings* while listening for your own resistance to or rejection of certain emotions is self-awareness. It's also the foundation for uncovering implicit bias.

In Chapter 3, we talked about how emotion concepts are developed based on your experiences in your family, in your culture, and in society. This includes how to recognize them, what to do with them, and understanding their related symbols. Sometimes children receive messages about certain emotions that are implicitly or explicitly reinforcing stereotypes. Often these messages are imbalanced due to the adult's attachment style.

Bicultural and/or bilingual families, blended families, and adoptive families are likely to be bringing different emotion concepts to their relationships with each other. Even if you share a social identity and/or a culture of origin with the person or people you're raising children with, you, too, can bring differences in emotion concepts. Teachers and families can have different concepts, too.

As we discussed in Chapter 3, children are capable of emotional biculturalism and bilingualism just as they are capable of learning other aspects of different cultures and languages. The healthiest way to teach emotional biculturalism is to embrace and emphasize that more than one way of being exists and that multiple sets of concepts are valid.

One year I had a preschool student, Peter, whose family culture regarding emotions was that feelings were to be shared only within the most intimate relationships. He would move through the day appearing calm on the outside and then share his feelings about what had happened throughout the day with his parents at home in the evenings. Sometimes they would share his stories with us if there was something that was unresolved. In the classroom, some of his most frequent playmates would express in a big way, and we had a classroom culture that allowed this.

As the year went on and Peter developed more intimate relationships with us as his teachers, and some of the other children as friends, he began to express his feelings to certain people, just 1:1. Yet he would get more upset if other children expressed curiosity about what he was doing. When that happened, we would help those children get re-engaged with play to create a space for Peter to express 1:1. This 1:1 approach was a good fit for Peter when he was experiencing big emotions because it matched his family culture of moving through emotions within the most intimate relationships. With our support, Peter was able to move in and out of these variations in emotion processing culture.

Your emotion socialization processes were influenced by your caregivers' unconscious biases about your unique social identities; this can in turn unconsciously affect your current behavior with children. I teach about emotions to an extremely culturally diverse adult student population. When students reflect on their experience of their own emotion socialization, their stories are equally diverse. Some people's cultural contexts when they were children encouraged them to express their feelings in a big way and with whomever they needed to. Other people's cultural contexts encouraged them to process quietly and only within the most intimate relationships when it was absolutely necessary. Sometimes someone's identity (particularly gender, race, and birth order) impacted the way the adults and other children in their childhood responded when they didn't express their feelings in accordance with cultural expectations.

For example, anecdotally it seems that people are more comfortable when girls express sadness and boys express anger, rather than the opposite. What did you learn about emotions, and how to express them, from your family or childhood caregivers?

We are hopeful that with CEP our children's emotion libraries will be more robust and granular than our own as they develop. If you are bilingual or bicultural, you may have more than one set of emotion concepts; you can rely on this knowledge as you decide what you want to teach the next generation. All of this is why uncovering, acknowledging, and addressing our unconscious biases is crucial to equity in emotion processing skills development.

Social Identity–Related Biases

In the mid-nineties, Mahzarin Banaji and Anthony Greenwald started inviting the public to participate in their research online, using the Implicit Association Test (IAT). What they found from the data they received is that even people who consciously believe that they are unbiased in certain categories, such as gender or race, are often biased *unconsciously*. Unconscious bias is also known as implicit bias. If you search online for "Project Implicit," you'll find a link to take social attitude tests about the following topics related to social identity and/or appearance: Arab-Muslim, Race, Gender-Science, Native, Skin-Tone, Age, Disability, Religion, Sexuality, Asian, Gender-Career, and Weight, and they continue to add additional groups. The more data that they collect via the IAT, in addition to other behavioral science research findings, the stronger the evidence for the presence of implicit bias in our society. At a 2018 public talk in Cambridge, Massachusetts, Banaji said that even five-year-olds show the same biases about race as thirty-five-year-olds in their racial identity group.

At the same time, *explicit* attitudes—the ones we are conscious of—about race are improving, which means that our conscious values and our unconscious behavior can be in direct conflict with each other. Plus, biases don't have to be overtly hurtful to be classified as bias. In fact, it's notable that one way that unconscious biases manifest is in who we choose to help compared to who we don't help. Helping members of the "in group" and not helping others is a form of hidden discrimination and it compounds at a societal level.

There is plenty of evidence to show that African American children are treated differently than other children, especially when it comes to emotions. Black boys are most likely to be labeled as having emotional and behavioral disorders, and Black girls are perceived to need less support and comfort.[18] Teachers, regardless of their race, are more likely to anticipate challenging behavior when looking at Black children, especially boys, as compared to white children.[19] And misinterpretations of emotions that lead to a cascade of anger and punishment are observable.[20] These are studies related to school, but we can assume that implicit bias doesn't turn off when we go home or when we are out in public.

Implicit bias about who should feel what and how they should express it goes beyond race. The way that children are emotionally socialized in different cultures can be related to the child's gender.[21] A quick web search on expectations and children with disabilities will provide plenty of anecdotal information about the adult struggle to maintain appropriate expectations for this group of children at home and in school. Adult unconscious (or conscious) biases about race, gender, and ability affect the way adults support (or do not support) children's social and emotional development. As you work to uncover implicit biases, you might notice discrepancies in your perception of when kids should cry, stop crying, how/if they should be comforted, or how/if certain emotions should be expressed.

During one of our workshops, a parent asked, "But when will he stop crying about everything?" "When do you expect him to?" I asked. "He can't be going off to kindergarten crying all the time," the parent replied. Aha! An age bias for emotional expression. This parent went on to share a fear of the child getting bullied for crying at school. In that parent's cultural context and lived experience as a child, it wasn't safe to cry at school. The fear makes sense based on the parent's childhood, yet was resulting in a bias.

It probably goes without saying that a child's development outcomes are better when adults have high and developmentally appropriate expectations, and this applies to social and emotional development.[22]

Attachment Style and Unconscious Bias

Our attachment style (see page 28 for a refresher) can affect the way we respond or react to kids' emotions, too.

If we learned an insecure attachment, because our primary caregiver was anxious about being able to meet our needs, it is possible that we will have the same anxiety about meeting the kids' needs. In the presence of insecure attachment, a child's crying can set off this trigger/fear in the caregiver of not being able to meet the child's needs—in other words, they fear that they will not be able to handle the child's emotions. In contrast, avoidantly attached parents might brush off or depersonalize the emotions of their children or interpret them as bad behavior. Securely attached caregivers may have an emotional reaction to children's emotional expression, and they may be uncomfortable with it, but they are able to experience that discomfort without rushing the child's emotions away to return to their own, adult comfort.

If you have an insecure attachment style, you may be wondering if your child will also have an insecure attachment. This can happen, but it doesn't need to! Daniel J. Seigel presents a compelling explanation of how a parent's attachment style relates to the attachment style of their children in *The Neurobiology of "We."* His research points to the correlation between the parent's *ability to make sense of their childhood* and a secure attachment with their own child.[23] Therapy is a common context for making sense of your childhood, having a story to explain how and why it was the way it was.

As I was beginning to explore the idea that my attachment lens could be impacting my relationships with students, I realized that I was allowing certain children to express in a big way often, while simultaneously invalidating other children's expression during transition times. I had gotten very good at anticipating the kind of emotional support that someone would need if I knew they had special needs, were known to express in a big way, and/or struggled with behavior. These children got all of my patience for emotion expression and all of my coaching for emotion processing energy.

But there was one child who would keep it together through transitions and otherwise, rarely asked for anything, and mostly managed her emotions independently. One day, to my surprise, she began to express frustration or sadness by tearing up and resisting cleanup. I told her, "I know you don't want to clean up, but there will not be a teacher inside and I can't leave you here alone." This sometimes worked to get her to *comply*, but as I said those words, I realized I was missing an opportunity to teach her about *emotion processing*.

The irony—or significance—is that I was just like her as a child. My teachers always reported that I was shy and a good listener. So perhaps I was not allowing her to express in the same way that I had not been allowed to express as a child. (In my family, a common phrase that was said when we were emotional was "Turn it off"). I decided to spend some time processing with her that day instead of rushing outside, and I think it was meaningful for both of us.

By uncovering and working through implicit bias and the assumptions that come along with it, we can become open to a child's unique emotion processing development needs. If you have more than one child and/or teach, we'll get into what this looks like—balancing the needs of multiple children, CEPing with a family or group, CEPing in public, making sure no one's falling through the cracks—in Chapter 10.

Even though we can't see our implicit bias, children can . . . or at least they take it in unconsciously and make it their own. As Mahzarin Banaji said during her Cambridge talk, "What do you do when one part of your brain doesn't know what the other part is up to?" We have three suggestions:

1. Mindfulness and self-awareness

Once we get into uncovering implicit bias, it can be evocative. In revisiting my experience with my teammate in that underfunded, under-resourced school system (page 77), I saw that we had approaches to teaching that were drastically different due to differences in our identities and experiences. I sought to teach emotion processing so that children would be comfortable with their emotions, learn to identify adults who were safe to process with, and learn how to self-regulate. I was committed to changing the system and

I also realized that I couldn't change the system by the time my students entered kindergarten. At the same time, I completely understood why my teammate prioritized teaching children to be obedient, so that they would not end up in confrontation—or what was perceived to be confrontation— with someone who might hurt them emotionally or physically.

I found myself tangled in my own and others' biases, and my co-teacher and I were especially tangled in assumptions about one another. When we become aware of biases, mindfulness can help us recognize judgment that often comes along with it. And a sturdy self-care practice will help to sustain you as you go deeper over time. It's okay if not every place is safe to process in. Children can learn to differentiate a safe space or person to express with from an unsafe place or person to express with.

2. Accountability buddy

Who is your safe person to express with? Who are you that safe person for? To stay accountable while addressing your own implicit bias work, team up with a trusted friend, colleague, or family member. Together, you can help each other see where your behavior doesn't line up with your values. The trickiest thing about implicit bias is that we don't know we have it. It's a lot easier to recognize it in someone else. My husband attended a professional development training on implicit bias recently, and the trainer used the analogy that just like we would simply and humbly tell a good friend, "Your slip is showing," our accountability buddy might let us know, "Your implicit bias is showing." As you build your self-care village, be on the lookout for potential accountability buddies.

3. Discretion elimination

When Anthony Greenwald, one of the creators of the IAT, was asked what actually works to reduce the impact of implicit bias, he explained something called "discretion elimination." This is a systems-level approach to reduce or eliminate subjective decisions about a people, which often lead to bias in behavior. "But when those decisions are made based on pre-determined, objective criteria that are rigorously applied, they are much less likely to produce disparities."[24] Over the years I've created a tool for making decisions about challenging behavior with discretion elimination in mind. It's called the Addressing Challenging Behaviors Tool, and we'll go over it carefully in Chapter 10.

With practice and in community, uncovering implicit bias starts to feel more comfortable—or at least less *un*comfortable. That's because, as Ruth King reminds us, "Every time we weather the storm of inner racial discomfort or distress—whether numbness, confusion, or aversion—we are quite literally reprogramming our minds, rewiring our brains toward more stability, well-being, and confidence."[25]

Implicit Bias Resources

Websites
- Take the Implicit Association Tests: https://implicit.harvard.edu/implicit/
- Implicit bias articles: https://outsmartinghumanminds.org/
- Podcast: https://www.sceneonradio.org/seeing-white/

Recommended Reading
- *The Neurobiology of "We,"* by Daniel J. Siegel
- *Attached: The New Science of Adult Attachment and How It Can Help You Find—and Keep—Love*, by Amir Levine and Rachel Heller
- *Blindspot: Hidden Bias of Good People*, by Mahzarin Banaji and Anthony Greenwald
- *The Origin of Others*, by Toni Morrison
- *Mindful of Race*, by Ruth King
- *Blink: The Power of Thinking Without Thinking*, by Malcolm Gladwell
- *Social Justice Parenting: How to Raise Compassionate, Anti-Racist, Justice-Minded Kids in an Unjust World*, by Traci Baxley

King is talking specifically about race, but the same concept applies to discomfort or distress about all kinds of biases. We can rewire our brains to see not only our biases, but children's expressions and intentions more clearly.

Scientific Knowledge

Scientific information is not easy to access, yet it has been a major game changer for us in our relationships with children. This is one of the reasons we aim to make it available here. Scientific knowledge is always evolving as research methods and technology advance. We've researched the time-tested theories as well as the most recent scientific developments to design a method that will be helpful today. We took a deep dive into the science of emotions in Chapter 3. What were some key takeaways that you want to remember as you continue this work? Make note of them and put them in a special place where you will see them regularly.

To build on what we shared in Chapter 3, you hold an incredible amount of power in your body language, tone, and general behavior when you approach someone who is feeling something, especially a child. That's because of two processes that are going on inside you.

The first lies in the limbic system, which is a section of the brain that includes the amygdala (fight, flight, freeze, and fawn brain) and hippo-campus and "plays a role in self-regulatory behaviors including emotion, personal memories, spatial behavior, and social behavior."[26] When we share space, your limbic system and mine are talking to each other, with or without our consent. We need to keep this dynamic in mind when working with kids. When we encounter a child whose battery is depleted, or is dys-regulated, or is experiencing a big emotion, using the coping strategies that calm our limbic systems (along with proactive self-care) is welcoming to a child. If, on the other hand, we rush over with an activated or dysregulated limbic system, the child's limbic system is going to respond with the same level of intensity—it reads our energy as unsafe. Adults with calm limbic systems are safest for children, and their limbic systems know it.

We'd also like to explain the very cool concept of mirror neurons. When you see someone doing something and automatically mirror it—such as when a baby laughs and you find yourself smiling—you do that because there are neurons in your brain that are doing the same thing as the baby's neurons. Perhaps this is why modeling is such a powerful way of teaching. In the same way that the baby's joy is contagious, so is the child's meltdown. When a child is having a meltdown in Aisle 4 of the grocery store, internally your limbic system is also having a meltdown in Aisle 4. **You can either be the thermometer and read the temperature of the room and join it, or you can be the thermostat and set the temperature. You have the power to bring the calm.**

Resources and Exercises for Scientific Knowledge

Website
- Harvard University's Center on the Developing Child: https://developingchild.harvard.edu/

Recommended Reading
- References from Chapter 3 (see page 278)

Adult-Child Interactions

Let's be real—it's the adult-child-interactions section that you came here for, right? While we've taken Part I of the book to explain the foundation of the CEP method, we will dedicate Part II to adult-child interactions. In the following chapters, you're going to see what it looks like to do this work with kids. Just remember to take your self-awareness, self-care, implicit bias work, and scientific knowledge along. Let's dive in . . .

Collaborative Emotion Processing with Tiny Humans

Chapter 5

What to Do in the Moment

*Appropriate responses are those that are aimed at
encouraging expression of emotion, which is what we
need when we are emotional.*
—SAL MEDAGLIO[1]

For many of us, there's a shift from how our emotions were responded to when we were kids to how we as adults want to respond to children's emotions. But how do we do that? How do we stay in the moment? How do we help them learn healthy ways to cope? In Part II, we will walk you through the Phases of Emotion Processing as they apply to emotion coaching.

Emotion coaching was introduced formally in 1998 by John Gottman and Joan DeClaire as an alternative to behaviorist-style discipline. In *Raising an Emotionally Intelligent Child*, they made a direct connection between parenting and emotional intelligence, and provided a new way of looking at behavior, based on the assumption that there were emotional roots beneath it. They offered parents the tools to help children identify their feelings, receive validation, and then move on. The five steps presented by Gottman and DeClaire are:

1. Be aware of a child's emotions.
2. Recognize emotional expression as an opportunity for intimacy and teaching.
3. Listen empathetically and validate a child's feelings.

4. Label emotions in words a child can understand.
5. Help a child discover appropriate ways to solve a problem or deal with an upsetting situation.[2]

As you read this book, you will see how influential Gottman and DeClaire's five steps have been in the development of the CEP method, and we build on their work in a way that affirms this significant contribution to the world of child development and interpreting behavior through an emotional development lens.

Children don't ask, "Hey, do you have spare time for me to have a hard emotion, let it all out, and work through it?" Emotions are spontaneous, they're unplanned, and often . . . inconvenient. Kind of like flat tires.

When I was a nanny, I had a friend who was a nanny for a child about the same age. We enjoyed taking the kids to the local reservoir. On this day, the sun was shining, both kids were awake, and we agreed to meet in the reservoir parking lot. After a short delay, Raina pulled into the lot, rumbling along because she'd gotten a flat tire on the way. So disappointing! Determined, Raina and I got the kids ready in their strollers, where they could safely see what we were doing, spent a minute grumbling about the tire, and then got to work. Raina pulled the tools out of her trunk, and we changed the tire, telling the children about the work we were doing until the doughnut tire was on the car. After that we followed through with our intention to enjoy the sun and the geese on a walk around the reservoir.

"Hey, do you have spare time for me to have a hard emotion, let it all out, and work through it?"

Perhaps the most significant part of this story is that there were tools in the trunk to change the tire. No one plans to get a flat tire, but the idea of getting one without having the proper tools to handle it is uncomfortable enough to warrant that most people carry these items around wherever they go! This is the idea of planning for spontaneous response. We can't plan when, or who, or how someone will have a big feeling, but we can expect that it *will* happen. Depending on the personalities and development of your children, it may even happen every hour! There is no use pretending that big emotions will not happen—it's like driving around without a jack and a spare tire in your car. If you expect that it will happen and know how to use the tools, then you will feel more prepared when it does.

It makes sense for you, as the adult, to have a reaction to the child's emotion. When you envisioned parenthood, you probably didn't picture your morning with your child protesting their diaper change, crying at your feet as you tried to prepare breakfast, dumping their smoothie cup on the ground, poking you in the arm with their fork, melting down because how dare you ask them to wash their raspberry-covered hands after they ate? When you envisioned mornings together, you imagined ease, moving through the steps collaboratively and calmly, enjoying making and eating breakfast together. Now you find yourself living with a tiny human who has so many big emotions. It can be similar for teachers and nannies—maybe you envisioned playing all day with cute, fun little ones.

It's natural to resist the reality of big emotions. We talked about mirror neurons in the last chapter and how your nervous system will fire off your child's unexpectedly. We want to emphasize that the expression of big emotions is usually spontaneous, unplanned, and unexpected. It helps to have prepared for these moments—we've got the tools ready to go whenever we need them. Think of it as bringing along a diaper bag with a spare change of clothes. We don't know if/when that blowout will happen, but we'll be ready when it does.

In Part II, we'll walk you through Collaborative Emotion Processing when big emotions come up for your tiny human(s):

- **Mindfulness:** pausing to allow us to *respond* instead of *react*
- **Self-awareness:** turning on our "monitor" to recognize thoughts and feelings, and to be on the lookout for implicit bias

- **Scientific knowledge:** figuring out whether it's a moment to calm or a moment to teach
- **Adult-child interactions:** coaching through emotion processing phases

Mindfulness

A pause for mindfulness allows the adult to *respond* instead of *react*. This pause gives you a chance to allow and notice your own feelings and prepare to understand the emotions of the child with more clarity. When our body reacts to a child, sometimes that survival part of our brain turns on. Mindfulness allows us to recognize that we experience the child's behavior as a threat, get back into the driver's seat, and move toward experiencing the child's behavior as an invitation to connect—even though it feels inconvenient or hard. (Of course, if something poses a threat to the child, such as a car coming down the street, or the child is badly injured, please react as quickly as possible. These are the moments when your survival brain shines and there's no time to pause and think, "Hmm, should I pick them up?" Reaction can be lifesaving here!)

Dysregulated Adult Mindset	Regulated Adult Mindset
My child is unruly.	Their body needs movement. I can guide by offering sensory input.
My child is defiant.	There's an underlying big feeling. I can guide by holding space for their emotions within my set boundaries.
My child is needy.	I can guide by empathizing with the need, offering choices, and holding personal boundaries.

After making sure no one is injured or about to get hurt, your job is to **find your calm** so that you can decrease rather than increase the intensity. As Stuart Shanker explains, "Our limbic system is hardwired to respond in kind when confronted with someone else's aroused limbic system, positive or negative. This is why laughter is contagious, and if someone shouts angrily at us, we instantly want to shout back."[3] This can be a win for us, because if we present a calm limbic system when approaching a child (or person of any age) who is triggered or dysregulated, we feel capable and the child will be more open to receive what we have to offer.

Time for mindfulness doesn't have to be long—thirty seconds makes a big impact. Take a breath and set yourself and the children up for success by bringing a calm limbic system. That means your facial expression will be relaxed and so will your limbs. What do these thirty seconds of mindfulness look like?

- Pause. Take a breath. Deep breaths, with long, slow exhales (try one now) are always a good start.
- Prioritize the children's physical safety, and then take a moment to assess what is going on within you.
- Scan your body for any physiological reactions. Notice any reactions; perhaps verbalize them ("Wow, my heart is beating so fast").
- Embody a sloth's pace and sloooow dooooowwwwn. Take another breath.

If you do one of the above and notice your calm is still nowhere to be found, then choose a responsive coping strategy such as lowering the lights, stretching, taking a drink of water, or any of the other self-care ideas discussed in Chapter 4 (page 83). Pick something you can do wherever you are at that moment. Once you have practiced mindfulness, plus self-care if needed, then you will be more likely to operate from your logical thinking brain, having access to your scientific knowledge and awareness that your implicit biases exist. It's no use having all that knowledge and understanding if you can't access it when you need it most. Pausing for mindfulness, and any necessary responsive self-care, sets the stage for self-awareness.

Self-Awareness

With self-awareness, there is space for the rational thinking brain to come online and talk to the survival brain. Here's where we practice moving toward experiencing the tiny human's big emotions as an invitation to connect. We get to shift how we experience their emotions and behavior. It's truly powerful. And it's helpful to remember that this transformation doesn't happen overnight, so simply giving it a try is a good place to start.

Now that the rational brain is online, you can use it to recall anything you're working on. You can ask yourself any of the following questions to get focused in the moment:

- What is my role as the caregiver?
- What have I decided I will do when this happens?
- Are there biases I'm working to interrupt?

Scientific Knowledge

When children's emotions erupt, we can use our scientific knowledge to decide "Is it time to calm or time to teach?" It was the afternoon after a long day and four-year-old Jonah kept pushing his younger sister's buttons. Taking her toy, teasing her, bumping into her . . . it was constant. I turned to Jonah ready to say, "Can you just leave your sister alone for four seconds? Why do you have to do this?" and got this glimpse of toddler Jonah, poking me with the fork at dinner when he wanted to interact. Aha! Connection. Jonah is dysregulated, and before he can engage in any problem-solving conversations, he needs support with regulation—he needs calming.

"Jonah, want to race over to the fence and back? I bet I can get there first! On your mark, get set, go!" Off I ran and there came Jonah, following, passing me, and heading back with a smile saying, "I beat you!" "You did! You're so fast." Let's do another race. This time to the tree. Ready, set, go!" After a few races in the backyard, I tapped out and started timing him.

"How many seconds do you think it will take to do five kangaroo hops, one somersault, and then jump up to touch the hammock?" After moving his body and simultaneously feeling connected to me, he was ready to engage in conversation about how to play with his sister while respecting her body and her play space. He needed calming (movement and connection) before I could teach social skills.

Remember the Triangle of Growth, discussed in Chapter 3 (page 52)? The base of the triangle is sensory regulation. We know that when someone is in distress or dysregulated, they will not be able to learn something new or access tools they may have when they're regulated, so it does not make sense to attempt to teach social skills or challenge them while they are in that state. Children can do emotion processing work while in some forms of dysregulation, but not when they are in distress.

When someone is in distress, they are not ready for emotion processing and complex communication, and are in need of co-regulation, or soothing. Distress can look like: vomiting or having a bowel movement from excessive crying, uncontrollable sobbing, complete disconnection/disengagement, tornadoing, or flailing around. The nervous system can be dysregulated, however, without going into distress. Dysregulation can look like: defiance, silliness, fidgeting, meltdown, bouncing off the walls, zoning out, or disconnecting.

If the child is demonstrating dysregulation, then they are not ready to learn social skills yet. Instead, when a child is dysregulated, we connect with them and support them with co-regulation so they can learn skills for self-awareness and self-regulation. They're able to practice emotional regulation skills. We call these calming moments as we help their nervous system learn how to recognize its alarm bells and practice calming and feeling safe.

The tricky part about identifying a calming moment is that challenging and triggering behaviors often arise when a child is dysregulated. Responding with calming may trigger a part of us that feels like we are condoning "bad behavior" and that supporting the child in response will breed that behavior. If there are other children or adults around, you may feel the natural urge to say something to the child, such as "It's not okay to hit," but that phrase won't lead to decreased hitting. It's most likely you have the urge to say something like that because you want the other children or adults to know you don't condone hitting, but they probably already know that about you. In this moment try to give yourself permission to prioritize calming, aka co-regulation. Calming can look like:

- Engaging your child in a shared physical activity (such as the earlier example of the race with Jonah).
- Getting down at the level of the child, putting your hand on your heart, and saying, "I can feel my heart beating [*actually feel for your heartbeat*]. It's beating fast, so I'm going to take some breaths [*take some nice, slow breaths*]. If you have a strong attachment, you can ask if it's okay for you to feel their heartbeat.
- Getting down at the level of the child, asking, "Want to hear the story of Maxine?" If they say yes, then tell a simple story very slowly while giving squeezes to the parts of the child's body as they're named, such as "Once upon a time there was a child and her name was Maxine. Maxine had two arms. Each one had an upper arm, and a lower arm [*repeat for the other side*]; at the top of each arm there was a shoulder, and at the bottom of each arm there was a hand. The left hand had five fingers, 1 . . . 2 . . . 3 . . . 4 . . . 5," and so on.
- Announcing, "It seems like a good time to take a break. I need some help moving this heavy box—I think we can lift it if we do it together." [*Try to lift the box, and pretend it's too heavy for you. The child will likely sense that you are pretending, but this is a form of play that is a sign to the nervous system that they're safe.*]

There will be time to proactively teach social skills later, and we'll talk about that in Chapters 7–9.

With babies, it usually feels natural to provide co-regulation because they are small and dependent on us for everything. We might hesitate to provide co-regulation with older children because they might have started to develop some self-regulation skills and we think they should be able to use them anytime they need them. Where did we get this idea that when someone graduates from infancy, they automatically know how to and should handle big feelings on their own and self-regulate?

Societal messaging is a strong influence, including the messages and opinions we heard growing up and still hear from the people in our lives. Many of these messages are based on outdated ideas about how learning and development happen. They show up in our unconscious, implicit bias processes and have a snowball effect on our behavior, in what's referred to as the Ladder of Inference. At the bottom of the ladder, we take in what's happening: "My child is shouting and flailing on the ground at the grocery store." On the second rung we select information to focus on, "Those people are looking at us," and unconsciously ignore other information, "Those other people are not looking at us and are carrying on with their grocery shopping." One step up now and we're making meaning, or assumptions based on what we think we know. Some societal messages that may impact this meaning-making process might be: "children should be seen and not heard," "temper tantrums need to be nipped in the bud," "kids who have temper tantrums are bad kids," "that must be a bad parent if their kid is flailing around like that in public; imagine what they're like at home." If we assume that the people looking are thinking any of these things, and if these thoughts pop up in our own head, then this information will affect the conclusions we draw, such as "I need to make this stop ASAP." This can lead to a belief, the next rung, such as "I need to make this behavior stop right away in order for my kid to be perceived as 'good' and for me to be perceived as a 'good' parent," which affects the action we take.

Suppose we back up to the second rung to select different information to focus on, such as "My heart is beating fast, and my child's muscles look like they're contracted and their eyes are scrunched closed." Then when we go one step up to making meaning, or assumptions based on what we think we know, the assumption might be "My nervous system is heightened, and my child's is dysregulated." This would lead us to a very different conclusion, maybe "This is a calming moment rather than a teaching moment," which would lead to our belief, maybe "If I take a

Instead of . . .	Try . . .
Making demands. ("Stop running!" or "Share with your brother!")	Regulating first. (If the emotion is in response to a basic need being met, such as diapering, you can decide if you need to take a pause to regulate first or continue on, providing validating support as you go.)
Allowing the child to hurt themselves or others, including yourself.	Protecting them within their environment. • Removing objects that can harm them. • Providing a physical barrier to areas that aren't safe. • Moving them to a less stimulating area or, if possible, asking others in the area to give some space. • Cueing safety with your body. • Squatting, kneeling, or sitting so that your eye level is at, or below, the child's eye level. • Softening your face. • Opening your chest and hands. • Slowing your speech or using less verbal communication. • Deflecting any attempt to hurt your body, while maintaining the message that you are not going to fight back.
Teaching new coping strategies.	Focusing on allowing the emotion and connecting.

breath, I can figure out what to do." This can lead to an action, such as "I will take a breath so I can bring the calm and co-regulate with my child."[4]

Remember, as discussed in Chapter 3, that when the amygdala gets in the driver's seat, these skills can get hidden or overridden. That means that toddlers and preschoolers need and deserve co-regulation at times. Even older kids need it sometimes. Some children need it every day throughout the day! It is through practicing co-regulation that a child learns how to self-regulate.

Once you have determined that the child is not in distress or is no longer in distress, and they are expressing an emotion, the next step is coaching through the Phases of Emotion Processing.

Adult-Child Interactions

The big emotion expression was the serve—now it's time for you to return in a way that says yes to secure attachment relationships. The following are some of the roles that you might play with this in mind:

- Witness
- Mirror
- Facilitator
- Toolbox provider

This is *not* the time for law enforcement or delivery of justice. Thanks to folx like Mister Rogers, it's become more mainstream to hear adults say that all feelings are welcome. That's a great start, but our actions can speak louder than our words. If we tell a child their feelings are welcome, but we try to make their feelings go away as fast as possible for our own comfort, what we are really saying is "Only some of your feelings are welcome," or "My comfort is more important than your feelings."

In order to create a culture where children are allowed to experience their feelings rather than suppress them, we use the Phases of Emotion Processing. These five steps will help a child get through an emotion and learn that it's okay to feel that way, that they're loved even when they're having a hard time, and that they can build coping strategies to navigate hard things in life. They'll learn how to have healthy conflict and solve problems with resilience. They'll build a toolbox for navigating whatever life throws their way by practicing it with you now.

The first four phases are aimed at helping the nervous system feel safe and calm. In these phases, children are practicing sensory and emotional regulation, which allows them to build language and communication skills. You might notice an urge to jump to Phase 5—to problem-solve, move on, or get the conflict over with. That makes sense. It's uncomfortable to be with someone who is having a hard time. Notice that urge to jump ahead and make it all go away. You get to practice your self-awareness and self-regulation skills here, too.

Phase 1: Allowing one's emotions to exist

It sounds pretty straightforward and simple, right? Allow their emotions to exist. Yet this can be extremely challenging. You might feel uncomfortable with a child's expression of sadness or frustration and feel the urge to actively distract them when they begin to express. There can be a general sense of dread or worry that the feeling will overwhelm the child and/or yourself.

This phase might be best defined by what it's not. When someone does not have the skills to allow emotions, it looks like distraction or deflection/rejection. When children are nervous about an adult's reaction (shame, guilt, anxiety, etc.), they can stop themselves from allowing their emotions and try to suppress their feelings. Most of the teaching and learning for this phase starts with us, as the caregiver, holding space for the child's big emotions. During your mindfulness practice, you started by observing your heart rate and breathing. Then with self-awareness you may have noticed your own emotions or thoughts in reaction to the child's initiation of an emotional expression. If so, take a deep breath. Resist the urge to stop the child from expressing. Please avoid teaching surface acting. Remember that crying is a normal and healthy way to express.

Allowing includes boundaries. Amaya had been having big emotions at school, specifically during free play time, when she was often hitting,

Holding Space for Big Emotions

In order to teach our kiddos to process emotions, we first have to *allow* the emotion by holding space for it.

- Accept their feelings without solving the problem.
- Give them time on their timeline, not yours.
- Keep their body safe without punishing them for feeling out of control.
- Engage in active listening to connect rather than explain.
- Maintain your regulation and model how to calm your body.

kicking, or biting other children. When I popped in right before morning snack, I saw things start to unfold. When she opened her snack container, she erupted in frustration, slapping the top of the container on the table and flailing it around in the air, yelling, "I TOLD MY MOM NOT TO SEND A BAR!" A teacher zoomed over to her and started to problem-solve, "You can choose something else from your box. You don't have to eat that cereal bar. Want to find something from your lunch for snack?" I could feel the teacher's fear of this emotion growing and what might happen if it did.

The teacher looked relieved as I asked to step in. "You didn't want your mom to send a bar and she sent it anyway! *Ugh*, that's so frustrating!" I empathized. I didn't agree that I would feel frustrated in the same situation, but I knew what it was like to feel frustrated and that it's hard. As Amaya grabbed the top of her container, I held her hands and said, "You sound so frustrated, and I won't let you hurt anyone's body. I'll stay here with you." In this way, I allowed Amaya to feel and express, while keeping her and her peers safe.

A child may be expressing for a range of reasons. Are they hungry, tired, overstimulated? Do they need a diaper change? Are they feeling an emotion, or yearning for connection? You know how when you're hungry you can get snippy or rude? Maybe you get overwhelmed more easily or have a lower tolerance for frustration. It makes sense when we think about the Triangle of Growth—the sensory systems are at the base. When our sensory needs are not met, when our battery needs to be charged, emotions can amplify. When you're in the allowing phase, check in with the battery questions first to see if a low battery is the root of your child's really big feeling.

When will they be ready to eat next? When will they be ready for sleep next? When was the last time they went to the bathroom? When was the last time they moved their body? When was the last time they had downtime? When was the last time I connected with them without screens or distractions?

We don't have to have all the answers to navigate this process with them, but understanding what else is going on in their body can be helpful for moving through the phases.

Phase 2: Recognizing the perceived emotion

When someone validates what you're experiencing, it allows you to feel seen and thus feel connected. You can feel understood, like "Ahhh yes,

Empathy is . . .	Empathy is not . . .
✓ An opportunity to connect	X An opportunity to problem-solve
✓ Accepting the perceived emotion	X Feeling sorry for the person
✓ Taking their perspective	X Using reasoning to avoid the emotion
✓ Understanding and validating	X Imagining you know best

they get it!" Feeling seen is sometimes enough for kids. When their nervous system is activated, feeling seen can help them return to a sense of safety or calm. Sometimes the root of dysregulation is a need for connection, and feeling seen and connected to you can be enough to regulate. In some instances, children calm and feel safe in this phase and are ready for Phase 5. Phase 2 is less about saying the "right" words and more about really understanding where a child is coming from.

If someone comes in when you're crying in front of a broken vase and says, "I see that you're feeling sad," it might feel different than if they came in and said, "Ugh, that was the special vase from your mom. It really sucks that it broke. That's sad." Phase 2 is about empathizing to connect.

After holding Amaya's hands, I repeated, "You didn't want your mom to send a bar and she sent it anyway! *Ugh*, that's so frustrating!" This is the beginning of me entering into Phase 2. This is a connection point. I see you. I understand. She went on to scream, "Yeah! And I told her it doesn't taste good when it breaks and she did it anyway! Now it's broken and it won't taste good!" Her eyes came toward me, and she yelled "Yeah!" when I recognized her perceived feeling. Even though she was still dysregulated and yelling, we were connecting.

"Oh man, you told her it wouldn't taste good if it broke and she sent it in your snack box and now it's broken. I get your frustration, Amaya." It's not my job to decide whether or not she should be feeling frustrated. It isn't my job to say, "It's not a big deal. It will taste the same." She already *is* feeling frustrated and never, in the history of feelings, has dismissing them made them go away. It's not my job to lecture her right now about hitting the container top on the table or flailing it around in the air. It's not my job to figure out how to solve this problem with her yet either. Her rational thinking and problem-solving brain is not fully online yet. This is still a calming moment.

This phase has two parts for the adult: looking and providing. The first is *looking* for signs of recognition that the child associates symbols with feelings when they are presented. It's that "Aha! Yes, I feel seen. My adult understands what I'm experiencing" moment. Signs of recognition

Details on Development

Recognition

Infants

Presenting a symbol to an infant

- Ask a question, such as "Are you feeling sad that Papa went?" or "Are you feeling angry that you have to wait?" Then, take it a step further and validate that child. "It can be sad to say goodbye," or "It's hard to wait when you're hungry."
- Hold a feeling card where the baby can see it and say something that combines an observation and a feeling vocabulary word, such as "I see your tears. You look sad," or, "You sound mad."
- Use sign language in combination with a question or observations.

Infant recognition

- Infants do not show recognition by using words until they can say yes and no. So, as with everything else that you do with your infants, eye contact and body language will be the primary modes of expressive communication. For this reason, as well as the pace of infant processing time, it is crucial to be able to detect recognition of a symbol that you have presented.

Toddlers

Presenting a symbol to a toddler

- If as infants, your toddlers have been offered symbols for emotions, then they will quickly learn to use emotion vocabulary as they start talking. Presenting a symbol to toddlers looks the same as for infants (described opposite in the box). The response you can expect from them, however, will evolve as their cognitive, motor, and language development grows.

Toddler recognition

- Individual children will demonstrate recognition in a wide range of expression when you present a symbol. Some children will give only subtle cues, while others will be very vocal and obvious about their feelings, or the response may be anything in between.

Preschoolers

Presenting a symbol to a preschooler

- This might be accomplished by bringing the cards and offering symbols, or it may include an extra sentence, such as "That's a hard feeling," or "It makes sense that you feel angry."

Preschooler recognition

- A preschooler might indicate recognition by nodding or shaking their head, or by saying yes or no when you present a symbol. Accepting the card in their hands and studying the image is a form of recognition (as opposed to tossing, turning away from, or bending the card). If someone is flapping their arms in an agitated way or tightening their muscles or screaming, then beginning stages of recognition look like a slowing or pausing of the movement.

may be subtle in a child of any age (or adult, for that matter!), especially if being offered symbols for emotions by adults is brand-new to a child. In response to symbols, recognition looks like:

- Eye contact
- Leaning in
- Relaxing muscles (that were tense just before)
- Reaching arms up toward you
- Nodding
- Verbal recognition. Note: The quality of the verbal sound of recognition might embody the emotion being expressed. For example, if anger or frustration is the emotion, the yes might be shouted.

This list is not exhaustive, and you will notice that signs of recognition vary from child to child, within cultures and age groups, and with different grown-ups.

The second part for the adult is *providing* explicit recognition that we see and validate their feelings. Having the words and symbols to express a range of emotions is powerful in a society that emphasizes verbal and written language as a common way to connect with others. The most common symbols for feelings that many parents and teachers are already using are words. Pictures are starting to be more available to children, especially if they have a relationship with an occupational therapist. Pictures help everyone, especially kids who have trouble making sense of verbal communication, sequencing, and planning. (We created the CEP Deck of emotion cards for coaching through the phases for just this reason. While the cards are not always accessible, they are designed to help build the child's emotion concepts and for caregivers and children to communicate about emotions as they come up. See page 274 for more about this deck.)

Many people we work with wonder, *What if I give the child the wrong name for the emotion they're having?* Using the theory of constructed emotions, which we introduced in Chapter 3, can co-create the definition of emotions in our families and communities. As the adult, you have more experience with naming emotions than the child and you've reflected on any cultural differences to help you interpret their expressions, so it's okay to offer what you know, just like you do with your knowledge about nutrition or the best way to accomplish a task.

There is no way to ever know for sure if you understand someone else's experience. When you offer the vocabulary and name the feeling, there is a bit of guesswork involved. There are ways to phrase the symbol for recognition that send the accurate message that you are making your best guess. You can identify objective information first with certainty in combination with your guess. For example:

- "I see your tears. I wonder if you're feeling sad?"
- "He's crying. Sometimes when I feel sad, I cry, too."
- "Your muscles are all tight and your voice is loud. I think you might be angry. Are you angry?"
- "It looks like you're worried she's going to take that toy from you. Can I put it on the shelf to keep it safe while we talk?"

If someone calms down as soon as you come to help, you can ask a question about how they're feeling or if you got it right. When someone is very upset, keep your question-asking to a minimum. In that case, their brain is already overloaded with the task of processing the feeling, and it may be frustrating to be asked to process a question and be expected to produce an answer. If you find yourself doubting the emotion vocabulary you're offering, then it might be helpful to spend more time using mindfulness and self-awareness to understand your own experience of emotions in relationship to symbols better.

There will be children who spend a long time preparing for Phase 2. You might notice that when you mention an emotion, they ramp up. Sometimes naming the perceived emotion is more supportive for some children when you make it less personal by removing them from it. Rather than, "You sound sad," you might try, "It feels sad to say goodbye to Daddy. I understand that." The right way to respond is the way that works best for the unique child in front of you.

Phase 3: Feeling secure in experiencing a range of emotions over time

When a child has reached this phase, you will have already observed them allowing a range of emotions without reaching the point of distress. You have also observed signs of recognition when the child is presented with words, signs, or pictures for emotions.

We want children to know about the impermanence of emotions. When we don't have security in a feeling, we might try to rush out of it or make it go away for fear of getting stuck in it. But this is like quicksand—the more we try to dig out, the more we get stuck. Security in our feelings means recognizing that we won't feel this way forever so it's safe to feel it for now. I like to tell children that it's like clouds in the sky. The rain cloud above us right now is slowly moving and a new cloud will be overhead soon. Our goal is to help them see the emotion they're experiencing right now as one out of many that they might feel over time. Whether we enjoy the feeling or not, we know it won't always feel like this.

Pictorial cues are also helpful in this phase. By showing kids pictures of characters who are feeling something in a book, or on emotion cards, or even emojis while saying or signing, "Are you feeling scared? Worried? Disappointed?" we are reminding them that there are different emotions that humans feel. Once we find an image and/or word that they identify with, then we acknowledge and validate it. Sometimes this experience is enough for a child to feel calm and steady again. Others will feel or continue to feel distressed at this point. We can show them something that makes us think of the words "calm" or "safe"—another picture from a book, an emoji, an emotion card, or even a hand-drawn picture—and ask them how they might feel calm and safe again. This helps them acknowledge that they will feel different at some point, which can provide security in the feeling they are currently experiencing. Pictures related to emotion concepts are not always handy, and that's okay—you can do this without them. You can think of them as a bonus tool, a helpful visual that aids in this process, but not mandatory.

Another way to stay with and explore an uncomfortable emotion is for the adult to share a story of a time when they felt the same emotion and moved through it. The key part is moving through it. Don't tell a story that has a scary ending or in which you felt abandoned. My preschoolers' favorite was always the one about the time I was about four years old: "My babysitter brought me on a special walk to the ice cream shop. I picked my favorite ice cream flavor—chocolate. I was so excited! As I took the first lick of the ice cream, the whole scoop fell off the cone onto the ground. I felt so sad! I think I may have even cried. My babysitter gave me a hug and then took some mint chocolate chip off her own cone and added it to mine. I never had that flavor before, so I didn't know if I'd like it—I felt a little nervous. I took a taste, and I *did* like it! It turned out to be my favorite flavor for years." Childhood memories are especially salient to children, but adult memories are good, too. If you don't have a lot of these stories, don't be afraid to repeat stories—children will ask for them! You can also use examples from books you've read together. If we aren't afraid of getting stuck in our own emotions and if we feel confident about supporting the child when they get stuck, it's easier for everyone to be at peace with the present emotion. We can study, play with, and get to know each one as well as develop granularity, which means we can distinguish between more nuanced emotions. Developing security requires the practice of mindfulness, self-awareness, and sometimes social skills.

"I'm here to help you feel calm when you're ready . . ." I told Amaya. By using the word "calm" in there, I'm signaling to her that calm exists, that she won't be in her feeling of frustration forever. For Amaya, I went on to add the phrase "when you're ready to solve this problem." It can be helpful to know that we *are* going to solve this problem together. I'm signaling to her and helping her get in the practice of calming before trying to solve the problem.

As the adult, if you struggle to be with an emotion when *you* experience it, you may notice the challenge to be with a *child* who is experiencing that emotion. For instance, if feeling fear can lead to anxiety for you where you are stuck in the fear, trying to escape it, you may notice yourself trying to keep a child from feeling fear. Start by noticing what emotions you try

Details on Development

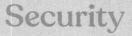

Infants

Infant security looks like secure attachment. The baby starts to calm down when the caregiver responds. Or they crawl to the caregiver if they see someone they've never met entering the room. This is because infants are in the co-regulation phase, so their emotional security is deeply connected to their relationship with their caregiver, and how/if they respond to co-regulation.

Toddlers

Toddler security also looks like secure attachment. Some toddlers are beginning to feel secure in their emotions without co-regulation. An example would be a child who expresses a little sadness (maybe some tears) when saying goodbye to their parent at drop-off, and they watch their parent go. They might linger at the door for a few minutes, and then they move on to begin playing. Another example would be a child who comfortably transfers from their parent's arms into the arms of one of their teachers at drop-off, even in the presence of tears.

Preschoolers

One example of security in preschoolers is when the symbol is recognized and followed up with a question about why the character on the card is feeling that way. You can ask the child what they think. If they have an answer that could make sense, then this is a good example of security. It means they are able to think about how different contexts might affect someone's emotions. This requires perspective taking, which is one of the seven essential life skills that every child needs that Ellen Galinsky names.[5]

to avoid or rush away and which emotions you feel stuck in sometimes. Noticing is the first step to creating a different pattern. You can practice security by reminding yourself, "Emotions are not problems to be solved. I'm safe to feel this."

Phase 4: Seeking support through coping strategies

"But I told her not to do it and she did it anyway," Amaya brought up again. "Ugh, you really wish she didn't put that bar in your snack box. Now it's broken and won't taste good to you," I acknowledged. "I see your shoulders up by your ears and your tight fists. I hear your loud voice. I hear your frustration. It makes sense," I told her. We are still in a calming, soothing moment.

Now let's bring in Phase 4: Coping Strategies. "Would you like to do ten big jumps with me? Ready, set, go!" Amaya and I jumped up and down ten times together. After jumping, she wasn't yelling anymore and her muscles were starting to relax, but her shoulders were still up to her ears and her jaw was tight. "Before we solve this problem together, would you like a hug?" She collapsed into me, and I held her snug until I felt that big exhaled "Ahhh." She pulled back and her face relaxed.

Remember the two types of coping that we identified in Chapter 4, coping mechanisms and coping strategies? Coping mechanisms are the coping tools that numb our nervous system temporarily. They are what we will automatically turn to if coping strategies are not taught. Experiencing an uncomfortable feeling is hard, so we inherently try to make the discomfort go away as fast as possible. Coping mechanisms result in the production of dopamine, tapping into the reward center of the brain. This provides temporary relief from the hard emotion, which is like hitting the snooze button on an alarm: we find the temporary relief but are not regulating the nervous system in order to process the emotional experience and problem-solve or navigate conflict resolution.

Coping strategies help the body slow or halt the production of adrenaline or cortisol and start to produce serotonin or oxytocin to calm the nervous system for a longer period of time. This also allows the child to work on processing the emotion rather than pushing it down inside just to pop up again later. We can expect that before a child reaches Phase 4, they may rely on mechanisms such as a pacifier, an attachment item such as a lovey or blanket, distraction in the form of a toy or screen, or food. That's okay. It's not fair to ask a child to give up their mechanisms before they've experienced security. Find a list of coping mechanisms, as well as coping strategies, below. Head to www.seedandsew.org/more for a more comprehensive, downloadable list.

As you can see, some of the strategies require social skills, such as sharing feelings, entering play with a close friend, or asking someone for a hug. Not every child will gravitate toward all the examples listed. You can help a child develop their personal Coping Strategies Toolbox by noticing what activities help them recharge their battery proactively. Do they benefit from climbing and jumping? Awesome, let's do ten big jumps

Coping Mechanisms	Coping Strategies
To numb feelings, push them beneath the surface, and feel temporarily better faster	*To process emotions, leave the reactive brain, and enter the rational thinking brain*
• Being distracted with a toy • Giggling/smiling when someone is having a hard feeling • Hurting someone else to feel powerful or in control • Using a pacifier to stop expression • Having a snack/feeding in response to a hard feeling • Trying to solve the problem • Offering a lovey/security item without coaching	• Drawing/coloring/ painting • Breathing • Moving/exercising • Playing calmly with a toy that involves small finger muscles • Free writing/practicing gratitude • Playing music • Reading a book • Hugging

in the moment or run down and touch the door and come back. Do they love to hang upside down or go on the swings? Great, let's spin on a chair or do upside down dips in my arms. They are learning how to self-regulate with these strategies by first co-regulating with you there to support them.

Leaving all mechanisms in the dust is not the goal. They can be really powerful tools to tap into. There is research to show that some neurodivergent humans, especially those with ADHD, may have low dopamine function.[6] Using coping mechanisms that elicit dopamine can be a bridge to then offering a coping strategy for neurodivergent folx. For instance, being playful and distracting, such as using a silly voice, can connect the adult with the child enough for the child to be receptive to a strategy, such as swinging or jumping into a pile of pillows. What's key is to be mindful of when we are turning to coping mechanisms so that we can work toward pairing them with a strategy, such as using a screen as a coping mechanism and then coloring together or playing a movement game afterward as a coping strategy.

We aren't tapping into coping in an effort to stop experiencing an emotion. Instead we're using a coping strategy to get the body and the brain working together in the interest of emotion processing. Remember that means having experienced and fully integrated emotions. It allows us to experience an emotion and make sense of it without being consumed by it. When the body gets back to feeling safe or calm, it doesn't mean we stop experiencing the emotion. You can bring the brain back online and still feel the emotion. A Coping Strategies Toolbox can include some tools that involve another human, such as a hug or talking to a friend, while others can be achieved independently, such as going for a walk or taking deep breaths. This is important because we want children to feel empowered in knowing that even if you aren't there, they have tools to tap into.

We learn to self-regulate first by co-regulating. It makes sense to begin with coping strategies that involve you, their trusted, safe caregiver. We can scaffold this growth by offering suggestions if they appear to be looking for a way to cope. This might sound like: "Mama left for work. You didn't want her to leave. Would you like a hug while you're feeling sad?" or "You were climbing and fell down. You sound scared. Would snuggling your lovey help you feel safe?"

But what if they get angrier when they're offered coping support? "When I support my daughter through the Phases of Emotion Processing, she now yells, 'NO CALM, MAMA!' What should I do if she's refusing coping support?" one of our Seed & Sew village members asked. We know the phases and it's tempting to rush to work through them to get to problem solving and be done with this feeling. However, emotions can take time to process. Sometimes kiddos need time to practice feeling their emotion and aren't ready to cope and move on. If you've guided them through the phases and see them stopping at one point, pause and give them time and space to feel and express before returning to offer coping support. Tom Petty nailed it: "The waiting is the hardest part." The waiting phase might sound like: "I'll be here if you need me." "I'm here with you. I love you." "You are safe to feel your emotions." With practice they will become less resistant to coping strategies and eventually embrace them.

Phase 5: Moving on

Woo! The child is in a regulated state, can access their rational thinking brain, and is ready to problem-solve, navigate conflict resolution, or let it go. You've made it to a social skills teaching moment. That might mean solving whatever problem precipitated the big emotion, or letting it go because it turned out not to be that important after all. For you, it also means identifying additional skills that need to be developed before the next attempt at emotion processing, or specifically problem solving, is made.

Problem solving can come in many forms. Children are fantastic at navigating it collaboratively when they're in a regulated state and have access to the rational thinking, problem-solving part of their brain. All emotional intelligence skills (self-awareness, self-regulation, empathy, motivation, and social skills) can be exercised in this phase.

"Amaya, I noticed there is five minutes left for snack. You do not have to eat that bar. The next time food will be available is at lunch. Your body may be able to wait until then, or it might get hungry. I'm not sure. What do you think we should do next?" I asked her. "We could tape it together!" she brainstormed. "Your bar? Sure. How do you think the tape

Problem Solving

Once everyone is regulated, conflict resolution can begin. Initiating problem solving might sound like:

- "How can we solve this?"
- "I wonder what would happen if . . ."
- "Hmm, this is tricky. I'm not sure how to solve this."
- "What do you think we could do?"

would taste?" "Ugh, disgusting," she said as she pretended to gag. "We could glue it!" "We could. I'm not sure how glue would taste," I stated. She paused. "There's three minutes left for snack. You don't have to eat it. I trust you to listen to your body," I told her. "Ugh, fine, I'll eat it," she said with an eye roll.

Amaya couldn't have navigated that problem-solving process, even with my support, until she was regulated. She wouldn't have been open to or able to see the different options available. When we rush to Phase 5, we send the child the message that their hard feelings are uncomfortable for us or inconvenient to us and that we simply want them to go away. Or we risk sending the message that it's not safe, or that it's bad, to feel emotions. It is only now, after the first four phases, that a child (or any human) can problem-solve.

Problem solving may look like:

- Using a timer for kids to take turns
- Setting a timer for when something will be all done (such as watching TV or playing in the tub before bedtime)
- Repairing something (i.e., the block structure that fell over)
- Making a plan to try again after nap or tomorrow
- Making a special place to save works in progress when it's time to put toys away

- Resolving conflicts between multiple kids (more on this in Chapter 10)

Once you have completed the moving-on phase, you're finished with emotion processing for now. In between big emotions there is other work to do, which we'll cover in Part III.

How Do We Know What Response Will Work for This Child?

The short answer is we don't. Getting to know these tiny humans' temperaments plays a large role in knowing how to respond to them, though. Then we work with trial and error, using what we know about how the brain works and how humans learn. We have to commit to approaches for at least two weeks to learn whether or not they work, as we will undoubtedly see emotional expressions from a child when we first respond to them without trying to fix their problem. It's normal for your child to express in a bigger way because their brain is trying to correct for the fact that you're not reacting like you usually do. It takes a little while for them to learn the new algorithm.

Sidra was two months postpartum with Charlie, feeling overwhelmed in trying to meet the needs of this new babe alongside her two-year-old's needs. The guilt was creeping in . . . "Did I ruin things for Hannah?" "Can I give them both what they need?" "I'm not enjoying this season." If Sidra stood up to change Charlie's diaper, Hannah yelled and cried, trying to climb Sidra's body. Words of affirmation and support weren't filling Hannah's cup. Honestly, Sidra found herself avoiding doing things because it was emotionally exhausting to engage in this dance with Hannah.

She tried telling her what she was going to do before doing it, and then coming right back to Hannah as she promised. She tried talking to her through the emotional expression, validating what she was feeling.

If there was an approach, she tried it. Nothing was working. As a last resort, she tried validating her emotion, doing what she had to do, and then continuing to give Hannah space after, not rushing to touch her, but letting her know she could come over if she needed support. Sidra stayed in the room, close enough to monitor her without hovering, largely working on managing her own feelings as Hannah expressed. She played with Charlie, and every few minutes would acknowledge Hannah's feeling and again offer comfort if she wanted to come over. The more Sidra tried to get Hannah's expression to stop, the more it grew in size.

Finally, it was clear. Hannah needed to be heard, but then needed time and space to express without being rushed through the process, as well as a way to positively reengage when she was ready. Sidra would validate her emotion and move away while still being present, saying, "I'll be here with you when you're ready." Once Sidra consistently applied this approach, Hannah's "tantrums" shortened, her ability to self-regulate strengthened, and eventually she was able to process what would happen without being debilitated by her emotions. She received the message that her mom could handle her big emotions even with the new sibling in the house. For Mom, handling Hannah's big emotions meant not rushing the process and, instead, holding space for Hannah to experience them.

A small percentage of children require physical space to express. This should remain a last resort because it can be easily mistaken by the child as a rejection of their emotions. When a child needs space to express, it's important to check in with them and also verbalize that you are there with and for them when they're ready, just as Sidra said, "I'll be here when you're ready." For Sidra, after over a month of trial and error, it was such a relief to find a strategy that worked for her to develop the skills she will carry with her. She had to accept the failed attempts in order to see what Hannah was asking for. Failure and reflection are frequently a part of this process. You get to fail! You get to say, "That was a bust." You get to look at things you could change, and you get to try again. This is self-awareness.

Anxiety

As an infant, Sage refused every bottle. We tried every type of bottle, nipple flow, temperature of milk, reheated versus freshly pumped, formula versus breast milk, this position, that time of day—you name it, we tried it. One day, four months postpartum I was nursing him alone in the house when I started to panic. What would happen if I died? How would he survive? Would they syringe-feed him? Who would help my husband figure it out?

The spiral began and continued, but I looked down at his sweet little face and snapped back into the present moment, recognizing that familiar feeling of diving into the depths of fear. Hello, anxiety, my old friend. I used to fight it. I'd try to run from it, coping mechanism my way out of it, and try like hell to make it stop . . . until I started practicing CEP. When we are able to build awareness of fear as it's bubbling up inside of us, we get the opportunity to be with it rather than be consumed by it.

When I started to see my anxiety for what it was, I needed to learn what to do with it. I started to notice that racing thoughts had become the norm in my mind. My proactive and responsive coping strategies weren't working anymore, and even sitting for meditation was excruciating because I didn't want to be left alone with my anxiety. I experienced panic attacks. I was overwhelmed, so I went back to therapy. Therapy has been a helpful coping strategy for me over the years. With the support of my therapist, I was able to learn how to identify my emotions as they were emerging instead of after they'd overwhelmed me. I made some new coping strategies, and my old favorites started to work again. I learned that a little self-validation for my underlying emotion plus a slogan like "We don't have enough information yet" help me stay present.

This whole experience reminded me that feeling worried is different than experiencing anxiety. Worried is an emotion that can be processed, while anxiety is a nervous system reaction to an emotion. When I use mindfulness to notice my thoughts, and then my self-awareness monitor to distinguish anxiety from worry, I can name and disarm it with a coping strategy.

Anxiety and the fear at its roots are a powerful teacher because they alert us that we have something that we don't want to lose. If fear comes up, it might be because we also have hope—the hope of keeping something that's dear to us. In the absence of hope, we experience despair, which can make us lose the will to continue. Anxiety is a fighter; it's a nervous system reaction that is fighting for survival. When we shift from trying to get rid of anxiety to having self-compassion when we're afraid of losing something, it's monumental.

There was a study from Yale released in 2019 that dove into anxiety in children. It looked at three treatment approaches: medication, therapy, and caregiver/parent support to respond in the moment.[7] Overwhelmingly, parent/caregiver support had the greatest long-term effects. This isn't to say that therapy and medication aren't helpful tools, but instead to acknowledge how impactful your role is in a child's life. There were three takeaways in the parent/caregiver responses that made a vast difference:

1. Allowing the fear without rushing it away. Instead of "You don't have to be scared at bedtime, I'm just downstairs." Try, "It can feel scary to be alone. I get that."

2. Separating the sensory regulation from emotion processing (remember the Triangle of Growth, page 52). Before we talk about what's happening, we first help them regulate. "Your heart is racing, your hands are shaking, your voice is getting big! You sound anxious." Pause and then support them with coping strategies. "What helps your body feel safe when you're feeling anxious?" Depending on where they are developmentally and in their Phases of Emotion Processing, you may suggest or model coping strategies. "You can place your hand on your heart, drop your shoulders down from your ears, and open your hands while we take a deep breath."

3. Emotion processing. We can support them by being a safe space for them to process the experience and to enter into Phase 5 and discuss it when they're ready. A factor in how trauma is stored in the body is whether or not we feel alone in it. When we have a safe space to turn to process afterward with someone who isn't afraid of our big

feelings, then we can learn how to do hard things without the body experiencing it as trauma.

The first step in supporting a child with anxiety is to allow ourselves to experience fear. As you practice CEP in your moments of anxiety, you'll develop a skill set to lean on when a child is anxious. Imagine what it would be like to learn these skills early in life! You're changing the way they get to experience the world. How powerful is that?

The Five Phases Belong to Us, Too

How do you model moving through your own emotions? Do you maintain self-care routines? Do you rely on coping mechanisms, or do you have coping strategies? Are you engaged in a process of reflection and self-actualization that allows you to share personal emotion anecdotes? Do you feel empathy in such a way that you can model it authentically? When we practice these five Phases of Emotion Processing, we model them for children. And if we know anything about kids, it's that they are more likely to repeat what they observe us doing than what we tell them to do.

Resources for Adult-Child Interactions

- The CEP Deck (emotion flashcards designed specifically for CEP; see page 274 for details), created by Lauren Stauble and Alyssa Blask Campbell.
- Children's books that tell stories of children expressing emotions and utilizing coping strategies or that illustrate emotion vocabulary. Visit www.seedandsew.org/more to see a list of our favorites.

Chapter 6

How to Set and Hold Boundaries

We were sitting in my young toddler classroom during morning drop-off. Three moms and I were surrounded by their toddlers playing around us as we chatted before they headed off to start their workday when Mika threw a block into our group. My instinct was to say, "Mika, we don't throw blocks. That could hurt someone. Go pick that up and put it back." But she knew this already. She could have told me in a regulated moment that she wasn't supposed to throw blocks and that doing so could hurt someone and they might feel sad. She had that information, but she wasn't able to access the skills for what else to do in that moment to meet her need.

Instead, I watched a wave of embarrassment come over her mother's face just before I responded to this behavior by sliding my body next to the child, saying, "Mika, I won't let you throw more blocks in our classroom [*my body next to hers, ready to stop her from throwing another one*]. If you want someone to play with you, then you can say, 'Play' [*signing "play"*], or touch someone and say, 'Play.'" She paused, looking at her mother and then back at me. We all held that space filled with silence. After longer than felt comfortable, Mika walked over to me, pulled my hand, and said, "Play." Mika's mother stated in disbelief, "*What?* How did you get her to listen? She would have never done that for me."

What Mika's mom meant by "listen" was "obey" . . . "How did you get her to obey you?" The thing is, obedience wasn't my goal. Setting and holding a safety boundary was my goal. What if Mika had tried to throw another block? Honestly, that was my prediction. It's why I moved closer to her and was prepared to stop her to keep others safe.

It's our job to set boundaries, and it's a child's job to push them, to see if they're real, to see if we will *really* keep them safe. Boundaries are designed to create an entryway, not to put up a wall. If I had simply told Mika what she *couldn't* do—no throwing blocks—without telling her how she *could* engage, she wouldn't have known what to do next. In her book, *Set Boundaries, Find Peace: A Guide to Reclaiming Yourself,* Nedra Glover Tawwab shares, "Unspoken boundaries are invisible, and they often sound like 'They should've known better' or 'Common sense would say . . .' Common sense is based on our own life experiences, however, and it isn't the same for everyone. That's why it's essential to communicate and not assume that people are aware of our expectations in relationships. We must inform others of our limits and take responsibility for upholding them."[1]

Boundaries are essential for secure attachment relationships. They communicate our expectations, what we will accept, and how others can show up in relationship with us if they choose. For recovering people-pleasers like myself, you may notice a desire for others to like and understand your boundaries. What a doozy this one is with kids. For a long time I felt like if I connected with a child first, then they would understand the boundary and be compliant with it. That they wouldn't push it. The reality, however, is that I've never set a boundary for a child and had them respond, "Great, I can't wait to follow it!" Shifting my expectations around their response has helped me feel better prepared for how to respond to them. When I set a boundary, I expect the child to be curious about it—to wonder if they can depend on me to hold it. They're so good at asking (through behavior), "What should I expect from you when I do/say . . . ?" When my goal moved from obedience to curiosity, my internal response softened. I was no longer mad at the tiny human in front of me for being curious and could thus move into the role of their regulated adult. I could respond with intention and model for them what it looks like to set and hold a boundary.

When Mika threw the block, I felt my emotions rush up and my instinct was to respond differently than I did. My response was possible because I practiced self-care and built my awareness. I felt that rush of emotions—embarrassed that this was happening in my classroom in front of parents watching my every move, angry that she knew better yet she still threw the block, and disappointed that she wasn't using her words to communicate with me instead. I paused and took a breath, allowing myself to move from my reactive brain into my rational thinking brain. Then I could respond to her with intention, addressing her emotions rather than reacting to my emotions. In a perfect world I would've added an emotion for her in my response: "Mika, I won't let you throw more blocks in our classroom. [*My body next to hers, ready to stop her from throwing another one.*] It looks like you're feeling lonely. If you want someone to play with you, then you can say 'Play' [*signing "play"*] or touch someone and say, 'Play.'" Thank goodness perfection isn't the goal.

What's the Difference Between a Boundary and a Threat?

Boundaries are about personal power. They state what you are willing to accept. A boundary works alongside consequences, letting someone know what to expect if the boundary is pushed. A consequence is in direct relationship to the boundary.

Boundary: I won't let you hit my body.
Consequence: If you hit my body, I will move to keep myself safe.

The boundary outlines your guidelines, and the consequence enforces them. Thus, if you'd like to stay near my body, you are responsible for not hitting me. A threat is about power or control over someone. It is used to manipulate someone to do what you want them to do. Threats jeopardize someone's physical or emotional safety.

Threat: If you hit me, I will spank you.
Threat: If you hit me, I will feel sad and won't talk to you.

Threat: If you hit me, you won't get a doughnut when we go to the bakery later.

Threats are in the punishment family. We will dive deep into punishments, rewards, and consequences in Chapter 8. What's key to note for the sake of boundaries is that clearly stated boundaries + clearly stated consequences = expectations. For now, just notice that threats are not part of the equation. When we know the boundary and the consequences of pushing the boundary, then we can know what to expect as a result. One of our favorite phrases to use just before stating a boundary is "I'm not mad at you. You're not in trouble." Then proceed with the boundary.

Consistency Is Key

Consistent boundaries and consequences help the brain know what to expect in a given scenario. Similar to the way routines become subconscious habits—where you open up the cabinet, grab your coffee cup, pour the coffee, and take a sip without consciously thinking about each step. When a boundary is consistently enforced, we come to expect it to be enforced.

When I was newly dating my now husband, we got in an argument, and I started to yell, and he walked away. It absolutely threw me—isn't yelling how we argue? I yell, you yell, there's a big explosion, and then we come back together. Well, that's not how he navigates conflict, and his boundary became clear right away—*I won't continue a conversation that involves yelling.* Every time we had a conflict, if I yelled, he walked away. I learned that if I wanted to navigate conflict resolution with him, I had to do so without yelling.

We push boundaries all the time, so why don't we expect kids to do the same? Consistently holding boundaries sets an expectation. It's our job to set up a boundary and theirs to be curious about when we will hold it: Is it the same on Saturday as it was on Monday? How about when a co-parent is not home? What if I'm sick? Or you're sick? Is it still the boundary when you're tired? At the end of the day and the beginning? The hardest part is always the beginning because anytime we set a boundary, we must be emotionally prepared for children to push it. It's their job. Laying this foundation can be challenging but it makes the rest of your days much less exhausting.

If Mika had thrown that block in the first few weeks of school, her response to me would have been very different. She may have tested the boundary to see whether or not I would hold it. Maybe she would have thrown another block, perhaps while looking me dead in the eyes, almost daring me to do something about it. That was *my* prediction for the first month of school. I trusted that when I set a boundary, she would likely push it, but if I held that boundary, she would push it with less frequency. Mika threw that block to see if I would hold the boundary when her mom was present. She learned that I would. She also knew from my previous reaction to her throwing blocks at the beginning of the school year that I would move my body close to hers so that I could stop her hand if she tried to throw another block. I consistently sent the message that it was my job to keep her, and everyone else in the classroom, safe, and this time that meant not letting her throw blocks.

Just as important, I gave her two options for what she *could* do to engage with me, or the group, both a verbal and a nonverbal option. We

No Statements	Yes Statements
We don't run inside.	Walking feet, please.
Stop throwing toys!	Set the toys in the basket, like this.
Quit kicking me!	Please be gentle with my body. You can touch my arm like this.
No more TV time.	TV time is over. Would you like to turn it off or should I?

often tell children what they can't do, but what if we included what they *can* do? We can find the yes. "I won't let you climb on that table. You could climb on the couch if you need to move your body." If they climb on the table, then it's your job to hold that boundary, rather than letting them stay on the table. You can help them down and say, "The table is not for climbing. You can climb on the couch." You might even stay by the table to redirect them to the couch if they try again. They are looking to see where that boundary lives. Will you actually hold the line? Or are they really calling the shots here?

You find a new banana bread recipe to try out. You do it once, and it's delicious so you make it again and again. By the third time, you've got all the ingredients out ahead of time, you remembered to preheat the oven, and the measuring tools along with your favorite mixing bowl are already clean and ready to go. You might not even need the recipe to look at because you've made it enough times already to have it down. Now imagine how many times your tiny human would have to make that bread before they understood all the logistics and planning that go into it. Their brains learn new things faster than ours, but a majority of what they encounter on a daily basis is novel, so they are actually working so much harder than us to remember and make meaning of it all. They're constantly soaking in the world around them, building a gazillion new neural connections and concepts; meanwhile, that recipe may have been the only new thing you did this week.

Expect them to need reminders. Anticipate boundary pushing, and be ready to hold the line, letting your child know that the boundary is real. Just like big emotions, boundary pushing can seem spontaneous—accepting this can help you recognize and mitigate an urge to react.

Expectation is something we are setting all day long; from how we let children speak to us, others, and themselves, to who dictates the routine and schedule of the day. "Don't let the inmates run the asylum," my dad used to say when we were kids to explain why we were not in charge. As I got older, I started to wonder, at what age do you stop being the inmate? Is this power structure always true? If my parents make the rules in my house with a "because I said so" mentality, is that how my boss at work will act, too?

This approach of top-down, authoritarian rule came from a desire for control and order. Parents and teachers knew it was their job to make the rules and believed the only way to do this successfully was to make it seem as though they always had control. This idea of control is an illusion. Anyone who has ever tried to get a child to sleep, eat the dinner you served them, or potty train on the adult's schedule knows that the adult does not always have control. (See: My child pooped in the bath last night. Become a parent, they said. It'll be fun, they said.) We see much greater success in children's development when we work with them rather than against them. This doesn't mean that everything is a negotiation, however.

How to Set Boundaries

Boundaries can help the nervous system feel safe. It can be very overwhelming for children if they feel like ultimately the decisions are always up to them. That is far too much responsibility for a child. Boundaries begin with clarity about what the child can expect from us.

Boundaries can sound like:
"I will not let you hit my body. I will hold your hands if you hit my body.
   If you want me to notice you, you can say, 'Play!'"
"I'm going to flip the sand timer. When it empties, you can put your
   pajamas on yourself or I will help you."
"We will spend five more minutes outside. I'll set the timer. When it
   beeps, you can walk or I will carry you."

Children will push the boundaries in order to see their flexibility, and can find comfort in knowing that there are firm rules in place for their security. Many children will ask questions about the boundaries to try and understand what may feel arbitrary to them. Without a doubt, they will express their frustration, anger, disappointment, and/or sadness when they don't like being given a boundary. When this happens, you can connect and empathize with them while holding the boundary. "It's so much fun to get to hang out with your cousins and you didn't want to leave. I get that, babe. I'll be with you on the drive home if you want to talk about it."

When you hold the boundary in this way, they find comfort in seeing that they aren't responsible for the adults' emotions, and that we can handle whatever they are feeling. There is a calm that comes with knowing you are in a safe space to express your emotions. If we can create this space for our children, then we will see immense growth as they trust us enough to be open, honest, and raw. Perhaps the greatest challenge is keeping our calm, letting them know they can feel disappointed/mad/sad about it, and that we can handle their emotions. They are not responsible for your feelings about *their* feelings.

They are not responsible for your feelings about *their* feelings.

Boundaries are also about distinguishing the how from the what. The adult chooses *what* is going to happen and the child chooses *how* it will happen. The following are some examples:

What: We are going to school.
How: We get ready to leave.
The child can choose how to leave: "Would you like to choose your shoes to go to the car, or should I pick them today?"

What: We are leaving the playground.
How: We get to the car.
The child can choose how to get to the car: "The timer beeped. It's time to go to the car. Would you like to fly like an airplane in my arms or hop like a kangaroo?"

What: It's time for teeth brushing.

How: Who brushes your teeth?

The child can choose who brushes their teeth: "It's time to brush your teeth. Would you like Mama or Mommy to brush them tonight?"

Visual aids are helpful for communicating expectations that have a timeline. We'll go in depth on visual aids in Chapter 9 with lots of examples.

Why is the child pushing the boundary?

In order to see the root of the boundary pushing, we have to acknowledge and be mindful of our feelings and energy in the moment. Breathe. Pause. Observe. What's coming up for you? Are you assigning meaning to their behavior and preventing yourself from seeing the bigger picture?

Behavior Reframes

Reframes for promoting teaching without judgment

"She's *so* whiny! I feel like I'm telling her to stop constantly."	"He drew on the wall again! I don't understand it; he knows better!"	"She's *so* naughty. I can't keep up with her!"
↓	↓	↓
"She's advocating for her needs right now. How can I teach her a way that works for both of us?"	"His behavior is communicating something to me. I wonder if he was trying to connect with me while I was on the phone."	"She tests the boundaries to know what is safe. When I set and hold clear boundaries, she can feel safe and empowered."

Here's what that could look and sound like:

- Their behavior feels like disobedience.
- You think they should know better.
- You think they need to learn how to follow the rules.
- Their behavior feels disrespectful.
- You think they're trying to push your buttons.

In many ways, it's natural to see boundary pushing as a form of disobedience—for many of us, that's how we were raised. But now we know so much more about why children behave the way they do, and it's your job to act as a detective to figure out what's at the root of this boundary resistance. If you hear yourself think something like the examples above, remind yourself: "My child is doing the best they can with the tools they have in this moment. They need my support." Now we can step back and get curious: What is the child trying to communicate?

How do you know if they are pushing a boundary versus exhibiting signs of distress?

The following are some signs of physiological distress. This list is not exhaustive.

- Red face
- Vomit
- Bowel movement
- Infant sitting with their hands out appearing overwhelmed
- Toddlers and preschoolers tornadoing around—unable to focus and/or sobbing uncontrollably

Before you can hold that boundary, you need to address the child's underlying stress first. Otherwise, this will not be a successful learning moment. Revisit Chapter 5 for techniques to help soothe them before moving forward.

How do you balance respect with physical boundary holding?

There are things we need to do to keep children healthy and safe that may not make sense to them. Some clear examples of this are taking your child to the doctor for a vaccine or changing a diaper to prevent diaper rash, buckling them into the car seat to keep them safe when they don't want you to do it. Sometimes these things require us to physically move or hold our children even when they resist, even if they say no. It feels bad to bust through someone's boundary, especially a tiny human's boundaries. You may recognize their confusion or feelings of betrayal and have your own feelings and parts of you triggered in response.

First, notice how you feel when they resist, and allow your own feelings. *I feel my heart racing and I'm getting sweaty. This feels overwhelming for me.* Take steps to move through them so that you can bring your calm. *I'm going to breathe and remind myself that it's my job to keep them safe, even when they don't like it.* Then emotion-coach with an emphasis on validation. You can let them know you don't like it either if that's true for you. I have said the following words to my child multiple times: "I know, buddy. This doesn't feel good right now."

When you can't do anything about the sensory experience—the temperature of the wipes, the sensation of the seat belt straps, the feeling of being grabbed to prevent you from running into the road—you have to move through it. See if there are any choices that you can provide as a coping strategy, such as:

- "Would you like to stand or lie down for your diaper change?" (Recommended for wet diapers only.)
- "Would you like to open the tabs on the diaper while I wipe, or no?"
- "Would you like Oma to hold you or me to hold you for this one?"
- "Do you want to put your arm through the strap or shall I?"

Obviously, there are no choices to offer if a child is running into the road or something dangerous like that—just grab them and explain later.

Don't ask twice; just go with the answer they give. If they don't answer, then be clear that you're taking the next steps by narrating in a literal way: "Okay, I'm going to put your right arm through the strap. Okay, now your left arm." There is no need to draw out the process any longer than is helpful. You'll need to accept that they may not get to the moving-on phase until *after* the task is completed. If you can accept this, it will be easier for the child to accept it (over time) because their nervous system will be taking cues from yours.

Before the next time you have to accomplish this task, do some preparations:

- Pre-teach, aka let them know what's coming up—this can help a child learn about the task while they're calm. (We'll go into detail on this in Chapter 9.)
- Use some visual aids—these can help reduce the number of words that you use so there is less information for the child to process. (We'll also go into detail on this in Chapter 9.)
- Take steps to prepare yourself for next time, such as moving through the Phases of Emotion Processing if you didn't get to do that before going through the task or logistical planning with the new information you have. How can you support your child differently next time? You might figure out how to load the car *before* putting your child in, and choose a calm moment to alert them in advance that they will be going in the car seat. You can make sure the wipes are open *before* the diaper change, sing a song or tell an engaging story before starting the diaper change, arrange for a support person to accompany you to the pediatrician's office for vaccines, or practice breathing and prepare a mantra to help you find your calm through the process.

You might be wondering, if children learn from modeling, how will they learn consensual touch when their most trusted caregivers bust through their no? The most important thing here is to be trustworthy. Don't take advantage of your physical power, and advocate when they can't or don't know how. The following are some of the ways you can do this:

- **Honor the no when you can.** In situations of hygiene and safety, it is our job to make sure that children get what they need. Sometimes they don't like it, and that's okay. When it's not a matter of hygiene or safety, then engage your self-awareness monitor to pause and consider what your job is at that moment and whether it's necessary to force them to do what you're asking. My mom loves to tell the story of when I was eighteen months old and she laid out an outfit and I said, "Another one." Sure, she could've pleaded with me and ultimately wrestled that outfit on me, but instead she said, "Okay, it's cold outside so you can choose something that covers your legs and arms." She opened the two drawers of clothes where my pants and long-sleeve shirts were, and I chose my outfit. It would've been faster and easier for her if I'd worn the one she chose. But this was an opportunity to honor my no and empower me to learn self-advocacy skills. If you honor the noes when you can, the child will learn that there are times when you have to do the task even when they've said no, and they'll trust that you are making those decisions with good intentions if you are consistently respecting their physical boundaries whenever you can.

- **Tell children what you're doing as you're doing it.** Our tiniest humans get moved around by us a lot. Give them the respect of letting them know what's coming—for example: "I'm going to pick you up now and bring you to the changing table." Pause to let them process the sound of your voice and then pick them up. Emmi Pikler and Magda Gerber are most well known for teaching this to caregivers in the context of orphanage care in Hungary. Their approach was revolutionary when Pikler opened her orphanage in 1946, but it has since become a recognized approach to infant care in the United States, called the RIE method, through Gerber's teachings on it, and was introduced to mainstream pop culture by Janet Lansbury.

- **Amplify the child's voice if you notice they're uncomfortable with someone else's touch or potential touch.** Each year at least one of my preschoolers confided that they didn't like it when someone specific tickled them. This resonated with me because as a child I was tickled and hated it. Like my preschoolers, I couldn't help but laugh when tickled, which grown-ups interpreted to mean that I liked it. I would ask them if there was anyone who they liked to be tickled by and almost all said the only person they liked to be tickled by was their mother. Seed & Sew posted a video on Instagram of my dad giving my toddler a "zerbert." My little guy was laughing and having a grand ol' time. After the "zerbert," even though he was laughing, my dad paused and asked my child if he wanted another one. My toddler shook his head no and my dad stopped. Practicing consent is possible for a child this young, but it requires us to observe nonverbal cues. Seed & Sew's podcast, *Voices of Your Village*, has some episodes on teaching consent, including how to use big-body, rough-and-tumble play as an opportunity for teaching consensual touch boundaries. Head to www.seedandsew.org/more for the list of episodes.

Even after all these efforts, your little one might still cry the whole time you're changing their diaper. If you've taken the steps to support the child's understanding about the process, the intensity of resistance will lessen over time. Sometimes it takes the next phase of development before it lessens. For example, when the child has learned how to say some of the words you use for the process. My toddler, Sage, learned the sound "Brrr" to anticipate the cold wipes. This helps him communicate about his experience, and in turn helps us let him know we understand why he doesn't like the diaper change. He gets to feel seen and understood in the process while we hold the boundary and change his diaper.

If the intensity of resistance doesn't lessen over time, it could be worth asking for help from the pediatrician or your child's teachers. "Over time" is different for each child and each situation, which is why it's helpful to connect with other people to figure out what the child (their body and brain) is attempting to communicate. I had a four-year-old student, Jessica, who cried and went limp when it was time to go outside in the winter. She logically understood that it was cold outside but insisted a sundress was warm enough. We had tried emotion coaching and other strategies consistently for more than three weeks and nothing worked. Our OT consultant suggested a sensory integration screening, which led to an evaluation. It turned out that this child's sensory system needed some help learning to make sense of the feeling of the snowsuit on her body. The OT provided a soft bristle brush to stroke Jessica's arms and legs with every day before it was time to get the snowsuit on. Jessica loved the sensation of the brush. After a couple of weeks, she was willing to put on her snowsuit and try it outside. She started to enjoy playing in the snow with her friends and didn't need the brush anymore. We were so grateful to have the help of a village beyond our team because we never would have known about this technique otherwise!

Is the behavior attention seeking? If so, how do you respond in a positive manner?

We will often see children push boundaries in an effort to get attention (aka connect with us or a peer). This is great! They are using trial and error to learn how to best captivate their intended audience. We can acknowledge their desire to connect, choose to ignore the boundary pushing for now (if they are safe), and create an invitation to interact in a positive manner.

Jazmine returned to school from a one-week vacation with her family. From the minute she arrived, she had a captive audience, maintaining her teacher's attention as she ran around the classroom taking toys from other children, climbing on surfaces she knew were not safe and were thus not allowed to be scaled. If there was a boundary, she pushed it. The teachers started the morning chasing after her, having her return toys she took, and helping her down from surfaces she wasn't allowed to climb. Not long into the morning one teacher exclaimed, "Wow, she came back fired up. She's driving me crazy."

Here is where mindfulness comes in: breathe, pause, and observe. See if you can let go of judgment—it's not helpful to get stuck in whether or not this *should* be happening. It *is* happening. When the teachers zoomed out to look at what was happening with a different lens, they acknowledged that Jazmine had just spent one week with family, where she had one-to-one adult attention most of the time. Perhaps the transition back to school was challenging for her. Maybe she was looking for more adult interaction like she had just had. Maybe she was sad to leave vacation and family time to dive back into school; that's how I feel every time my vacation ends. Either way, she may have needed more support than usual while transitioning back to school and engaging in a positive manner. Enforcing the boundary was just leading to negative interaction. She may have needed a different approach.

The teacher decided to ignore the negative behaviors as addressing them just seemed to be calling attention to them, and instead provided an opportunity for Jazmine to engage positively with her. Knowing the child's love for reading and music she said, "I'm going to read *Barnyard Dance*." (Thanks to Sandra Boynton for this hit!) The child paused her running and glanced toward the books in the classroom. Then she went off and took a child's toy and ran away with it. None of the teachers acknowledged this behavior. The teacher started reading the interactive book with one child who was singing along. By the second page, Jazmine started filling in the animal noises in the book from across the room. Aha! It was working; she was engaging. Then she climbed onto a table she knew she wasn't allowed to climb on, still pushing those boundaries. The teacher kept reading, and by the end of the story, the child was in the book area participating in the storyline and laughing. When the teacher finished the book, she said, "That was fun! Jazmine, would you like to pick another book to read together?" Jazmine smiled as she ran to the book basket, picked out another one, and brought it to the teacher. If the root of boundary pushing is connection seeking, it will not dissipate until the child feels connected.

Certain children, most commonly around four to five years old, find a physical boundary—such as an adult staying near the table to redirect them as they attempt to climb it—a fun challenge. They need help finding a different activity that will be more appropriate yet still fun. Their physical boundary pushing is an attempt to connect with the adult through play, and when this is the case, the adult needs to reciprocate in order to prevent the deepening of neural pathways related to pushing the physical boundary.

I have countless examples of times I had to interrupt a fight or a boundary-pushing action and the responsible child looked positively happy. There was a group of five-year-olds who looked delighted when I took away a toy that had been the focus of conflict. They were no longer upset as they saw the situation as a happy game of keep away. There was a child who knew we had to respond if they stood on the table, and when he climbed on the table, he was always beaming with joy as we approached because he knew we would need to be present with him to help him down.

Kids want to connect with us, and sometimes the way they subconsciously try to connect can feel annoying or inconvenient. It might feel mischievous or seem like they're pushing our buttons intentionally. In reality, they are signaling a need for connection. When we set boundaries that interrupt a child's intention to connect with us, it's helpful to provide another avenue for connection. If they attempt to connect with you in a physical way that is a mismatch with your boundaries, then try to offer a physical avenue that's a good match. For example: I won't let you climb on my body. Would you like to sit in my lap to read a book?

Life Changes and Boundaries

We are going to dive deep into changes and transitions, such as a new sibling, starting school, moving, and death, in Chapter 12, but let's take a look at boundaries in these seasons of life. Through transitions we sometimes feel the urge to be flexible with boundaries. We know that there is a lot of change happening that a child is adjusting to, and we want to be mindful of how much stress they may be under already. Ironically, this is the reason they need us to *hold the boundary* the most at this time. Locating boundaries is hard work. Knowing that there are firm parameters that are staying the same creates a safe space for children, a sense of comfort so they have some energy to move through the transition.

"Because I Said So": Changing the Boundary After It's Set

Raise your hand if you grew up hearing the phrase "Because I said so." I'm over here with both hands in the air. There was nothing more infuriating for me to hear than this. I always want an explanation. I want to know the why. And you know what? I'm not alone. So many of us, including our tiny humans, want to know the why. This does not mean our answer changes, but it can mean that we change *how we phrase* our answer. It is a constant balancing act of mindfulness of children's autonomy, giving space for innovation, setting guidelines to keep them safe and healthy, and being aware of our internal reactions and narratives. Cultural norms play a huge role in what "balanced" means in this context. In some cultures, children's autonomy is central. In other cultures, respecting elders is gold. There are many correct answers on this scale. How is it for you in your culture? What does balanced look like on your scale?

Sam came over to Amelia and reached for the fire truck she was using. Amelia yelled, "*No!* I'm using that!" Sam started to cry. I was busy making lunch and I popped my head in, saying, "Amelia, you can share the truck with Sam. You can play together." I saw the disappointed look on her face, but I was in the middle of making lunch. As I headed back into the kitchen, I heard a little voice in my head that said, "She doesn't have to share if she doesn't want to." Another voice quickly came back with, "You already set the expectation. If you change it now, they'll expect wavering boundaries."

Hello, ego. I wanted to be seen as in control. I wanted to have the right answer the first time, every time, but I didn't, and I don't. Instead, I paused the lunch prep for two minutes, went back into the room, and said, "Amelia, you do not have to share the truck if you don't want to." Her face softened and she said, "Okay, it's because I have a rescue mission and I need to go to it now." She zoomed off with her truck. Sam started crying again and Amelia looked back, possibly wondering if she would have to share when he cried. I turned to Sam, validated his feeling of disappointment in wanting to use the truck. I co-regulated with Sam for two minutes while he cried and then calmed. Amelia brought him an ambulance, saying, "You can go on your rescue mission and save the person." Sam didn't seem thrilled, but he accepted the ambulance and off they went. I was wrong in my initial reaction, and my fear of inconsistency almost prevented me from changing course.

As frustrating as it feels when we don't do the right thing from the start, this is actually a great teaching moment. We get to model for children how to make mistakes and what to do next. Children will never have all the answers or move through the world perfectly—and neither will we. They'll learn how to stumble and then get up and try again by watching us. It's okay to listen to those voices inside your head and decide for yourself which one will be in the driver's seat.

Sometimes we set boundaries and afterward realize we don't know why we set them. When children question the boundaries, we can get in this place of control, wanting to assert the "because I said so" mentality even though there is no valid reason.

During a meeting at work, Stacey's boss called out her project in front of the team. He picked it apart, and then told her he wanted the revisions on his desk by tomorrow morning. When she got back to her office, she looked at the clock to see that it was 3:36; she had to leave in an hour and a half to get her kids from childcare, and there was no way she'd have enough time to finish the revisions before then. Well, it would be another working-after-the-kids-go-to-bed kind of night. As Stacey was getting dinner ready at home, her wife, Jen, called to say she would be late and was hoping to be home by bedtime. Three minutes later, Stacey walked into the living room to see her three- and five-year-olds had pulled the cushions off the couch and were jumping around the room on them. "Clean up the cushions," she said. "They go on the couch, not the floor, Chase." "But Mama, the floor is the ocean, and if we put the cushions back, we will sink!" "The cushions aren't toys. They go on the couch. Put them back, please." "No, Mama, we will fall in the water!"

Sometimes we set boundaries because we are in go mode, not pausing perhaps in fear of feeling, and that feeling might lead to crashing. It's as if we just keep powering through, then we will make it another day. Sometimes we set boundaries in a desire to control our environment, the classic "because I said so." The thing is, the kids had pulled the cushions off before, and to be honest, Stacey genuinely didn't care; it wasn't really about the cushions, but now what? If she goes back on what she said, will they think that all boundaries are negotiable? In short, no. We can make mistakes, too; in fact, adults making mistakes and talking about it shows kids they are free to fall down and get back up, as well.

Stacey tapped into mindfulness; she practiced self-care in the moment and paused to breathe. You will have hard feelings, hard days, and hard seasons of life, and now you have tools to navigate them. Perfection is not the goal here. Stacey's self-awareness and ability to pause, give herself space, and enter her rational thinking brain was the best choice for her tiny humans, deciding to not hold the arbitrary boundary about the cushions that she'd formed as a reaction to her feelings.

One of the concepts I studied in yoga is "boundaries = freedom." It may seem counterintuitive, but as you start to gain clarity on where your own boundaries are, the children will, too. You won't have to work so hard to establish them every time. And children won't have to do as much research to find out where they are. There is more freedom for both of you. Plus, you'll be able to see the emotional nature of children's responses to boundaries, which will open up a chance to connect through CEP.

Chapter 7

When and How to Talk About the Behavior

Many of us grew up in households where behavior was addressed immediately. There's a belief that we need to talk about it right away, so children know what they did was wrong.

Before diving into when and how to talk about their behavior in a way that supports long-term behavioral change, take a minute to ask yourself something really important: What's your goal? Why do you want to talk to the child about their behavior? Is it:

- **Accountability:** Do you want to hold them accountable for their actions to teach them about how their behavior affects others?
- **Skill building:** Are you trying to help them build a new skill in order to make a different choice in the future?
- **Skill access:** Do you know they have a skill, but they didn't use it in that moment, and you want to help them learn how to access that skill in future moments?
- **Inclusion and connection:** Are you trying to help them learn how else to communicate their needs so they can feel connected to others and be socially included?
- **Personal responsibility:** Do you feel like your success is modeled through their behavior?

Every single one of these reasons makes sense and hits home. We want kids to access skills we know they have, build new ones, understand their impact on those around them, and feel connected and included. We also understand the very real personal work of acknowledging how others perceive us based on our child's behavior.

Sometimes strangers will comment, "He's such a good kid," about my son, Sage. What they mean is "He's so convenient." **All kids are good kids.** All kids want to feel safe, connected, and secure. And all kids are learning about the world for the first time. They're learning how to be in relationship with other people. They're learning cultural norms and how they're "supposed to" act at home versus a restaurant versus Grandma's house versus a grocery store. When we believe they are doing the best they can with the tools they have in that moment, it can help us reach a place of compassion and curiosity. We can become collaborators rather than entering into combat with them. They *want* to show up in the way that helps them feel safe and included, so if they aren't doing so, they're letting us know they need help. How we help them matters.

Self-Esteem versus Shame

Self-esteem is how we value and perceive ourselves. It's defined by *Merriam-Webster* as "a confidence and satisfaction in oneself." Brené Brown, *New York Times* bestselling author of *The Gifts of Imperfection*, defines shame as an intensely painful feeling or experience of believing that we are flawed and therefore unworthy of love and belonging. Shame is a powerful tactic for short-term behavior change, but it has devastating, lasting effects.[1] Self-esteem is about the behavior. Shame is about the person.

Shame: I am bad.
Self-esteem: I'm a kind human who made a bad choice.

Shame: I am lazy.
Self-esteem: I am unengaged and feeling unmotivated right now.

Shame: I am annoying.
Self-esteem: I am lovable and do annoying things sometimes.

As we dive into how and when to talk about a child's behavior, we will look at shame and self-esteem and the impacts they can have.

How do you talk to yourself when you make a mistake? The other day I was visiting a friend who was reflecting on a text she'd just sent. "I don't know why I wrote that. I guess I was upset. I'm so stupid . . ." I know my friend is not stupid, so I reminded her of that, and we agreed that a mantra like that would not help the situation. It takes an empathetic person to recognize that their words might have hurt someone else. It's a lot easier for me to acknowledge that with someone else than it is for myself. Sometimes, when I feel shame about something I said or did, I replay the situation over and over with better ways I might have responded in the moment. I'm always afraid to talk to someone about it because of the shame. When I finally push myself to talk to a dear one or a trusted colleague, that shame gets named and disarmed. I can learn from the situation instead of getting stuck in it—all because of the way they show up for me.

We all say things we regret, and make mistakes in general, no matter how thoughtful we are. Often it's because of our nervous system reaction or that our self-awareness monitor is asleep at the wheel. It matters how we talk to ourselves and to children when that happens. Until recently, the traditional approach to teaching how to "be nice" to other people included shaming to try and change behavior. "Look how sad you made them. That's not nice. You made them cry." Or, "How would you like it if someone took your toy?" Remember the '80s car seat? Here is another example of how generations of parents who came before us were doing the best they could with the tools they had at the time. With mindfulness, without judgment, we can try something different, but it means changing the way we talk to ourselves and children, too. As Peggy O'Mara says, "The way we talk to our children becomes their inner voice."

When to Talk About the Behavior

The most significant indicator that it's a good time to talk about the behavior is that the child feels calm; your nervous system is disarmed and so is the child's. Mindfulness and the five CEP components are your best tools to get there and to assess the situation. The following are a couple of questions to ask yourself in order to figure out the best time in each situation with a child:

- **What do words mean to them?** Have you ever started talking to a child about the behavior and they seem to ignore you and get distracted? Maybe you've tried to address it and it seems to go in one ear and out the other and you're wondering how to make it stick. Sometimes some kids benefit from more than an adult just talking it through with them. Maybe you'll snag the emotion cards or coping visuals, or perhaps there's a book you have that addresses this behavior or challenge. Visual aids can be a really helpful tool, especially for neurodivergent humans. Using visual aids (emotion cards, coping visuals, schedule, etc.) is not essential, but it's helpful to provide it as an option if you can. Telling a story about a time you experienced that same thing can help your child work through what it means for them. Before diving into the discussion about the behavior, you can gather the visuals or think about the social story you'll tell. When we gather our thoughts and plan as the adult before entering into the conversation, it can help us move through it in a regulated state and connect with the child.
- **How do they remember?** I've heard plenty of people say, "I have such a bad memory." But they're not all talking about the same thing. One person might be talking about dates or numbers, someone else might be talking about childhood moments, and others are talking about remembering what happened yesterday. How long will a child be able to remember something that happened? It depends on *how* they remember and *what kinds* of

episodes they remember. Some children will remember the little details from every single grocery store trip you've ever taken. Others will remember how key events felt. Pay attention to the child's way of remembering in order to figure out if it's worth talking about something that happened yesterday. Do they recount events or bring things back up from previous experiences? Note: If the child is four years or older and doesn't remember what happened (or seems genuinely bewildered) right after a challenging behavior happened— and often—then talk to the pediatrician, teachers, and/or school admin about types of screenings that might help figure out the best strategies.

- **Are they regulated?** When a child has hurt someone, or they run away, their nervous system is not regulated. Wait until they let you approach them for CEP and after you've helped them through the five phases to process their feelings.
- **When there is a chronic behavior, then a good time to talk about it is out of context.** Choose a time when both of you are calm and there is a natural lull in activity. For some children, it helps to reduce vulnerability if both of you are using your hands to work on something enjoyable and not making eye contact (i.e., food prep, building with Legos, drawing, folding laundry). If you're in the car for a while together, that could be a good time. Be mindful not to "trap" the child into talking with you. If they resist, this is the child's attempt to communicate something like "I'm afraid you're mad at me"; "Your words are reminding me that I was 'bad'"; "I'm having a feeling, but I don't know what it is or what to do with it"; etc. You can stop and let them know, "I love you always, even when you make mistakes or have a hard time." And let the conversation pause there for a later time.

Don't try to talk about the behavior when your child is still in their reactive brain. They are not able to retain the information at that time. If you try to talk to them about what happened and they yell or scream, they may need more time to regulate. If it's been a little while and every time you revisit the behavior, they react or say they don't want to talk about it, try letting them know they aren't in trouble and you aren't mad at them. It can also be helpful to share a story of a time when you did something similar to normalize making mistakes and model how to move forward.

As a part of our nap and bedtime routine in my household, we touch base about the day. I mention things I noticed like "I saw you give Alice a turn with the lawn mower toy. That was kind of you to include her." Sometimes I mention certain behaviors or a hard moment from the day: "When you were trying to put your shoe on, it kept getting stuck. It's frustrating to work on a new skill sometimes." [*Pause.*] "Instead of throwing the shoe, you can squeeze your fists and say 'Grrrrr!'" Sometimes they will practice it then or sometimes they just take it in. It's like journaling to offload the experiences from the day. As kids get older, adding in a journal or notebook for them to draw in can help process those daily challenging behavior moments.

How to Talk About the Behavior

Have you ever understood something intellectually but struggled to take action or feel it on a visceral level? For example, any of my friends or family will tell you that I do too much. It's true. I say yes to work (I really like my work) and DIY projects without considering the number of hours in a week, and I understand this on an intellectual level. I'm starting to learn what I need to do to change, but I don't feel it in my body yet. I'm working on embodying my intentions with my proactive and supplemental self-care techniques, and I've learned I need to have patience with myself. Just because I know in my mind doesn't mean I know in my body. There is more than one kind of knowing.

Maybe your child just threw their cup at you—again. You think the child *knows* you don't want them to throw things at you—and it's possible they do know on an intellectual level. But it's possible they don't know it in their body yet. If their behavior doesn't line up with what you think they know, it's not because they consciously chose to do the opposite. The task here is to excavate beneath the surface, to translate the behavior as communication. What would cause the child to do the thing you just asked them not to? What would cause a child to run away instead of listen? What would cause a child to scream instead of put their coat on or allow you to put them into the car seat? What would cause them to throw a chair? They may be saying No to you, but what are they saying Yes to? Lead by example by finding your physiological calm, so you can reframe their behavior, interpret their attempt to communicate, and coach through the Phases of Emotion Processing.

In 2010, Ross W. Greene gave us the concept of Plan B in his book *The Explosive Child.* Greene described Plan A as situations where the adult makes a decision about how to solve a problem (a top-down approach to emotions and behavior). Plan C refers to situations where the child is in control and the parent defers (a passive approach to emotions and behavior). Plan B is when you notice in a nonjudgmental way what happened and then ask your child, "What's up?" Like "I noticed that every morning when we're getting our coats on, you scream. What's up?" After that, you set the stage to solve the problem *with* the child. By asking about this behavior in a nonjudgmental way, you might find out that the wrist elastic on the child's coat feels too tight. Collaboration in problem solving with children happens in a developmentally appropriate way during Phase 5 of Emotion Processing. The only way to get to Phase 5 is to coach through Phases 1–4. Practice nonjudgment as you coach by reflecting back what you see and hear. For children who are verbal, add a check-in phrase such as: "How are you feeling?" "What's up?" "Are you okay?" or another open-ended question. The goal is to let the child know it's their turn to talk and share their experience. The following are some examples:

- "I saw that you threw your cup just now. What's up?"
- "I noticed you've been running and bumping into us a lot this morning. Whoa, your heart is beating so fast. How are you feeling?" (Secure attachment and comfort with physical touch will help by putting one hand gently on their chest and the other gently on their back.)

- "I noticed that you've screamed at Maddie a couple of times just now. Are you okay?"

If they don't know what's up or don't have words, you can provide your best guess—for example:

- "Did you throw your cup because you were disappointed that I said no cookies today?"
- "I see your tears. Are you sad because you miss Mami?"
- "Are you feeling mad because Maddie is playing with your favorite car?"

During Phase 5: Moving On, you can talk about alternatives to the behavior:

- "Since throwing your cup isn't safe, I wonder what you could do the next time you have a big feeling . . . How about squeezing your hands really tight and saying 'AHHHHH!' next time you have a big feeling?"
- "I miss Mami when she's gone, too. Sometimes I send her messages when I'm missing her the most. I know that you love painting. When you miss Mami, how about making a special painting that we can send her instead of running around and bumping into us?"
- "It seemed like talking about this helped you feel better. Next time you're mad and feel like screaming at Maddie, how about you come and get me right away?"

Make space for children to reject your ideas and share their own. Also, be prepared to think of a couple of other suggestions if they don't have any.

An indirect, less vulnerable way to talk about a behavior is to bring it up during play at a later time. You could play a character who needs help moving through a similar big feeling, or the doll could be having the feeling. Two Lego people could be having a conflict and need the help of a third Lego person. The key here is to really get into character. Children can often sense inauthentic play. Make sure that you play with children at other times, too, not just when addressing behaviors.

No matter when you talk about the behavior, keep your tone and words nonjudgmental and keep the messaging simple. It's okay to introduce a new word, especially because it can engage the child's curiosity, but use mostly words and concepts that the child already knows. Remember, they are working hard to learn emotion concepts and processing in this moment, which is the priority. Giving too much information to process and/or learn will take their energy away from the goals of this moment.

One last thing to help you decide when and how to talk about the behavior is the development of the moral compass. Most children who are younger than five years have a binary moral compass. Things are good or bad. Even at eight months they have an association with helpfulness as preferable and unhelpfulness as unpreferable,[2] and they also rely on our responses to behaviors (theirs and others') to understand what else is good and bad. By age seven, most children have started to develop their own internal sense of ethics and might be able to articulate why they think something is good or bad. As with all developmental milestones, there are exceptions here, too. Use this information as a general guide to figure out if it's more likely you're talking to someone with a good-bad binary moral compass or someone with a beginning sense of their own about why something might be good or bad.

Repair: A Key Ingredient for Secure Attachment Relationships

One of the cornerstones of secure attachment is repair as a crucial component to a safe, healthy relationship. Inherent in the acknowledgment of repair is that mistakes are welcome. I've never left the day as a parent or teacher and said, "Wow, I was perfect today." Perfect isn't the goal. We can't say to children that they are allowed to make mistakes but then hold ourselves to a binary standard of perfection or failure. Pause for a minute—let's say that again: We can't say to children that they are allowed to make mistakes but then hold ourselves to a binary standard of perfection or failure. You aren't failing if they make mistakes. You aren't failing if you make mistakes. Everyone will have moments of dysregulation, losing their cool, yelling, reacting instead of responding with intention, and that's okay. What's important is what we do next.

Big Little Feelings co-founder Kristin Gallant shared a story about her eldest child's first day of kindergarten. In the weeks leading up to this big transition, Kristin shared her big feelings about her little girl heading off to kindergarten and all that comes with that transition. As they were getting out the door on the first day, Kristin wanted to snap that classic "first day of kindergarten" photo with her girls right after putting their new shoes on. It was precisely at this moment that everything exploded. All the emotions came thrashing out—meltdowns for the tiny humans and big humans alike.

> **We can't say to children that they are allowed to make mistakes but then hold ourselves to a binary standard of perfection or failure.**

In that moment, while her youngest (at the time) was crying, Kristin started fighting with her husband, and she yelled, "Can we just take one picture?! Just one nice picture?!" The older one at this point started crying and said, "Mommy, can we take a break?" At which point Kristin realized, *Damn, I messed up.*

She paused. She co-regulated with her girls, found their calm together, paused the pictures, and moved through it together. As they headed to school, they repaired: Kristin owned her part in losing her cool, connected with her children, and got the picture once everyone was regulated. Repair builds connection. It says, "Sometimes I'm going to drop the ball because being human is messy, and I will acknowledge and be accountable for how I show up in our relationship."

Repair is possible when we are regulated enough to see our part in a conflict or mistake. When we can truly acknowledge the role we played. Signs you are ready for repair include: your body is regulated; you're able to see the other person's perspective; you can acknowledge your reaction without placing blame or ownership on the other person; you are ready to connect; you are feeling curious and/or compassionate.

Repair with a child can sound like:

"We got home from grocery shopping and everyone was asking for things at once and I felt overwhelmed. I'm sorry that I yelled. Next time I'm going to take deep breaths to calm my body."

"This afternoon has been hard. Would you like to hit the pause button with me and read a book?"

"I was trying to finish the dishes when you asked to play with that toy and I answered quickly. I've changed my mind; you can use it if you'd like. Let's find a safe place to play."

During a genuine repair interaction is a good time to model how to use the phrase "I'm sorry." This will be a data point for children as they build their concept of "sorry" because it's real, it's in context, and it's happening within the attachment relationship. If you walked away when a child was having a hard time, repair is a time where you can connect over why, letting them know it wasn't a punishment. This might sound like "Sometimes when my feelings get really big, I need space for a minute to calm my body down so I can help you. It helps me feel calm if I go to the bathroom and take deep breaths. What helps your body feel calm?" If you leave this book with one thing, I hope it's that you know that you're allowed to be imperfect, learn, grow, and try again. Being in relationships includes making mistakes and making amends as you navigate the messiness of being human.

Does Giving Them Attention Reinforce the Behavior?

"Just ignore him and he will stop," my mom would tell me when my brother pushed my buttons as a kid. For some of us, the idea that ignoring the behavior will make it go away runs deep. Behavior is communication of an unmet need. This isn't to say you aren't meeting their needs regularly. It just may be your child's way of telling you they need you in this moment. When we can regulate our reaction in the moment to better understand why they are acting the way they are—what unmet need they are communicating—then we can recognize that we aren't reinforcing behavior by giving them attention, but rather helping our little ones develop a new skill for communicating that works better than the behavior. These are social skills, which we teach after we help them calm.

Attention-seeking behavior is connection-seeking behavior. Children don't often ask for connection by saying, "Will you connect with me?" They ask by pulling your shirt while you make lunch, throwing their cup on the ground, yelling, "You're the worst. I hate you!" You might have an internal reaction to these behaviors and notice a desire to disconnect, ignore them, not feed into the behavior, or even punish them. (We will dive into punishments in Chapter 8 and offer alternatives that are actually effective in building long-term, life skills for children.) For now, *notice* your reaction and remind yourself, "They are trying to connect and need help."

Children benefit from explicit and nonjudgmental teaching about what kinds of behaviors are effective ways to get an adult's attention. Tell them what they *can* do: "Instead of throwing your toy, you can say 'Play'!" At the beginning of each school year, I would have preschoolers attempting to get my attention in all kinds of ways. I would take the time to teach them how I wanted to be treated with some options they could choose from. The conversation always started with the child's attempt to get my attention, for example by hitting my leg forcefully. Then I would ask, "Are you trying to get my attention?" To which they would usually nod yes. "I want to pay attention to you when you need it. Here are some of the ways you can get my attention: You could tap my leg gently like this and say, 'Lauren?' Or you could say, 'Excuse me.' Or if you like hugs, you can come and give me a hug. Do you want to practice? Here, I'll pretend I don't know you're coming—which one do you want to try?"

I was visiting friends and their three-year-old daughter, Miley, was shouting and bopping around repeatedly as my friends and I chatted. We slowly increased our volume to keep hearing each other. I noticed Miley kept looking at me in the midst of the shouting, so I said, "Miley, are you trying to get my attention?" With exasperation she said, "Yes!" So I replied with a smile, "You don't have to shout—just come on over here and say, 'Excuse me, Lauren.' Then I'll know you want to talk to me." She came over with a big grin and told me about her new costume. My friends and I were able to get our conversation in after that. If the shouting for attention had happened again, I would have invited Miley to practice saying "Excuse me," but on this day, all she needed was the validation that her desire to connect was real.

Meeting needs for connection doesn't have to happen with 1:1 time. You can fill their connection bucket by noticing . . . "I noticed you made a path for us to walk by your train tracks. Thanks for being thoughtful." "I noticed you scooched over for Kana to sit by you. You're so kind." "I noticed you took space when you were feeling frustrated with your Lego earlier." This doesn't mean they won't ask you to notice them in other moments. Children will offer a bid for connection or utilize behavior to communicate their need for it.

Forced Apologies versus Genuine Acknowledgment

"You need to go apologize." "Go tell him you're sorry." If you grew up in a culture where these statements were present, you might hear those words coming out of your mouth out of habit. We want children to learn how to be accountable for their actions—we get that. It makes sense to want someone to apologize for what they've done because it acknowledges that someone was hurt in relationship to their behavior. As we talked about in the "Repair" section on page 161, owning *our* share of a conflict and our mistakes are crucial parts of secure attachment relationships, but there's a difference between a forced or obligatory apology and genuine acknowledgment.

Imagine your partner comes home from work after a long day and snaps at you moments after walking in the door, "The laundry is still in the basket and dinner hasn't even been started yet. What have you been *doing*?" Now imagine right after that, your friend who's over says, "Stella, that's not kind. You need to go apologize to Macy right now." Stella comes over, looks away, and mumbles, "Sorry." How does that feel? Do you feel more connected to your partner now? "A meta-analysis of 175 studies showed that an apology was one of the most powerful predictors of interpersonal forgiveness, greater than any demographic, personality, or relationship characteristic. However, an apology is not always effective in resolving conflicts. Whether or not conflict resolution occurs generally depends on the perception of the apology as trustworthy, genuine, and sincere by the injured party."[3]

In *NurtureShock: New Thinking About Children*, Po Bronson and Ashley Merryman discuss how we unintentionally teach kids to lie. One of the examples is forced apologies.[4] What does the word "sorry" actually mean? According to *Merriam-Webster*, it means "feeling sorrow or sympathy" and "feeling regret or penitence." If the child doesn't actually feel either of those things, then teaching them to say "I'm sorry" is setting them up for miscommunication in the future. Feeling sorry requires some already developed self-awareness and perspective-taking skills. It's an emotion concept that should be taught like the other emotions—when you perceive it in the child, when you're reading a book or watching a show that has a character who feels sorry, or by modeling when you feel it.

If a child makes the same mistake a few times, they'll need you to start teaching them (or change how you teach them) the skills that they need to navigate similar situations. Otherwise, you are just pointing out their failures again and again. This sends the message that there is something intrinsically wrong with them, which can lead to compounded feelings of

Is your reason . . .	Try this instead . . .	Why?
To show them that what they did is wrong?	Help them identify the feeling you think they were having when they demonstrated the behavior. Did they feel left out? Embarrassed? Lonely? Angry? (Phases 1 and 2.) Then let them know it's okay to have those feelings (Phase 3), but it's not okay to [*insert undesired behavior*]. Offer suggestions about what to do instead next time (Phase 4)—if your child enjoys pretend play you can even pretend to go back in time to practice the new idea (Phase 5).	It's inevitable that the child will experience this feeling again. So, our job is to help them get comfortable having that feeling so that they learn to regulate themselves when they experience it next time, and know what tools are available to them in order to help them process—building the Coping Strategies Toolbox. Remember: Problem solving (thinking of something to do differently next time in this situation) is the last phase of emotion processing.
To help the other child feel better?	CEP with the other child. Help the other child feel better with your help (regardless of where the child who made the mistake is) to identify their emotion, provide validation (Phases 1–3). Then help them seek coping strategies (Phase 4) and problem solving (Phase 5) if needed.	In the real world, people don't usually come and apologize right after they make a mistake. In fact, they may never return to apologize. Let's teach children that their processing and moving on is something they can control, and that it's not dependent on someone else apologizing. Also, we give children too much power/pressure if we lead them to believe they can control others' emotions (especially adult emotions).

(box continues)

Is your reason . . .	Try this instead . . .	Why?
To teach empathy?	Model empathy consistently, especially in your own interactions with children and in front of children. Chapter 11 is dedicated to the development of empathy so stay tuned for more strategies.	According to Bronson and Merryman, requiring an apology before a child actually feels regret will teach them to lie rather than to experience empathy. Also, when shame about making a repeated mistake is a factor, it may be even harder to learn empathy because shame is not a safe place. Eventually that may be appropriate, but kids who chronically hurt others need to take this step of learning about others' emotions in a less personal way first before they can experience empathy.

shame. When you feel the urge to have a child apologize, we encourage you to ask yourself why you are requesting this. If the reason is something in the left column of the table above, then we recommend an alternative CEP approach in the center column, along with the why in the right column.

A more recent and popular version of a forced apology is a forced "check-in" with the other child before moving on. The argument for this is often so that the child will learn how their behavior affects other people, or to teach them empathy. When the "check-in" occurs before the child is regulated enough to connect with you and with the other child, they aren't able to experience empathy yet. Empathy is not taught through shame, guilt, or embarrassment, but rather through safety and connection. We will dive deep into developing empathy in Chapter 11—buckle up.

It's never too late to start this practice. I was at a friend's gathering with adults and kids alike when a conflict between two elementary-aged children arose. After I popped down and supported the children through the conflict, one of their parents came to me and said, "Okay, I've been making her say 'I'm sorry,' but I like what you just did. How do I change from saying 'I'm sorry' to doing that?" As we learn new things, we can pull from Adam Grant's research on rethinking outlined in his book *Think Again* and model for kids the power of growth. The next time you have a calm moment together, you can say, "Hey, buddy, I learned something new about saying 'I'm sorry.' When we don't feel sorry in our bodies, then it doesn't feel good for the other person if we say it. Next time, if you're having a hard time, I'm going to practice helping you before we say 'I'm sorry' or check in with anyone else."

Chapter 8

Consequences, Punishments, and Rewards

*Punishment: the infliction or imposition of a penalty
as retribution for an offense.*[1]

We live in a punishment-oriented society. In fact, there is a humongous for-profit industry that is solely focused on it, called the prison industrial complex. We know that punishment affects behavior. Corporal punishment was alive and well in the '80s and was considered an effective way to "teach" kids what we don't want them to do. I was spanked as a child—maybe just once, and I think my mom cried afterward. But at that moment I became immediately determined to avoid ever being spanked again. This irony is that I have no idea what it was that I was supposed to not repeat. As it became clear that this was not the most effective way to teach, parents have tried to replace one kind of punishment with others. It makes sense, especially if punishment was our experience as children.

We have all kinds of curious approaches to "teaching" through punishment. Did you have to stand in the corner? Did you have to miss out on a chance to connect with your friends because you were sentenced to time out or you were grounded? I remember the day my cousin's parents got his seventh grade report card, and disappointed in his grades, they promptly removed his beloved stereo from his room. He was emotionally destroyed by this move, but it didn't help with his grades. It seemed like every year there was a different punishment for unsatisfactory grades.

Punishment removes children from the teaching and learning context by seeking to cause hurt, loss, and/or isolation in the hopes it will make the child think twice before repeating the same mistake in the future. Let's pause to remember why kids do stuff we don't want them to do using the Triangle of Growth, which we covered in Chapter 3—it invites us to look at sensory system regulation, emotion processing, and language. Punishment has nothing to do with teaching and learning sensory system regulation, emotion processing, and language. Punishment is not on the list of ways that humans teach and learn that we covered in Chapter 4: intentional modeling, active encouragement, exaggeration to make the qualities of the task more obvious, breaking down the steps of a task so they are clearer. In fact, when we punish, we are only teaching punishing behavior by modeling punishing behavior, and/or fear of retaliation within our attachment relationships.

Six-year-old Sasha came home from her first day of riding the bus to school. "There is a naughty seat at the front of the bus. If you don't listen, you have to go there for two weeks. So I won't be able to see you for that whole time," she told her mom. If you misbehave on the bus, you have to sit in the naughty seat for two weeks, and in her six-year-old mind, that meant you couldn't *leave* that seat for two weeks—you lived there. No school. No home. Nothing. How terrifying would that be? At six years old!

When we create punishments with the goal of controlling a child's behavior, we can send unintended messages. Punishments are often used to reduce "bad" behavior. We get that desire. We really do. But when we get stuck on the behavior we see on the surface, we miss the opportunity to meet the child's need that is driving the behavior. Until that need is met, we will continue to see new "bad" behaviors appear in other areas as the child subconsciously tries to get the need for regulation or connection met. Punishments can include time-outs, ignoring, threats, shaming, and taking away things that are unrelated to the behavior. Physical and emotional abuse are also a form of punishment.

Intrinsic versus Extrinsic Motivation

External reward: a thing given in recognition of one's service, effort, or achievement.

Suppose Sasha comes home from her first day riding the bus to share that "Every day that you are good on the bus, you get a sticker by your name. If you're good every day for the month, you get to pick out of the prize box at the end of the month." External rewards are often used to try and get more of the "good" behavior. Some examples are verbal praise, sticker charts, toys, sweets, and attention, which are only given after certain behaviors. It makes sense, right? When we reward the behaviors we want to see, we will see more of them.

The problem is that we aren't helping children build skills for communicating and meeting their underlying needs, plus we're undermining the brain's *intrinsic* reward system. What happens when there isn't an external reward? Will that "good" behavior still show up? Rewards often elicit a dopamine response in the brain. The tricky thing about dopamine is that when we get some of it, our body wants more, and then to feel as good as it did the last time, it wants even more, which can result in needing further and ever-changing rewards to continue to get the same behavioral result.

We also release dopamine when we've accomplished something that was challenging and when we make it through something risky. In these situations we don't need an external reward to reinforce behavior because our brain has already delivered the dopamine reward. For example, when we get through the really big emotions together, we've accomplished something that was challenging and that's an opportunity for our dopamine systems to naturally reinforce this hard work for both children and adults. The trigger for dopamine release was getting through something that was hard, not a sticker reward. So the unconscious result is "working hard feels good" rather than "getting stickers feels good." External rewards can interfere with the nurturing of intrinsic motivation.

Consequences

Consequence: a result or effect of an action or condition.[2]

Suppose Sasha shared about her first day riding the bus, saying, "The bus driver told us that it's her job to keep us safe. If someone is not being safe with their body or someone else's body, then they sit in the first seat buckled in for the ride so the bus driver can make sure everyone is safe while she's driving." The bus driver's expectation is safe behavior. The consequence for crossing this boundary is sitting right behind the driver, and buckled in. In an ideal world, there would also be a system in place to address the *root* of the child's "unsafe" behavior if it becomes a consistent theme on the bus. Consequences can be natural or imposed. A natural consequence is a direct result of an action, like getting wet after jumping in a puddle. An imposed consequence could be the adult moves the markers out of reach after the child draws on the wall.

It's okay if an imposed consequence feels natural to the child because it happened behind the scenes. This approach would be a good

Imposed Consequence	Natural Consequence
When a child repeatedly harms their sibling, you separate them to keep everyone safe.	When a child throws their cup to the floor, the cup is out of reach.
When a child runs away in a public space, you tell them they have to hold your hand.	When a child uses scissors to cut their pants, there's a hole in their pants.
When a child climbs on the kitchen counter, you move the child's body to a safe place to climb, like the couch.	After a child dumps water on their shirt while playing, they get wet.

fit if we had an expectation that turned out to be unreasonable for their development. For example, if the child who was drawing on the walls was eighteen months old, it would be questionable to leave markers out where they could reach them with the expectation that the walls wouldn't be drawn on. In this situation we can just put the markers up on the shelf and spend more time modeling and guiding how to use markers before we try leaving them within reach again. When determining an imposed consequence, make sure it's something that you'd be okay with and/or able to follow through on. For example, would you actually keep your kids home from the family gathering (which requires you to miss it, as well)? If not, then it's not a helpful consequence. Also, if you feel a hint of revenge or find yourself trying to think of a consequence that would make the biggest impact, you may actually be seeking a punishment. If so, practice some responsive self-care to regulate your nervous system before you make that determination. When you choose a consequence, it should be directly related to the situation, and without emotional investment on your part.

Scenario: Child pours excessive amounts of maple syrup all over his plate during a pancake breakfast.

Punishment: Now you have to eat at the small table by yourself.

Imposed consequence: I will help you pour the syrup on your pancakes next time.

Scenario: Child is stalling at bedtime, not putting on pajamas, brushing teeth, etc.

Punishment: I'm not going to lie with you at bedtime if you don't put your pajamas on now.

Imposed consequence: We have ten minutes left until bedtime. If the timer beeps before your pajamas are on, we won't have time left for books before bed.

Emotionally supportive parenting or teaching includes both natural and imposed/logical consequences as a way to help a child in the moment of either dysregulation or skill building. Imposing consequences allows kids the freedom to choose their actions, but it does not mean the adult is permissive with boundaries. Expressed boundaries + consequences = known expectations.

How to Navigate Consequences and Discipline in a Punishment-Reward System

We live in a punishment-reward culture: punitive approaches to discipline in schools, mass incarceration, and workplace compensation and promotion systems, to name just a few examples. Society at large is waking up to what many of us have known for a long time—that people are punished or rewarded differently depending on their social identity. How can we set kids up to enter a world where they will regularly encounter punishment-reward systems while we're valuing and teaching something completely different? Author of *How We Do Family* Trystan Reese once told me, "We have to prepare children for the world we live in, while empowering them to change it." We do have a responsibility to teach children how to navigate the systems they'll encounter, and what we decide to teach will be rooted in our own experience with these systems. The way we teach it can be the same way we teach social skills:

- Reading books together and talking about the character's experiences
- Preparing children for the spaces they will enter (if you scream in the movie theater, an employee will tell you to leave rather than asking you how you're feeling)
- Getting curious with children as they notice or encounter punishment-reward systems
- Discussing the system's goal(s) and asking for their input on another way it might be reached

If you believe that these systems are not fair, then you can talk about that with children, too. The second edition of the book *Anti-Bias Edu-*

cation for Ourselves and Our Children[3] and *Raising Antiracist Children: A Practical Parenting Guide*[4] are our two favorite resources for learning about how to discuss unfairness and how to change it in a way that makes sense to tiny humans. The first is designed for teachers, and the concepts apply to parenting, too.

We can be with children through the process, letting them know that while different spaces, people, and environments may have different rules and expectations than we do at home, we will maintain a safe emotional space at home for processing.

Connecting with Children to Clarify Expectations

When people start practicing CEP, they sometimes wonder if they are unintentionally reinforcing negative behaviors. You don't have to worry so much about figuring out what *negative* behaviors you're reinforcing if you focus instead on connecting with children—letting them know you see them—when they've done something that matches your values. Some ways to connect and let children know you see them include mini-parties (silly dances or jumping up and down), high fives, hugs, big smiles, a thumbs-up, or praise such as: "You did it!" "Wow, do you feel so proud?" "Yay!!!" Tom Drummond's "Guides for Enterprise Talk" (linked at www .seedandsew.org/more) is a great resource if you want help thinking creatively about phrasing and body language.

As you're coming up with some ways to connect over positive behavior, please take these things into account:

1. "The thumbs-up gesture is commonly used in many cultures to signify a job well done. However, if it is used in Australia, Greece, or the Middle East—especially if it is thrust up as a typical hitchhiking gesture would be—it means essentially "Up yours!" or "Sit on this!"[5] When your family is bicultural or you're interacting with a child whose primary culture is different from your own, it's important

to educate yourself about social cues that are related to that other culture.

2. Studies show that if you say "Good job," kids are likely to think that means they're done with something and stop doing it. Also, because it is not specific, the child may not know which behavior you were excited about. Try something like "Wow, look at how much space there is to walk after you put all your books away so carefully! Thanks for cleaning them up so we don't trip on them."

3. Studies show that if you praise a child's personality trait after they work on a math problem—for instance, "You solved that problem quickly. You're smart!"—then they are less likely to choose a more challenging math problem next, perhaps for fear of actually not being "smart." But if you praise their hard work—"You solved that problem quickly. You worked hard!"—then they are ready for the next challenge and will choose a more challenging problem. This acknowledges what they can control in the moment—how hard they work—rather than traits that they either have or don't have—something they don't have control of in the moment. It also emphasizes the value of the process rather than the end result.[6]

Strategies for making your expectations more accessible to children are:

- **Acknowledge their prosocial gestures.** We often catch kiddos when they are doing something that is undesirable, but what if you *acknowledge them* when they are exhibiting pro-social behaviors? "Thank you for helping Sarah clean up those blocks. That was so kind of you." This is a great way to build trust with children and help them feel seen as collaborative members of society, the family, or the classroom. Imagine how it would feel if someone said, "Hey, thanks for doing the dishes tonight. I really appreciate it."

- **Notice the way that you phrase expectations.** Reflect on the expectations you have decided to create. Stating expectations positively makes a huge difference. If you haven't tried that yet, start there. For example, if the child is starting to climb on the table, you could say, "Please keep your feet on the floor," rather than, "Don't climb on the table." It seems some humans, of any age, prefer to do anything that someone tells them not to do!

Negative Command	Positive Reframe
Don't climb on the table.	Feet on the floor, please.
Stop yelling!	Can you make your voice match mine?
No more snacks. We're done eating.	Snack time is over! Should we wash up together?

- **Break down the steps to accomplishing the task.** "Let's get ready to go" might not be enough information. More information in that situation could be "Let's put these toys in the basket, and then go over to the door to put our shoes on." You might need to slow down even more and give more detail as you go. "Please put the car in this basket [*while holding the basket out*]." Or you can practice Enterprise Talk, "When I clean up the cars, I put them in the basket [*while demonstrating*]."
- **Be mindful of your nonverbal cues.** The body is constantly scanning the environment to look for threats in order to keep us safe. Nerd alert: This is called neuroception. If you run into a bear in the wild, it may growl and get up on its hind legs to send a "back off" signal. As animals ourselves, we send similar nonverbal cues that convey either safety or threat messages. To convey messages of safety: lower your voice, open your chest and shoulders, slow down, breathe, and get on a child's eye level. These actions will regulate your nervous system and help the child feel safe and thus more likely to connect and collaborate.

- **Make it interesting.** We know that when children are emotionally involved, they are more likely to be engaged with the material presented. If the expectation is that we don't throw toy cars, but the children want to play a game about cars that crash and then sail through the air, then show them how to do slow-motion flying cars while you hold on to the car the whole time. Figure out what about their ideas you can say yes to.
- **Sing your expectations!** I still remember my eighth grade math teacher Mr. Sheridan's song about equations. Singing engages the heart, mind, and memory. You don't have to be good at singing to try this out, and silly voices are encouraged, but not required. Choose simple, easy-to-repeat phrases. A common song in my classroom when transitioning inside from the playground was "Put my coat in my cubby and wash my hands," which worked for most of the group.
- **Notice when someone chronically seeks your attention.** Is it during a certain transition every day? Is it when you are paying attention to someone else? Is it on the days they need to be woken up instead of waking up on their own? All children need attention, but there is no magic amount or type of attention that every person needs. If you're noticing a pattern in the *when*, then it can help you feel prepared to provide it or build it into your routines.

Sometimes a child's connection-receiving cup feels leaky. Like you spent all morning together and they still need more. Five hot tips for filling a child's connection cup:

1. **Screen-free time.** Screens off. Your phone on silent and truly away, not buzzing as a reminder that it may pull your attention from them.
2. **Child-led play.** Let the child call the shots. They get to tell you how they want you to play with them (as long as it's within your boundaries), from what stuffed animal you will hold to what that animal will say.

3. **Do an activity you know they like.** My toddler loves to be a part of any cooking that's happening in the kitchen. Honestly, it's hard to include him. It's easier to just bust it out, prep, and make the meal without toddler curiosity. However, when we show him what's happening in the pan for thirty seconds and then give him a task like taking the stickers off the fruit or mixing with a bowl and spatula, he feels included and connected.

4. **Notice the little things.** Set yourself a goal of acknowledging one small moment in the morning and one small moment in the afternoon when you notice something they're doing. "I saw you help your sister get the top off that container. Thanks, buddy." "I love listening to you play your instruments." These little acknowledgments go a long way.

5. **Set a timer.** Let a child know what to expect by using a timer as a tool for communication: "Before I get dinner ready, I would love to play with you. I'll set the timer, and when it beeps, I'll go make dinner." It's okay to set boundaries around how you connect after filling their cup. When the timer goes off, they may want more. You can direct them to what that could look like. "I had fun playing with you, too, bud. Would you like to pick a song for us to listen to while I get dinner ready?"

What Is the Goal?

There is much research and general awareness of behavioral reinforcement available. Remember Pavlov's dog? While punishment was central to Pavlov's dog study, positive reinforcement is the focus of contemporary uses of the behaviorist approach. Applied Behavioral Analysis (ABA) is a widely respected approach to teaching kids with autism. Positive Behavioral Interventions and Supports (PBIS) is a nationally recognized and utilized approach to behavior in school systems.

We want to be clear that the goals of CEP do not include behavior reinforcement. We also want you to know that CEP is not in conflict with

ABA or PBIS, and you can use them together. Programs like ABA and PBIS work to elicit more prosocial behaviors by reinforcing them or rewarding them. The goal of CEP is supporting the development of emotional intelligence. Addressing behavior with punishment or external rewards may elicit a desired short-term outcome—like getting a kid to do something to avoid punishment or in search of the reward—but it won't build a child's toolbox for emotional intelligence.

When we see that children aren't giving us a hard time, but that they're *having* a hard time, we can respond with compassion, curiosity, and connection.

The CEP method is about seeing the whole child, while simultaneously seeing ourselves, particularly the *why* behind our urges or desires. Maybe you have a desire to control the behavior through fear and punishment. Maybe you are leaning toward a reward system that is more about *things* than connection, to try and elicit certain behaviors with positivity. When we tap into mindfulness, practice self-awareness, self-regulate, and acknowledge our biases, it's easier to see the whole child in front of us with emotional intelligence.

The CEP method is a path to connection and collaboration with a child rather than disconnection and control. It creates a foundation for a relationship of mutual respect and trust, where the adult sees the behavior as a communication of a need that the child does not yet know how else to express. When we see that children aren't giving us a hard time, but that they're *having* a hard time, we can respond with compassion, curiosity, and connection.

Chapter 9

Ending Meltdowns Before They Start

We've been talking about what to do when big emotions and unexpected behaviors are happening—those often stressful, spontaneous moments. Now we want to share some strategies that reduce the frequency of "meltdowns"—in other words, the unplanned distress and/or dysregulation moments. The key word here is "reduce." Please be kind to yourself and let go of any vision that doesn't include big emotions and dysregulation sometimes.

Pre-Teaching

Imagine you got a new job, but all you knew was that you got a new job. You didn't know what the job would entail, who would be there, or what your day would look like. Would you get lunch? What time do you get there and when do you head home? What should you pack? What can you expect? How stressful would that be?

Now imagine how children may feel when they have to face a new experience or activity without any preparation. Pre-teaching sets those expectations. It gives children respect, by providing them with information about what's going to happen and making space for them to ask any questions they might have.

My cousin, a million weeks pregnant, called to say she had a stomach bug. "Any chance you can take Pierce today? I just can't parent a three-year-old right now." "Sure," I told her, "I'm heading to an early childhood rally [because of course I was], but he can join me." Pierce is not a big-group kind of dude. He is curious and observant, and when he feels overstimulated, he generally has big emotions to let us know he is overwhelmed. We were heading to a rally . . . with a whole bunch of people he didn't know . . . I know, right? It was a bold move. We had a half-hour drive, and the entire way over we chatted about what to expect.

"Hey, buddy, when we get to this party, it will be at a big building with a ball on top called the State House. When we arrive, we will walk inside and have lunch with some of my friends before the party starts." [*Pause. Let him take that in.*] "My friends have never met you before, so they might be excited and curious about you. When you meet someone new, what's something they might ask?" "Do you like chocolate?" he answered. "Yeah, they might ask that. What would you say?" "Yes, of course!" he replied. "What else might they ask?" "Hm, what's your favorite dinosaur?" "And what would you tell them?" "T-rex! It has sharp teeth, but teeeeny tiny arms." I smiled. "It sure does. Sometimes when we meet new people, they ask what your name is." "Pierce!" "You got it! They might ask how old you are." "I'm three!"

Now that he had an idea of what to expect from social interaction at the beginning, I wanted to support him with what to do if his nervous system felt overwhelmed, even if he felt prepared. "When we are there, if you are feeling overwhelmed or nervous, you can squeeze my hand and I will listen to you and help you."

I went on to let him know what to expect after lunch and how he could ask me for help. When we walked into lunch, he announced, "Hi! I'm Pierce and I'm three!" Like, aha! I will head all the questions off at the pass. It was adorable. At one point during the day, someone was talking to me and turned to ask him a question. He started making silly noises and spinning around my body. "Do you need to squeeze my hand?" I asked him. "Mmhmm," he said as he squeezed and I popped down to connect with him and help him regulate.

We can pre-teach before big transitions, such as a new school, a new classroom, a new sibling, or a move. But just as helpful, as impactful, is pre-teaching in the day-to-day. The morning routine, en route to the grocery store, heading to a restaurant, before we get to Grandma's, what to expect at the birthday party . . . And it starts as young as infancy. We'd rather give them the respect of communicating what's coming next even if we aren't sure how much they understand. Talking to them and communicating with them helps build the skills to understand and communicate back to us. As adults, we sometimes forget how much we know about how things go. Sharing this information can reduce the amount of trial-and-error research children need to do when entering new or new-ish situations.

After pre-teaching with an infant about getting dressed, they might be calmer throughout the process. After pre-teaching with a toddler about who is coming over today, they might be able to answer the question "Who will be here for dinner?" "Nana!" After pre-teaching with a preschooler about what to expect at the playground, they may be more prepared for what to do when someone is using the shovel they wanted. After pre-teaching with a six-year-old about what to expect at their friend's birthday party, they might be able to navigate feeling jealous if they don't get presents, too. Pre-teaching is your classic win-win, because as children feel more prepared for what's to come, they feel safer, allowing them to access more of their tools, which helps us all move through life together.

Proactive Solutions

One of my favorite proactive solutions is the "what if" game. We can brainstorm what to expect in different social scenarios to practice them. "What if we get to the playground and all of the swings are being used, what could you do?" Sometimes a child has the answer ready to rock. "I could say, 'Can I be next?'" And sometimes they need guidance. If they aren't sure or provide no response, you can offer up a solution. "You could say, 'Can I be next?' And when you're waiting for a turn, you could play in the sandbox or climb on the structure."

- What if Conley comes over and wants to play with your new fire truck?

- What if you're building with blocks and Quinn comes in to play, too, and knocks them down?
- What if you really want to have something in the store and Papa says no?

Social stories are another proactive solution. You can write or simply tell social stories. These are short stories that you make up where a problem arises and the characters navigate it in a productive manner, modeling a how-to for kids. If leaving school at the end of the day is a challenge for your child, you can make up a story about a child who *reeeeally* wants to stay and play more at school when their caregiver comes to pick them up. You can put real-life sentences in the story but avoid the child's name so they can take the story in without feeling embarrassment, shame, or defensiveness. You can tell these stories throughout the day; when there's a natural lull in play or activity, when there's a request for attention, during mealtimes, at bedtime. You can tell stories that include an inappropriate way to respond to a situation, challenging a preschooler to brainstorm other ways to solve it. Or you can have a story start with how the character used to react and then how they learned to respond differently, in a way that makes them *feel* better.

We make decisions based on how we feel, and so do children. It doesn't feel good to be mad and throw a toy. It feels better when we get mad and can process that emotion to try solving the problem. We cannot pull a tool we don't have out of the toolbox. So when we practice these scenarios outside of the moment, we can build their toolbox to pull from *in* the moment. Just like when we practice mindfulness, self-awareness, and self-care for ourselves in moments when we feel calm, we will be more likely to pull them out of our own toolbox during the more intense or tender times.

Visual Aids and Technology

Adults use visual aids all the time so they don't have to keep track of everything in their mind. Some people use technology in addition to or instead of visual aids. Calendars, to-do lists, clocks, alarm clocks, sticky notes, packing lists, grocery lists, emails marked unread, the reminder to bring the diapers to childcare, invitations to weddings, birthday parties, and gatherings. We are surrounded by visual aids and audio reminders. We can treat children with respect by giving them the same gift. Visual aids are especially helpful for children who are neurodiverse, as well as children who are learning more than one language, children who are deaf or hard of hearing, and children who are receiving services for speech or sensory integration. Six visual aids you can build into your day are:

1. **Calendars.** Is it a home day or a school day? Who is picking me up from childcare—is Nana coming or is it a Dad day? When are we going to the zoo? When is Mommy leaving for her work trip? And when will she be home? When do we leave for vacation? How many days will we be gone? Having a place to turn for this information can help a child feel grounded and safe. Bonus: Use pictures on the calendar to communicate what's happening. An airplane on take-off day and landing day. A picture of the beach on the first day of vacation and the last day. A photo of the school or teacher for school days and then a family photo for home days. A calendar doesn't have to be fancy. You can draw one or use one you already have at home. It doesn't have to be Pinterest perfect. If you are a parent who shares custody of a child, use the calendar to help them see where they will be staying that day and when they switch to another house. Even if the routine is the same every week, it's helpful to have a visual reminder so the child's brain isn't wondering what's happening next or when something begins or ends. For more on how to use a calendar with your child effectively, check out examples at www.seedandsew.org/more.

2. **Daily schedule.** Imagine you show up to work and you don't know what is in store for the day. All of a sudden you get a five-minute warning before a meeting or are told that you'll have an opportunity to eat in ten minutes. You're deep into a task when you find out it's time to leave and go on an adventure to the library, but you had no idea that was coming until *right now*. It's dysregulating to be unsure of what is coming up, even if the routine is generally the same every

day. You can write the schedule out on a whiteboard or a piece of paper. Again, nothing fancy is required. Bonus: Use a little picture cue next to the word, especially for tiny humans who cannot read yet. When using a daily schedule, break it up into digestible chunks. Rather than, "Okay, Zainab, you'll wake up, brush your teeth, go to the bathroom, change your clothes, eat breakfast, play with your toys, get your shoes and jacket on, grab your backpack, go to school . . ." all the way until bedtime, we want to communicate in snippets: A schedule for what to expect before you head out the door to go to school. A schedule for pickup and the evening routine. Or a morning schedule pre-nap or before lunch and an afternoon schedule. For some children, especially children who are neurodiverse, you can get more specific and have a series of smaller schedules like a "wake up" schedule, a "getting out the door" schedule, a drop-off at school schedule, a pickup routine schedule, an evening schedule, and a bedtime schedule. If there is a particular transition or time of day that is challenging, you can use a specific schedule for *just* that transition.

A S.E.E.D.-certified teacher reached out to say a child was having a hard time getting out the door. After creating a very detailed visual schedule for the child—including "Put on one sock, put on the second sock, put on one shoe, put on the second shoe, flip your jacket on, ask for help starting the zipper, zip your jacket"—she was able to get out the door with more ease. I love a good checklist to help me remember how to prioritize my to-do items. For children who also love checklists, you can consider making your schedule into a checklist for them to mark off as each step is complete. You'll find out right away if this is motivating or distracting for a child, because either they will want to check things off right away or you'll find yourself having to coach them to check each step off. If they need you to coach, then it's not a good fit.

Sometimes big emotional expressions are a result of not understanding the expectations or the order of events, and using pictorial cues can help you explain what you're asking them to do or what the plan is.

3. **Timers/clocks/countdowns.** "Hey, Sebastian, dinner is at five o'clock. So please clean up your toys in ten minutes to get ready to eat." But if you can't read a clock, that doesn't mean very much to you. "Hey, Sebastian, when the timer beeps, it's time to clean up for dinner. I will set it on the counter so you can see how much time is left." Maybe it's a timer on your phone, a sand timer, a visual timer that shows a countdown, or a microwave timer. Any timer you have available is great. I'm sure my parents would've loved a timer on our annual beach trip from upstate New York to the Outer Banks, when I would spend the entire eleven-hour drive asking how many *Barney* episodes (fifteen minutes in length each) until we got there. "Seven thousand four hundred and fifty-six, Alyssa, and here's the atlas to occupy your time." We don't use timers as threats. Louder for the people in the back: We don't use timers as threats. They are a communication of timeline expectation. Timers, and clocks if they're able to read one, let children know when to expect something—their turn with a toy, a transition, when you will be available for questions, how much longer until Mama comes home from work, when the next mealtime is, how long they have for screen time, when their friend is coming over.

Another way to communicate a timeline is with a visual countdown. "Is it beach day yet?" I'd ask, eager to embark on said eleven-hour beach drive. "How many rings are left on your countdown?" my parents would ask. "That's how many days until we leave." Timers help everyone get on the same page when it comes to timelines, as long as you hold yourself accountable to them, too. If you said you would come read a book in ten minutes, then you need to come read a book in ten minutes. If you need to adjust the time, then communicate that. Try to model the way you want your child to ask you for extra time. Here's a tip for introducing new tools like this: Plan to spend some time exploring the tool with your child if they are motivated to do so. Children, with their scientist minds, may be very curious: How does this tool work? What is it made of? How does that part move like that? Also, explain and model the rules for using it. These steps can help them get ready to use the tool. Otherwise, you might return to find the sand timer playing the role of light saber in a pretend play game instead of keeping track of time.

4. **Emotion cards.** After researching what emotions are, we designed a set of emotion cards to use in practice, called the CEP Deck (see page 274). These can be used for coaching through the Phases of Emotion Processing as described in Chapter 5, as well as proactively, outside of the big emotions.

5. **Coping strategies.** As a teacher, I kept Post-it Note messages in my classroom as reminders for myself. They ranged from "They aren't trying to piss you off," to "Breathe." In the moment, when your body is dysregulated and your brain isn't fully online, a visual can serve as a reminder. For kids, these reminders for regulation are tools from their Coping Strategies Toolbox.

In one of my infant/young toddler classrooms, Joey would throw her body on the ground in a loud tantrum, at times she would hit or bite, and the entire time she would cry and yell. She could get stuck in this pattern all morning, unable to communicate her feelings or needs. Even when what she wanted was something she had the signs or verbal language to communicate, she couldn't always access those skills.

After much reflection as a team on how to best support her, we tried a coping strategies choice board to help her regulate when she was unsure how to do so herself. Then, once she was calm, we could talk with her and build her emotional language in an effort to help her learn to communicate her feelings before they were too big to manage. The choice board was a piece of cardboard with Velcroed-on pictures of her and each of her choices. She could grab the card that said "lovey" and pictured her with her lovey, or she could grab the card that said "hug" with a picture of her hugging a teacher. We started with four choices and expanded to six.

When she had her next seemingly uncontrollable expression of hard feelings, we told her we wanted to help her, but weren't sure what she needed. We guided her to the choice board, where she paused and looked at it. She touched the picture of her lovey, and we showed her that she could pull it off and we could go find her lovey if she wanted. She nodded her head and off we went. Once calm, we said, "You sounded really frustrated. I want to help you. Can you tell me with a word what you want?" She paused. I demonstrated saying and signing a few words she knew: "Water? Diaper? Play? Eat?" Her eyes lit up at "eat" and she signed it back. Then she started to sign it and whimper. She was hungry! We had figured out what she wanted and now we could move forward and support her.

Over the course of the next month, we saw a drastic improvement in her ability to regulate and communicate. The choice board gave her a visual aid to help calm down, take deep breaths, and find her voice. Before we knew it, she was building her vocabulary, including her emotional library. While our goal wasn't for her to stop crying (and she didn't), it was clear that she was getting stuck there. She didn't know how to get our attention when her needs or feelings would get too big to handle until she had a tool to help her communicate with us.

Visual aids for coping strategies are little cues to the brain for what to do to return to feeling safe and calm. Use strategies that you already know help the child proactively. Do they love jumping off the couch? Great. A jumping visual. Do they calm from a snuggle? A hug visual. Is reading a book how they find their calm? A picture of a book. If they're old enough, you can create the visuals together. Bonus: Talk about coping strategies in regulated moments. When you're sharing a book and a character is scared: "Hm, which coping strategy could help them feel safe?" [*Pull out the visuals.*] When you're playing together and you can't figure out how to put on the doll's shoes: "Ugh, I can't figure out how to get these shoes on!" Turn to the coping strategies cards. "I'm going to do ten big jumps." Do ten big jumps. Model this in times of calm, pull strategies into your "what if" games—practice them outside of the meltdowns so they can be used during the big emotions.

6. **Books about emotions.** When we offer books about the impermanence or range of emotions while children are operating from their rational thinking brain, we give them an opportunity to

analyze the subject matter while they're not in the middle of feeling it. Books can help children step outside themselves and observe someone else experiencing something they are learning how to navigate. You can find a list of some of our favorite books about emotions at www.seedandsew.org/more.

If you want the aforementioned visual aids and don't want to comb the internet for them, head to www.seedandsew.org/more for our favorites.

Preventing Unnecessary Breakdowns: The Big Deal

What qualifies as a big deal? As "wise" adults with so much life experience, we sure think we know. We even think that explaining that something is not a big deal is an effective way of calming someone down. Once in a while this works. Some children have strong self-regulation skills and/or they understand what it means to have to wait your turn, and they hang on to your every word, like "I'm gonna be fine? We can fix this? It's no big deal? Okay, tell me more . . ." On the other hand, most of the time, even though we as adults can see that the problem is no big deal, it's still a very big deal to our kids. For example, one child is playing with a train that the other child wants to use. No big deal, right? You've totally got the solution—the other child can be *next*! But, alas, you are dealing with someone who has only just recently been introduced to the concept of "wait for a turn." They didn't want to be next; they were planning to play with it *now*. In addition, young children are masters of the present moment. At any given moment, the present is *all that exists*. Simply because "you're next" is not *right now* makes it sound like "your turn is *never.*"

Sometimes the big deal is that you are asking the child to stop doing whatever the present moment consists of, in order to do something else (most likely your agenda). Imagine you were in a flow state, working on something you were really interested in and your wheels were spinning, when someone came in and told you to stop and go eat. Your insides are screaming, "But I'm not hungry! I want to finish this. I'll eat after." This can be equally disturbing to a tiny human who is deeply engrossed in whatever material or activity they are paying attention to.

Let's say your child is on a playdate, and both kids want to play with that train. You tell Maya that it's Sarah's turn now, and she can be next. But now Maya is crying, maybe trying to grab the train from Sarah, maybe flopping her whole body onto the floor. Then you say something like "I see you're sad but it's Sarah's turn right now. You'll have a turn soon." You think you've done your job, but Maya is still screaming and flailing . . . and you're the adult . . . so what is the teaching opportunity in this moment? Good old-fashioned, wholehearted, authentic empathy—coaching through emotion processing. Right now it's not relevant that Maya will one day understand that waiting is an everyday occurrence. We know that the resulting feeling—most likely anger or frustration—is a normal feeling and that they are part of a human family that has experience with that feeling, too.

Here's the amazing part: You can validate the feeling *even* if you don't understand that feeling in relation to the events that have unfolded (waiting for a turn) in the same way that they do. Remember Amaya's big feelings about the cereal bar in Chapter 5? I

You can validate the feeling *even* if you don't understand that feeling.

didn't need to feel the same way about the broken cereal bar in order to validate the frustration. It's validating the existence of the feeling itself that's important.

Before we move on, let's spend a moment on the word "but." In the English language, this word is meant to be used to explain contrast. That means using the word "but" after naming an emotion is in direct conflict with validation—Phase 2 of emotion processing. The words following emotions are most productive if they help children move through all the phases rather than stop after recognizing an attempt to jump to the moving-on phase. The next phases, security and coping strategies, are important steps along the way. You may need to share a contrasting message eventually, like "It's okay to feel angry, *but* it's not okay to hit," and you can do that later. For now, try replacing the "but" with one of these validating statements:

- "That's a hard feeling."
- "I get that."
- "You're having a big feeling."
- "It looks like you're feeling it in your arms."
- "I can see your eyebrows are squeezing together."

Analyzing and explaining what you see helps reflect the child's body language back to themselves. It will also help you turn on *your* rational thinking brain instead of your survival brain. Once you validate, sending the message that it's okay for the child to feel that way, then you can coach through the next phase.

We have learned that when a child is having a nervous system reaction, like Joey (see page 189), *our* nervous system is likely reacting to theirs. The coping strategies choice board that we made worked because the pictures were prepared when everyone was feeling calm—before we were in the presence of a distressed child. Visual aids do not have limbic systems, so they are always ready and provide static visual information for analysis, to wake up the rational thinking brain. Prepare tools that will be helpful in the moment, as well as strategies for remembering that those tools exist, since you're less likely to remember when you're stressed. You don't have to wait until you have a moment without children. It can be beneficial for the child to be involved with making the tool since they'll be using it, too. This activity is a form of validation in itself.

What about ending *your* "meltdowns" before they begin? Keep circling back to your proactive and supplemental self-care strategies (see Chapter 4). Each time you realize your self-care routines have disappeared, start with mindfulness. Okay, that happened. It's not good or bad; it just happened. Then start again. Taking care of you will help you take care of them. And this part is worth repeating: Please be kind to yourself and let go of any vision that doesn't include big emotions and dysregulation sometimes.

Chapter 10

When There's More Than One Child

You might be feeling more confident about the CEP method—perhaps you've even started to put it to use here and there, recharging your batteries, becoming aware of your implicit bias, and working through the five Phases of Emotion Processing with your little one. But what happens when there's another child in the mix, or other children? Let's explore how to use this method when siblings and peers are involved.

Come Watch

Have you ever noticed that humans are intrinsically and deeply interested in suffering? For example, drivers who pass an accident on the road can be seen craning their necks to see how bad the accident is. Are there police? An ambulance? A fire? Are those people going to be okay?

The same is true among groups of young children. I worked with a couple of teachers of toddlers who knew this and demonstrated it by saying "Ooooh noooo!" to get the children's attention before coaching them to help with cleaning something up or putting a puzzle back together or checking out the next page in a book. It was extremely effective. When there is more than one child, it might feel more complicated to coach through the phases—how can you meet everyone's regulation and emotion processing needs at once? It is more complex, so we have some strategies to help you navigate the social world of children and emotions, and it starts with children's intrinsic curiosity about other children's big emotions and the behaviors that come along with them.

Before we jump into adult-child interactions with multiple children, let's practice self-awareness with implicit bias. Remember when we asked you to reflect on your implicit bias when it comes to attachment? And what you learned about emotion concepts within your culture? Depending on your experience, it's possible you associate the expression of sadness or anger with shame and seek to "protect" a child from shame by trying to prevent them from expressing these feelings. When there are other kids around, this urge might be stronger than when it's just the two of you. Maybe you fear that the other children will be confused or scared when one child expresses big emotions. Or perhaps you learned that it's polite to mind your own business and not to burden anyone with your own concerns.

No matter where the roots of our discomfort lie, we may be compelled to send other children away when one child is experiencing a big emotion, and that's okay! Start by noticing as these parts of you come up and get curious. What does that part want you to know? *If the child shows sadness, they will be made fun of.* What is that part of you afraid will happen then? *Then they won't feel connected to the people around them and may feel lonely.* Try some compassion for that part. *You felt lonely when you were sad and cried. It's scary to feel lonely and not have a safe space to turn. I will create a safe space for this child so their experience can be different.* Invite these parts of yourself into the process—it's the only way we can work with them or through them.

When we act on the urge to send other children away from one child's big emotions, especially if our survival brain is in the driver's seat, we send the message that emotions are meant to be handled in isolation. We send the message that they are not to be curious about other people's emotions. We send the message that big expression is shameful and/or scary and separate from "what we are doing." When instead we say to the curious or concerned child, "Yes, you're welcome here, too," we send the message that it's normal to express emotions, that we can choose to be a peaceful witness of emotions, that we can do this together, that we can hold space for and comfort one another in moments of big emotions. We show them that emotions can be processed collaboratively. We can actually capitalize on the intrinsic concern and curiosity of the witnessing children as a springboard for developing compassion and family or community relationships. We call these opportunities the "Come Watch."

The Come Watch is something I learned in my first yoga teacher training. The idea there was to focus on one aspect of alignment while teaching a class, and at some point during the class call the students over to one mat in order to watch one student go through a pose featuring that one alignment principle. There would be a demonstration of what *not* to do and then what *to* do, so that students could see the difference and then be able to practice more clearly on their own mat. With the help of the teacher, the student usually goes much deeper in the pose than they usually do because they got such specific instruction and support and attention from the teacher and the rest of the class.

The Come Watch uses all four types of teaching that we wrote about in Chapter 4: intentional modeling; active encouragement; exaggeration to make the qualities of the task more obvious; breaking down the task so the steps to completion are clearer. The Come Watch is a great fit for CEP with more than one child. I might even go so far as to say it has made moments that felt the hardest—such as when I felt like I didn't know what I was doing—the most beautiful.

I remember the first time I tried an emotion processing Come Watch. I was standing next to one of my preschoolers who was flailing on the floor and not letting me near him. I had taken a breath and let him know, "I'm going to stay here and protect your space. I won't let anyone come close to you until you're ready." I asked one of the teaching assistants to grab the emotion cards. (If I had been the only adult in the room that day, I would have skipped the cards because protecting the space of this tiny human was more important than having the cards in this moment.) I got down low and offered the angry card, asking, "Are you feeling angry?" He screamed, *"I'm not angry!"* and threw the card. By now there were a few children who had moved closer to us, watching intently. When I saw them, I felt worried that their attention would exacerbate the intensity for the flailing child. But I could see their readiness to learn. They had stopped playing because they had intrinsic motivation to learn what was happening for someone else, and they wanted to know how I was going to handle the situation.

In the midst of my pause, Sylvie, one of the children who was watching, asked, "What's wrong with Sonnie?" I explained that I thought Sonnie was upset because someone else was using the toy he wanted to use, and they weren't finished with it yet, so he had to wait. As I told the story of what happened, Sonnie's flailing slowed. I went on to explain that I had wondered what Sonnie was feeling, that I had offered the angry card, but he had thrown it so maybe that wasn't it. By that time Sonnie was no longer flailing and was instead listening to my conversation with Sylvie. I invited Sylvie to make a guess about how Sonnie was feeling. She guessed disappointed. Sonnie didn't readily confirm or deny disappointment and I didn't ask him to. I suggested, "Disappointment is a hard feeling." Sylvie nodded. There were two other children who had come over with Sylvie still watching this exchange. And there was a hush that had come over the room as all the children who could hear us from where they had been playing were now paying attention. After that experience I realized the power of group processing, and the power of a child feeling seen by another child.

This way of being with more than one child in a big emotion moment is often a good fit, but not always. What are the qualifiers for a Come Watch?

1. This particular child's culture does not exclusively address emotions in a private way.
2. This particular child's behavior does not get more intense as others approach.
3. This particular child's expression does not "disappear" as others approach.
4. The child's body is safe for other kids to be nearby.
5. Your rational thinking brain (as opposed to your survival brain) is in the driver's seat.

Conflicts Between Children

Sometimes the reason there's more than one child is because there's some kind of problem between them, like a conflict over toys or who's in charge of the game. You may have the urge to jump to problem solving, which is part of moving on in the fifth phase. This is completely natural, and with mindfulness practice, you'll start recognizing it as an urge. With self-awareness, you might be able to do something else. That something else is coaching through the phases.

Here's what stays the same as 1:1 coaching:

- Bringing your calm
- Figuring out if it's distress or dysregulation
- Moving in order through the Phases of Emotion Processing

You're going to have some extra decisions to make, such as: Who should I help first? Should I talk to one child or more than one at a time? Is now the right time to find out what happened? The following are some questions that might help you make decisions along the way:

- Is one of these children in distress? If yes, provide soothing for this child first.
- Is there a strategy that would help *all* of us calm down (i.e., taking breaths together, lowering the lights, taking a group water break)? If yes—do it!
- When I ask about what happened, are the expressions getting bigger or smaller or staying the same? If they're getting bigger, then it's not time to talk about what happened. Keep moving up the Triangle of Growth and coaching through the phases. You don't have to talk about what happened until everyone's ready. Hint: It might be tomorrow.

We were on the beach when Nell came running up to me crying and yelling, "Julian said I'm so stupid!" Julian was running right behind her saying, "I told you not to tell an adult!" I dropped down to face Nell, hugged her, and said, "Ugh, it's sad to hear words like that from someone you love. I'm going to talk to him, and I'll be right back to help you." Sometimes it's hard to turn to the one who caused the conflict because of the stories we might be telling ourselves in the moment—don't give them attention, they need to know that isn't okay, the crying child needs me most, etc. But I knew that if Julian said something hurtful, he was in his reactive brain and needed support.

Julian was fired up when I turned to him and was yelling about how she wasn't being fair, and he didn't say that to her. Now is not the time for me to address any lying or get to the bottom of what's true. Now is the time for connection and co-regulation. "Hey, buddy, I'm not mad at you and you aren't in trouble. I am here to help you. [*Pause.*] Do you want to tell me what happened?" "Yeah, I was making a tunnel that would go under the ocean like a submarine and she came over and took my shovel, but I was still using it. I just needed it again after I was digging with the other shovel, and she didn't even ask, and she just took it anyway." "*No!* He wasn't even using it," Nell chimed in. I turned to Nell and said, "Your story is really important to me. I'm going to listen to Julian and then I'll listen to you, too." I turned back to Julian and said, "Wow, that's really frustrating when you have a plan and it gets interrupted by someone else. You weren't done with the shovel when she took it. I get that."

His shoulders dropped down, his body started to soften, and he replied, "Yeah, I wasn't even done." "Okay, bud, I'm going to talk to Nell and then we can figure this out together. Nell, did you think he was done using the shovel because it was on the ground, and you wanted a turn?" "Yeah, and he didn't even include me one time when he was digging, and he always gets the shovels." "I get that. Were you feeling left out and wanted to feel included?" "Mmhmm," she replied. "Okay, Nell, Julian, my heart is beating really fast, and my body feels like it needs to move. Do you want to have a race with me and then we can solve this together? Let's run to the flag over there and run back. Ready, set, go!" We raced over and back.

As we returned, they were laughing together about being so much faster than I was. "Okay, Julian, it sounds like you had a plan for digging that tunnel and Nell thought you were done with the shovel and wanted to feel included. What do you think we should do?" "Well, she could have the shovel in three minutes and dig another hole by mine, but not touching it." "Nell, does that work for you?" "No, I want a turn in five minutes." "Julian, does five minutes work?" "Yeah." "Okay, would you like me to set a timer and let you know when it beeps?" "Yeah, then we will know when it's five minutes," Julian replied.

About ten minutes later, when they were deep in their play, I joined Julian and softly said to him, "I'm proud of you for calming your body to solve the problem. I know you are really kind and that it doesn't feel good inside when we say something hurtful. Next time, if you are frustrated, you can yell for help, and I will help you." He nodded and continued on with his play.

Here are some special notes on coaching through the phases with more than one child:

- **Phase 1:** Allow everyone to have their feelings. No one's feelings negate someone else's.
- **Phases 2 and 3:** Recognition and security may include finding out what happened *if* it allows you to provide some validation. Like "Oh, your tower was knocked over? And you had been working hard to make it so tall? That sounds disappointing." Two children may have very different stories about what happened. It's so important to *hear* all the stories even if you think they're not true. It doesn't mean you have to agree. You might even have the opportunity to validate how frustrating it is when someone says what you're saying is not true. Recognition may include children who were not involved. Even if the child with the big feeling is not ready to learn, like the child who was flailing at the beginning of this chapter, the bystanders are most likely able to use their rational thinking brain. They'll be able to guess how the child with the emotion is feeling by looking for observable signs. The child with the emotion may find this soothing because others have taken the time to attempt to truly *see* them without getting in their personal space. They can benefit from hearing others go through the process.

- **Phase 4:** The helping children have the opportunity to exercise their empathy muscle by offering suggestions for what might help an expressing child calm down. They have a chance to practice self-awareness by reflecting on what helps them feel calm when they are having that big emotion. In the reverse situation, children who struggle with Phase 1: Allowing will learn a lot by observing or helping someone else through emotion processing while they are regulated and *not* having a big emotion.
- **Phase 5:** If you haven't found out what happened yet, now is a good time. Once everyone's story and perspective have been validated, you'll have a team to solve the problem with.

Domino Effect

When I had a family childcare in my home, I spent my days with six kids from age six months to five years. When I was just starting out, learning to navigate nap time for my youngest was tricky because as the older toddlers and preschoolers played without my direct attention, they got louder and louder in a giggly way. I kept getting distracted by trying to get the older children to quiet down. Our nervous systems are talking to each other, and the children's are talking to each other's, too. That's why when one child starts to express, the others might follow.

An infant room in childcare at the beginning of the year is an amplified version of this when one child starts to cry. It's exactly like falling dominos, with one child after another joining the chorus of tears until everyone's limbic systems, including those of the teachers, are activated. Another way this might look is when one tiny ruffle between siblings snowballs into an all-out brawl. Siblings seem to know the exact words or behavior that will really set off the other. I remember riding in the back of the van with my cousins as the older one kept repeating the same insult along with "Yes you are," while my younger cousin was on repeat, too, only with more intensity each time, saying, "No I'm not!" As their older cousin (and an only child myself), I attempted to convince my younger cousin that she should just ignore her brother, the way Alyssa had been coached with her siblings. The thing is, that verbal advice doesn't go very far with an activated nervous system.

When you find yourself in the midst of the domino effect, the first step is to find your calm. I love this lyric by Brandi Carlile for inspiration: *"You can dance in a hurricane, but only if you're standing in the eye."* The situation might feel chaotic, like a hurricane, yet there is a way to the calm at the center of the storm. Usually taking a breath will get you started in finding it. Once you've found it, then choose one child to CEP with first. If any of the children are in distress, then work with them first. If not, it could be the child who is more likely to welcome your co-regulation or the child who started the domino effect.

Even if the children are dysregulated in an excited way, it's a good time to allow the feeling of excitement and then move through the phases, including coping strategies. Excitement is often perceived as a "good" emotion, something you *want* to be feeling, but for some people, this feeling is dysregulating or overwhelming in some way and they need help to experience it. You can read the temperature of the room, like a thermometer, or set it, like a thermostat. A thermostat will start at the room temperature and then regulate the space to the desired temperature. When everyone is getting loud, sometimes using a big, loud voice to draw attention to yourself can be helpful, and then you get to set the temperature by dropping your tone, maybe even whispering. In a big voice you might say, "WOW! THERE ARE SO MANY BIG FEELINGS AT ONCE!" and then move into a whisper: "I wonder who can make the quietest voice?" [*Pause.*] Still in a whisper: "Hm, I hear Maya using a quiet voice. Ooo, Alma is whispering so quietly, I can only see her lips moving but can't even hear the words."

Objects of Contention

Whenever possible, removing any object of contention from the immediate area will be crucial to the goal of helping the involved parties see one another, and by that I mean, listen to and hear one another's story. One of the children might not want to be a part of the conversation and may evacuate with or without the object. Sometimes they are running away because they feel embarrassment or shame about having made a mistake. Don't grab a toy out of anyone's hands. Trust me, I have tried this and never once did I feel proud about it afterward. It's worth waiting until everyone's nervous system is regulated, emotions have been identified and validated, and you're in the problem-solving phase.

If one child is expressing in a big way *because* the other child is holding the object, then you might try offering something like "Are you feeling worried that you're not gonna have a turn?" or "Are you feeling angry because you really want to hold that toy?" If they show signs of recognition, then you can validate, "Oooh, that's so hard! I wonder what we can do to help you calm down while we solve the problem . . ." and move through the phases.

Suppose you've tried to get the children's attention (with a calm nervous system) a few different ways and the two children are ignoring you as they continue to lunge at each other for the toy. As a last resort, it's worth prying the toy out of their hands. This is really a last resort. If it is used as a last resort, sometimes there is sigh of relief from the children after the object is put out of reach. It's like when one football player has already tackled the guy with the ball, but ten more players pile on anyway. Everyone has their eye on the prize and it's hard to switch gears. When the referee blows the whistle, it's like everyone can relax again.

Being Pulled Between Children

I recently received this message from an overwhelmed parent:

Valentina is four and has been really into preparing her own snack, a new-to-her skill. I was helping her prep all of the things and was about to cut up her apple while she got her plate and the peanut butter when I got a call from the bathroom. "Moooom! I pooooped! I need you to wipe!" my two-year-old, Marcos, called out. To add to the chaos, my newborn, Liliana, started crying as Marcos called for me, reminding me that it was time for her to eat. Everyone needs me at once and I don't know how to be in three different places at once, help!

When I read this message, I was immediately filled with empathy. The feeling of *is there enough of me to go around* and constantly triaging *who needs me more* is so real. It's okay not to have the capacity to respond to every child 1:1 in every moment.

If no one is in immediate danger, pause and breathe so you can assess. "Valentina would be alone with the knife. Marcos is currently alone with his poop. Liliana is hungry." Safety first. "Valentina, I'm going to come back and help you cut up the apple after I wipe Marcos. Can you get the plate, spoon, and peanut butter while I'm gone?" Then move the knife out of reach. "I'm coming right now, Marcos!" As you walk to Marcos, if possible, pause to tell Liliana, "You're hungry! I'm going to come feed you in two minutes." Once you're done with Marcos, you head back and cut up the apple. It's okay if Liliana is crying during this time. If she were older, she would be saying, "I'm hungryyyyy. I need a snack." It's okay if she feels hungry for a couple more minutes while we support the older kids. Once the apple is cut up, pop on a visual timer, and let the two big kids know, "I'm going to feed Liliana. When the timer beeps, I'll be available to help you again if you need something."

Sometimes this season might look like you feeding a newborn while reading a toddler a book or a child watching *Daniel Tiger's Neighborhood* while you help an older sibling with their homework. Children will practice being bored, learning patience, building new skills for independence, and knowing that you will return to help them. It's okay if it isn't immediate or on the timeline they'd like it to be on. You aren't failing if it feels hard. Raising children *is* hard. Notice the feelings that come up for you and recognize any parts of you that want you to be perfect or think you should be able to do it all. You can remind those parts, "I'm worthy of love and am doing enough," even when you make mistakes, lose your cool, drop the ball, or feel like your life is a constant juggling act. You are enough.

When You Should Step In

Throughout my ten years of teaching, I observed a pattern year after year among the girls. Some girls emerge as leaders by providing structure and delegation during dramatic play. They are optimistic and seem to solve problems easily, and rarely get upset. I found myself regularly praising these one or two girls in my class each year and counting on them in a certain way to keep the flow of play going. From a distance it seemed like their leadership was well deserved and that the other children respected them for their maturity and predictability, but over time I started to question it.

During the year we started working on CEP, I was observing in the block area (right next to dramatic play) when I overheard a discussion in dramatic play between Allison, the child I assumed to hold these leadership qualities, and one of her friends, Penny. She was carefully explaining why she didn't have to share the beloved ballet slippers to her friend, who explained she had been waiting for a turn for a "really long time." I could hardly believe that Penny, who had been waiting, sulked about it and simultaneously accepted the idea that Allison was in charge of the ballet slippers. I started listening in more and more to the dramatic play conversations to discover that Allison actually ran the show completely and on a daily basis. To my surprise, it was not because of her diplomacy but because of her threats! Threats that were made regularly and only when an adult was not paying attention directly.

I found myself wondering, did I give the other children the impression that this child was in charge with my regular praise and attention? That any behavior she presented was desirable? Did I give them the impression that this child should be popular? How was my bias interfering with the children's relationships? I started to consider my potential role in having set this child up for getting her way all the time. Certainly these were not the social skills that I was hoping my preschoolers left for kindergarten with. None of these children were demonstrating healthy concepts of friendship.

So I decided it was time to step in. One morning in dramatic play, Allison was using the ballet slippers. Penny said she wanted to have a turn with them. Allison replied, "Well, it's my game and I'm the mom so I have to wear these shoes." I started to wonder if this desire to control was coming from an underlying emotion. Was it that Allison was afraid of feeling discomfort, like disappointment, and avoidance of discomfort was what motivated her to think of a really "good" reason why she did not have to share?

Since Allison had the slippers in her possession, Penny had the self-regulation skills not to grab the slippers, and because she wanted to keep having the privilege of playing with Allison, she obeyed. Penny started to sulk with a sad facial expression, alone with her feelings. Allison's body, which had become tense, relaxed. No one cried, no one complained, and the play went on without help from a grown-up. But was everyone okay? Was Allison missing an opportunity to experience emotions? Was she going to avoid this for the rest of her life if I didn't address it now? What about Penny, who didn't know she had a choice? What if she found out that with a little support she could, in fact, have her turn with the ballet slippers and still play with her friend?

I interrupted the play in order to facilitate a sharing experience. Allison started to cry uncontrollably, holding on tight to the slippers. I was surprised and unprepared for the intensity of this emotional response. She was so upset that the game paused for a few minutes, and her friends paused to witness the event. Finally, I remembered the emotion cards, and together we looked at the cards to see if she identified with one for sad, worried, or disappointed in regard to having to share. Allison chose the worried card. We made a plan for Penny to take a turn with the slippers after the two-minute timer was up, and Penny was delighted that she would finally have her turn. The event was so meaningful to Penny that she started self-advocating regularly and continued to develop those skills for the rest of the year. And Allison got to learn how to process big emotions.

Have you noticed dynamics like these? Do you prioritize the emotions of the most expressive children over those who are more compliant with their peers? We mentioned early on that emotion regulation is not the same as emotion processing. Just because someone can regulate doesn't mean they can process. For example, if the toy a child is playing with suddenly gets snatched out of their hand by another child, they might have an internal emotional experience.

Remember in Chapter 7, when I said Sage was identified by another parent as being "good," but they meant obedient? This happens to a lot of children. It happened to me as a child. My teachers said I was a good student (even though academics were a bit of a mystery to me) and I was easy for my parents. I didn't complain and I was "good" with other children, but a lot of the time it was because I didn't understand what I was feeling or didn't have the skills to articulate it. Once in a great while, after my feelings all built up and became visible, I would fall apart. This was how my mom would know I needed her.

It wasn't until I had been teaching for ten years, and after discovering therapy, that I noticed the children who were like me—Penny from the story earlier, for example. Some children's nervous systems react by going into fight mode (hitting, kicking, yelling, biting) while others flee (running away), fawn (apologize or people-please immediately), or freeze (disconnect, go quiet, and maybe even seem regulated when they are not). If a child who freezes is uncertain about their rights to the toy or how to get help, they might distract themselves quickly in order to avoid feeling uncomfortable. They might look perfectly fine, not complain, or get involved with something else.

A regulated child is usually presumed to be high functioning and not need support or have to work on skills regarding social-emotional development. This child may seem very easygoing, when, in fact, they don't know how to self-advocate. Instances of advocacy often start with a feeling of discomfort, sometimes even despair or rage related to whatever the current circumstances are. So emotion processing is important for transforming a pattern of giving up into a pattern of self-advocacy.

When you were a kid, did you ever shout "That's not fair!" at your caregivers as they expressed a boundary? Maybe you heard "Life's not fair" in return? Should life be fair? Is that what we're going for? What is fairness anyway? *Merriam-Webster* says, "Marked by impartiality and honesty: free from self-interest, prejudice, or favoritism." Sounds pretty good, but sometimes this is interpreted to mean that everyone *gets the same*. Yuko Munakata, a psychologist and neuroscientist who studies the impact of parenting, points out, "The same parent could shape different children in different ways. One child might find it helpful when her mother provides structure. Her sister might find that it's stifling. One child might think his parents are caring when they ask questions about his friends. His brother might think they're being nosy. One child might view a divorce as a tragedy while his sister sees it as a relief."[1]

Emotion processing is important for transforming a pattern of giving up into a pattern of self-advocacy.

So, fairness—or at least fairness alone—might not be the way to go after all. Then, what about equity? When it comes to child development, equity means everyone gets *what they need*. What would it be like if everyone gets what they need? Some kids need more of our energy or need specific supports or tools that others don't—and that's okay. If James needed glasses to help him see and Pilar didn't need glasses, we wouldn't get Pilar glasses to make it fair. James would get glasses so he could see, and Pilar would be able to see without glasses. It's the same with attention, energy, sensory supports, and calming strategies—we observe and get curious about what the individual child needs as it differs from one unique human to the next.

Here's what to listen for when you're figuring out what a child needs and how much: Feelings of guilt or intense worry, on your part. Are you feeling worried that you spend too much 1:1 time with one of your children? Or guilty for pouring energy into one child more than others in this season? Try to avoid making decisions about what a child needs while you're experiencing these vulnerable feelings. Take a minute to remind yourself, "What they need is the right amount to give." If you have a child who needs more of you in this season, it doesn't just benefit that child, but the whole environment, if their needs are met. If that child's needs aren't met, the energy of that need will be felt throughout everyone else. Let's say it again—there's no need to be perfect here. When you experience guilt or intense worry, notice, practice self-care, and then get back in the driver's seat.

How Do I Know If They're Getting What They Need?

Flynn's teachers reached out for support because he was regularly scratching and hitting the other toddlers in their class. They'd tried explaining that this hurts the other child and showing him how to use "gentle hands" with no success in behavior change. It often seemed unprovoked, and a clear pattern was undetectable. It wasn't always when someone was taking Flynn's toy, or always when he was overstimulated from an activity. On the surface, the behavior seemed random.

The teachers started to track the behavior more explicitly than anecdotally. They'd observed and found out that the times when it happened were usually right after another child or a teacher turned down Flynn's attempt to connect. Sometimes it was that the teacher he wanted to connect with was changing another child's diaper and he needed to wait for her to finish. Although it was not a rejection, it was a delay in physical affirmation. Being turned down by peers for play or hug offerings was happening more and more after several children had been hurt. Teachers allowed children to say no to playing with another child if they wanted to play by themselves and the children had learned to use this strategy to say no to Flynn regularly.

These observations allowed us to zoom in on Flynn's feelings. We wondered if Flynn was feeling angry, disappointed, or embarrassed when these 1:1 connection rejections happened. We introduced some emotion cards, including ones for these three emotions, to the whole class. At the beginning, Flynn threw the angry card when the teachers presented it, but they were patient and didn't give up. After a few days, Flynn embraced the angry card. Now he was able to identify his emotion and the teachers could teach him what to do when he felt angry instead of scratch or hit. At home his family planned to talk about emotions, too, and they created a book with some personalized stories about emotions. Within two weeks of consistently supporting Flynn this way, he was able to identify his emotions and practice some simple coping strategies. The added community benefits were that the other children were also developing these skills and they came to see Flynn as a safe playmate again.

The teachers and I in that story were using a tool called the Addressing Challenging Behaviors Tool. Originally, I created it because my friends with kids had started sending their friends with kids to me when those parents were unsure if their child's teacher was doing enough for their child. In some cases, there was some speculation that implicit bias regarding racism was at play. The tool was designed to hold teachers accountable for planning social-emotional curriculum, and also to help teachers articulate what was going on for their students. I've started to share this tool with parents, too, so that you can see what teachers can do to address challenging behaviors in a collaborative way.

On a basic level, teachers should be able to explain how they teach social skills and emotion processing skills. If there is a chronic challenging behavior, then teachers need to be specific when describing the behavior: "She kicks other children when they approach her during free play," rather than "She's mean to the other children." Teachers need to be able to say how the behavior impacts a child's relationships, access to curriculum, and satisfaction of basic needs. And teachers need to be able to say what they've tried so far. If you're a teacher, then this tool will help you do all these things, and if you're not yet able to, then it will give you information about what to do next. If you want to check out the Addressing Challenging Behaviors Tool, you can find it at www.seedandsew.org/more.

Out in the Wild

We were at a playdate when my friend's three-year-old started taking every toy my child had, moving his body where she wanted him to play, and trying to control how he played. I watched at first, both taken aback and curious to see how he would respond. It can feel messy when the other child isn't yours and an adult relationship feels at stake. When I pictured playdates with my friend, they didn't include conversations about how her three-year-old was being rude and controlling, ya know?

I noticed my triggers first:

1. **The freedom to play and create.** I'm the fourth of five kids. I grew up having to share all my things and rarely feeling in control of what or how I got to play. Rather than the cartoons and kid shows my friends were watching, I watched *Dawson's Creek* and *The West Wing* because I didn't get to control the remote. Witnessing someone dictate how and where my child should play brought up those feelings of not having control over my own play as a kid.
2. **Consensual touch.** As a sexual assault survivor, these wounds run deep. Parts of me are hypervigilant around consensual touch, wanting not only for my son to receive it, but for it to be the expectation for how he shows up in relationships with others.

As I noticed these triggers, I was able to find the pause. I told those parts of me that I appreciated their concern for my little guy and that I would help him with tools so his experience could be different from mine. I turned to my friend and said, "I love how confident she is and don't want to tamper with her assertiveness. I would like to step in and help them figure out how they can play together as he is still learning how to use his voice for self-advocacy." "Oh, I know. She can be so bossy. I'm sorry, she's fiery," my friend replied. "No, her strength in knowing what she wants is a skill I wish I had at her age. I'm just going to guide them as he is still building that."

I popped down and said to my friend's daughter, "It looks like you have an idea of how you want to play with him. Can you tell me your plan?" The three-year-old shared her vision, including the role my child would play. "Wow! That is really creative. He might want to do that, and he might not. Before you touch his body or take something from him, you can ask him, 'Do you want me to move you over here?' or 'Are you all done with that?'" She agreed and went back to playing.

About fifteen minutes later, she took a spatula out of his hand, and he whimpered. I rejoined the play. "Oh, did you want to have a turn with the spatula when he's done?" I asked her. "Well, I need it for my pasta," she replied, mixing in an empty bowl. "Oh, you're making pasta? I love pasta. He was using it and you want to have a turn. I'm going to hold it while we figure this out together," I told her. She wasn't happy to let go of the spatula but did give it to me. "Next, next, next," my child said, reaching for it. "You were using it and want to have it back?" "Mmhmm, back." "Yeah, you can have it, and I will help her figure out her plan." She started yelling, "I NEED IT! I NEED IT! IT'S NOT FAIR! I NEED IT!" "You really want to use it to mix your pasta! I understand that. I'll be here with you to figure this out." "But he's using it!" she said as she tried to grab it from him.

I slid my body between the two of them to focus on supporting her while protecting his physical space. "I won't let you take it from him. You really want to use it and he's having a turn. When you're ready, we can take deep breaths or do ten big jumps together to calm our bodies before we figure out what to do next." "UGH! NO!" she yelled. I sat with her, allowing her to feel and express. It's not my job to rush her through this, I reminded myself. She is allowed to feel mad. After about three minutes of stomping her feet and telling us how mad she was, she walked over to a bin, grabbed a ladle, and went back to mixing. I stayed for another minute and then turned to my child and said, "When you're all done, you can ask her if she wants a turn." "Next," he replied. "Yep, she can be next," I validated as I moved away.

When I went back over to my friend, she said, "OMG, I thought she was going to lose it." I empathized, "Yeah, it's scary sometimes to be in that space where you aren't sure what their reaction is going to be when you're holding the boundary and empathizing." And she responded, "It really is. I was watching you, though, and think what I am going to try next time is just being there without giving her the new thing to stir with. I was shocked she got there on her own."

Listen, it's messy to parent alongside other humans who are parenting. It isn't always smooth, and we all have parts from our childhood that come into play. The two most beneficial things I've learned on this parenting journey with others are:

1. **To find the good.** My friend wants to be the best parent she can be. Her child has incredible confidence and assertiveness that can be great leadership qualities when supported with the social skills of seeing others' strengths, individuality, and abilities. By seeing the good, we are able to look beyond our triggers to notice and connect with one another.

2. **Perfection isn't real.** They see me as an imperfect parent with a messy house, rushing my child through emotions sometimes or reacting instead of responding. They hear me vent about the challenges, and we get to lean on each other knowing that we are worthy of love even when we make mistakes. Being vulnerable can feel scary. Letting folx see that we don't have all the answers and aren't confident in every single parenting decision often allows them to know they aren't alone, to feel connected, and maybe even to start having compassion for the parts of them that aren't always confident either. I feel like I need a doormat for my house that says, "Your mess is welcome here."

Part III

CEPing It Up a Level

Chapter 11

Developing Empathy

One of the five components of emotional intelligence is empathy, and boy, is it a big one. In this chapter we will explore what empathy is, and what it isn't. It's important to understand the differences between empathy, sympathy, compassion, and codependence. We will chat about how to foster empathy and create a culture of empathy in our environment without breeding codependence.

The Four Attributes of Empathy

Nursing scholar Teresa Wiseman's research identifies four qualities of empathy: perspective taking, staying out of judgment, recognizing emotions in other people, and then communicating about that. Let's explore what these look like in the context of CEP:

1. **Perspective taking** is an opportunity to get curious about what the other person is experiencing and what that experience means for them. It does not mean having the same experience, agreeing with how they feel, condoning behavior related to their experience, or deciding whether or not their experience is real. Perspective taking involves temporarily removing yourself from the scenario to observe their experience and trust that it is true for them.

   When a child is pulling at their shirt and saying, "It's scratchy. I don't like it. I want a different shirt," we can practice perspective taking by believing that their experience is true. "That shirt feels uncomfortable for you, and you want to change it." It's not my job to convince them that the shirt is perfectly comfortable and remind them that they've worn it before. It's my job to step outside myself and be a witness to their experience.

2. **Staying out of judgment** is practicing mindfulness of our biases and self-regulating so we can see the child's experience without a biased lens. Instead of responding with "You don't need to be so upset, it's just a shirt. We can fix this," staying out of judgment is noticing what *is*: "You're really upset that it's so uncomfortable."

3. **Recognizing emotions** is connecting with *what* they're feeling, not why they're feeling it. Remember when Simon's block tower crashed, and he was disappointed? I had that flashback to when the baby destroyed my laundry piles. If you know what disappointment feels like, you can choose to empathize with that feeling regardless of why someone else is feeling it. This is when you might recall a time you felt the feeling a child is expressing so you can connect with *how* it feels.

4. **Communicating** our understanding about the emotions is when connection happens, when we have the opportunity to say, "I see you. I get it. That's so hard. Ugh, yeah, I understand that. Damn, that stinks." The other day I texted my best friend, **I've been so tired the last couple of nights that the thought of us meeting you two for dinner tomorrow night feels exhausting. But also because my MIL is free to watch S and we haven't been out to dinner in a hot minute, I feel like we should**. She replied, **I get how exhausting that feels. Especially today looking at tomorrow.** She didn't try to convince me or minimize my experience. She was present to my pain because she recognized inside herself what that bone-tired exhaustion felt like and really listened to what I was communicating. Communicating about emotions that others enjoy experiencing is also part of empathy. A self-awareness invitation is to notice if it's easier for you to communicate when others are having hard feelings as opposed to enjoyable feelings or vice versa.

Teaching Empathy by Modeling Empathy

The most powerful way to teach empathy is to model it. This can be tough with tiny humans. One reason is that it's very easy to focus on the *why* rather than the *what*. The *what* is the emotion and the *why* is the experience. The *why*'s of children are so different from ours as adults. We might dismiss an emotion if the experience doesn't seem to warrant that emotion from the adult perspective, if we don't think it's a big deal.

Focusing on the experience might sound like . . .	Focusing on the feeling might sound like . . .
"It's just a block tower! You can build it again."	"Your blocks fell. Wow, that's disappointing."
"You don't need to be scared."	"You heard a loud sound. Did that feel scary?"
"It's not a big deal!"	"This feels like a big deal. I get that."

Sometimes "sympathy" and "empathy" are confused as synonyms, but they are two different concepts. *Merriam-Webster* defines them as follows: *sympathy* implies sharing (or having the capacity to share) the feelings of another, while *empathy* tends to be used to mean imagining (or having the capacity to imagine) feelings that one does not actually have.

The most powerful way to teach empathy is to model it.

Sympathy is disconnecting, as it separates one person from the other. It often comes with a "but" or "at least" and can be found in statements like "I can see that you're feeling mad, but . . ." Sympathetic responses can try to find the silver lining rather than holding space for the present emotion and experience. Sometimes when we deliver a sympathetic response, it seems as if we are imagining that we would have handled that moment differently. Sympathy is self-protective, as it allows us to think that we wouldn't feel that same way or to rationalize that we don't have to feel that emotion for a variety of reasons.

Remember when the freshly folded laundry was destroyed by the baby? Sympathy sounds like "You look frustrated. Don't worry, you can fold it again." Empathy sounds like "Oh man, that sucks to finish all that and have to do it again."

Sympathy might sound like . . .	Empathy might sound like . . .
"I'm sorry that you don't want to leave the playground right now, but it's time for lunch."	"It's *so* hard to stop playing when you're having this much fun. I'll be here with you while you're feeling sad."
"I can see that you're angry right now about your sister coloring on your drawing. You can draw on another page."	"*Ugh!* You were working so hard on that drawing and your sister colored on it. That's frustrating."
"I hear you crying. I'm sorry you don't want to go to bed. Don't worry! We get to play together again tomorrow."	"You and your brother were making the coolest fort. It's really hard to step away to get ready for bed. When I'm working on something I enjoy, it's hard for me to stop, too."

In these examples of empathetic communication, it isn't important that the adult agree that the experience was a big deal. This is where perspective taking comes in. Imagine what the experience feels like for this child—not a grown-up—in order to validate what they're telling you, their truth.

It's vulnerable to choose empathy and connect with someone. Sometimes vulnerability is really freaking hard. We don't need to feel the same thing in that moment in order to call it empathy—it might be surprising if we felt just as devastated as our friend who was just broken up with. In order to be empathetic, we just need to imagine, see, and honor what someone is feeling. It can help to consciously remember what you know about that feeling, and how it has felt for you in the past—these are your emotion concepts coming in handy.

When one person's feelings change at the whims of other people's feelings and with the same depth, it's not empathy, it's codependency. In this book, when we refer to codependency we are referencing when someone is reliant on another person being in a regulated state in order for them to regulate. If Tasha shares her hard feelings and is met with codependence from Winnie, it can become Tasha's job to regulate in order for Winnie to regulate.

In order to respond with empathy, you have to be in charge of your emotional experience and self-regulation tools. If someone is drowning and you jump in to drown with them, it's not effective. Our ultimate goal is to foster empathy—a skill set for feeling *with* someone, while teaching kids how to act with compassion. You want to be an *action*-based partner to empathy. Empathy is saying, "I get what that feels like." Compassion is saying, "I'll sit here with you while you're feeling it." Compassion builds on empathy as an action one person takes to help another person tolerate the discomforts of life. Sometimes it's holding space and allowing the hard feeling, which might feel like doing nothing.

This is particularly challenging for parents and caregivers, and understandably so. There is nothing harder for me as a parent than compassion when I could fix the hard thing and make it go away. For instance, it's hard for me to watch Sage navigate the frustration of trying to put the top on a container rather than jumping in to do it for him and rush the frustration away. It's hard when all you can do is offer a hug and listening ear when your child doesn't win in a game, score the goal, or get the part in the school play—it's hard not to try to fix it to avoid the hard stuff. If there was a world where our children never had to feel a hard thing, I'd sign up, but the truth is that all humans experience hard things. Rather than attempting to save them from all the hard stuff while they're under our care and then sending them off into the wild without tools for resilience, we build these tools together. We build the skills to tolerate and get through life's challenges collaboratively, and it starts with us modeling them for and with them.

What Happened to My Empathy?

When you're raising or looking after kids, it's likely your house has toys strewn about, there's seemingly constant noise, and the children have ever-evolving needs. The mental load of keeping track of what everyone is doing, needs, and has, while anticipating what's to come, can be absolutely overwhelming.

This environment can reduce our ability to think creatively. We feel less flexible and less open to unexpected events. Big emotions seem really inconvenient! If your little one is tantruming and you hear yourself thinking, "This shouldn't be happening," then it's a sign that you're judging, rather than practicing mindfulness. There's no need to judge yourself for doing that—just notice. Why would you be quick to judge? It might be that you're under-resourced and need to recharge that battery, even just for one minute. This could be one reason why we lose track of our empathy skills sometimes. We might act quickly in an attempt to make unplanned expressions of big feelings stop as soon as possible because we think the child shouldn't be feeling that, that they should be able to manage it without your help, or that it's inconvenient timing as we are late for a meeting or trying to get out of the door for school—in other words, the opposite of emotion processing Phase 1: Allowing. In the face of a quivering lip or a tense body, examples of trying to stop versus allowing feelings may sound like:

- "You're okay."
- "I'm sorry you don't want to put your coat on, but we are going outside now."

- "Who's got your nose?" (Said playfully, to distract in the absence of CEP.)

Yes, big emotions actually *are* inconvenient—but learning to process them is worth it. You're allowed to feel inconvenienced. If you explore a little, you might find a feeling underneath that experience, such as disappointment or frustration. After you process those feelings, you might find your empathy is within reach again. All that being said, it's unrealistic to imagine that you'll be able to allow and process any and all emotions that come up for children or yourself. This is a "leaning in" kind of practice. As often as we remember to allow, as often as we have a little bit of energy to share, we allow emotions and work through them together. Growth is uncomfortable at times, so pay attention to your expectations for yourself. It should feel like a good stretch.

Another reason your empathy might go missing is if other people's suffering is hard for you. If you felt like a burden to others when you expressed needs in your childhood, you might find yourself triggered when your own child has needs. You might feel that they are unlovable or high maintenance. You might feel the same about yourself. Remember, you and your child are worthy of having needs.

Personally, I have a hard time accessing empathy when someone is sick. Growing up, there wasn't loving compassion for me when I was sick. In fact, quite the opposite. I was raised with a "power through" mentality—go to school, play in the game, go to work, unless you need to be hospitalized, and even then . . . do you really need to? Now, when someone is sick, that part of me surfaces and wonders how sick they really are and expects them to power through. I can't gift them with compassion I don't first give myself.

When you were a child, if you were made to feel responsible for someone else's feelings through shame, you may have a hard time accessing empathy. A shame response might sound like: "Don't say that. It'll make Mom feel sad." "Dad will be mad if you do that." "Oh great, you made your sister feel scared." While shame might change a behavior, even for the short-term, it becomes a part of a child's self-talk and can result in lying, rationalizing, or defending down the road when they make mistakes or engage in conflict. If it isn't safe to have a hard feeling or make a mistake, then we develop self-protective measures that can make it hard to experience empathy. If you didn't receive empathetic, compassionate responses to your emotions growing up, start by practicing self-compassion. When we learn how to give ourselves compassion, it becomes easier to extend that to others. Kristin Neff, associate professor in the Department of Educational Psychology at University of Texas at Austin, and the author of several books including *Self-Compassion*, has tools for putting self-compassion into practice. You can find them linked at www.seedandsew.org/more.

I used to struggle to stay present with other people's big emotions. Through mindfulness and self-awareness, I've noticed my tendency to want to make their big feelings go away as quickly as possible. I'm starting to be able to practice staying present when a dear one is suffering, but it's still super challenging when I perceive or know that the person's emotions are in direct response to something I have done. I find myself going into "problem-solver mode" or rationalizing my own behavior before fully understanding the situation, specifically the other person's truth. Even though it's tricky and I feel like a beginner most of the time, it seems more and more valuable as I practice. When we stay present, we have the opportunity to get to know emotions better—our own and others'. When we know them better, we can communicate about them better.

It is important to notice when you feel inconvenienced or resistant to others' emotions, so that you can pause, practice responsive self-care, and choose empathy over negativity and defensiveness when you respond.

They Are Not Responsible for Your Feelings

Kids do things all the time that trigger us. They do things that are annoying and frustrating. They say things like "I hate you," "You're the meanest mommy ever," "You're stupid," or the latest one on the Seed team, "It's never going to be your birthday." The goal isn't to feel calm and serene when these things happen; it's to notice our internal reaction and work to build the tools to regulate and translate that behavior into what the child really means: I need help or want to feel connected to you.

Kids know that we also have feelings, but imagine if they knew we also had our own toolbox for our feelings? Imagine a world where all children had at least one person they could turn to, who they knew could handle their big emotions. No matter what comes their way in life, we want kids to have at least one person they can break down to, one person whose feelings they don't feel responsible for. Your relationship with them is different than a peer relationship. It's the foundation with which they will feel safe and secure in the world.

There is a difference between communicating to a child that they *caused* your feelings and communicating your feelings. This is also an excellent way to teach by modeling. When you allow yourself to feel a range of emotions, and demonstrate how to process them, children learn that all feelings are welcome and manageable. What's key is acknowledging how you process the feelings. "I'm feeling overwhelmed after coming in from the car with all the groceries and making lunch. I'm going to slow my body down and read my book for five minutes to get calm." "I'm feeling disappointed about the marker on the walls and need to take some space and move my body for a minute. I'm going to be right back." "It was thoughtful of you to make this picture for me at school. I feel loved."

Communicating your feelings is different than making your child feel like he or she *caused* your feelings. Consider these statements: "It makes me happy when you clean up your toys"; "It makes me sad when you hit." Phrases like these give tiny humans power over our feelings. What a big responsibility that is. What's your goal here? Is it to get them to clean up their toys? Let's try, "Thanks for cleaning up your toys. It's comfortable to walk through the house without stepping on them." Is the goal to get them to stop hitting? Great, let's help them feel safe and regulated in their body again so we can chat about what they need in the moment to make a different choice.

Instead of . . .	Try . . .
"Don't run in the parking lot! It scares me!"	"My job is to keep you safe. Let's hold hands in the parking lot."
"It makes me sad when you talk to me like that."	"You really wanted to keep playing outside. I get that, buddy."
"You used the potty! Yay! I'm so happy!"	"You used the potty! How did that feel?"

There are lots more examples in Chapter 9 about how to guide behavior without handing over responsibility for your feelings. You aren't failing if you've been using phrases from the left column. Remember, this journey isn't about perfection; it's about growth. Next time, you can let your little one see that you have emotions as you claim responsibility for them and model the use of a coping strategy. Modeling coping strategies can sound like:

- "I'm having a big feeling. I think it's frustrated. I'm going to take a break so I can help my body feel calm before we keep talking."
- "I'm feeling worried right now, so I'm going to take ten deep breaths to calm myself down before we talk. Do you want to take breaths with me?"
- "I want to feel calm so we can solve the problem, but I'm still feeling angry. Looking at the sky helps me feel calm. I'm going to look at the sky for one minute. Here, I'll set my timer. Do you want to look at the sky, too?"

In this way, you're demonstrating that you can use a coping strategy to find your calm when emotions feel really big, rather than requiring a certain behavior from the child to find your calm.

This may make sense and sound simple enough, but it's actually really hard to do. It's hard to be the person that someone can crumble to, especially when we feel like we *can't* handle those big emotions. Every single one of us carries our own beliefs about emotions, with our own patterns of what emotions we were allowed to express as kids, and what we weren't. We all have differences about what we feel comfortable experiencing, as well as what we do not have the toolbox to experience.

If every time you expressed an emotion as a child, you were told to get it together, get on your big girl panties and buckle up, man up, or told that you were okay, when you felt everything *but* okay, then it's really hard to wake up tomorrow and hold space for little ones to feel. It might feel like it isn't fair that no one allowed you to feel or gave you the gift of learning what to do with those emotions. Maybe solving the problem is how you kept yourself safe. Perhaps you grew up experiencing abuse, alcoholism, addiction, homelessness, poverty, or other toxic stress. You may have learned how to be small and quiet so as not to add to the stress. Now this tiny human is screaming because that isn't the shoe they wanted, and their problem seems so small compared to the ones you surmounted.

Give yourself grace. Know that this is hard work, and it takes time and intention. Remember, we're not looking for perfection. Parents, did you yell today? Did you cry? Did you ignore your child and zone out on your phone because it all felt like too much? That's okay. No one is perfect at this and being someone's person they give their everything to, especially the hard stuff, can be draining. You have patterns, habits, and learned behaviors that have been building long before that tiny human was in your world.

Teachers and nonparental caregivers, did you give in or distract because you weren't up for big emotions? Did you tell a child they make you sad when they [*fill in the blank*]? Were you constantly correcting instead of teaching? Learning to recognize your patterns, bringing awareness to them without judgment—just noticing them is the first step to moving into regulating and processing emotions in order to choose a different response more and more over time.

If I don't tell kids how their actions make me feel, how will they learn that their actions/words have consequences and effects?

This question comes up for me personally, too. Whenever this question arises, I pause to ask myself what I'm afraid of. When I make parenting choices from a place of fear, the fear seems to show up in other ways, spiraling more fear-based parenting choices. When I pause and ask myself what I'm afraid will happen if I don't tell my kids that their actions cause my feelings, I realize I'm holding on to a fear of them growing up and not being socially successful because they are unaware of how they impact those around them. Social skills are one of the five components of emotional intelligence and are a key component to navigating the world. When I am able to acknowledge that fear, then I can reframe the original question for myself: "How do I teach children empathy?" The answer is in a million other ways, but not in a way that makes them feel like they need to monitor their expressions in fear of how you, as their safe-space person, will feel. Let's take a look at six ways you can increase empathetic awareness:

1. **Model self-compassion out loud.** As a recovering perfectionist, I've had to reckon with my fear of making mistakes, especially those that let people down. This was one place that I could practice self-compassion with children. In the busyness of the morning, I would sometimes forget that I had told one of the children I would put out the material they'd requested or that I would start circle time earlier so we could have more time on the playground. These were low-stakes situations where I could apologize that I'd made a mistake, "Oh no! I made a mistake. I'm sorry I forgot to get the pink paper out of the closet." Then, looking up instead of making eye contact to suggest I'm talking to myself, "I guess everyone makes mistakes sometimes." The last sentence is self-compassion because

I'm acknowledging that I'm part of a larger group of people who this happens for—everyone. Then I could move on to supporting the child with disappointment or whatever they were feeling, if necessary, or make a new plan to follow through on their request.

2. **Practice holding space without fixing.** When children learn that it is safe to experience an emotion, then they can learn how to hold that space for others, as well. This is the first phase of emotion processing—Allowing. See Chapter 5 for a refresher. Empathy is something we can engage in only after we understand what emotions feel like inside ourselves. As we allow children to experience emotions, notice what they feel like, and move through CEP, they learn how to recognize emotions in others and connect without fixing.

3. **Teach empathy by showing it.** Just as we build self-regulation skills by co-regulating with a child first, we teach empathy by responding to children with empathy. Connect with them and imagine what the message underneath their behavior might be. Trust that they are kind humans and allow them to make mistakes without teaching them that your love for them is conditional. Pause to say I love you; it's impossible to spoil kids with love. You can never say those three words too much, we promise. A six-year-old boy had bounced from one foster family to another, totaling four in his short time on this earth. He was in a first grade classroom at circle time with an infant as the focus of the morning meeting. After a while, he asked if he could hold the baby. With hesitation, the teacher passed her precious baby to this little boy. The infant started to cry and the teacher nervously tensed up, unsure what the boy would do. He naturally swayed the baby back and forth in his arms as she calmed. He looked up to the teacher and asked, "If no one has ever loved you, do you think you can be a good daddy when you grow up?" We assume these kiddos know they're loved because of what we provide, but please never ever stop saying it to them.

4. **Model perspective taking.** We were playing on the beach when my son came up to smash the sandcastle my daughter had worked

so hard to build. As I saw his leg wind up, I stopped it from crashing down on her creation. "I won't let you smash her castle. She worked really hard to make that." He looked at me, surprised and wordless. Then he tried again. I repeated my response and followed it up with "Put yourself in her shoes. How would you feel if you worked so hard to build something and she crashed it down?" "Sad," he replied. "Stomping on sandcastles is really fun. Would you like to build one together that you could crash?" "*Yeah!*" he exclaimed as he ran to grab a bucket. We can encourage kids to put themselves in someone else's shoes starting in toddlerhood, yes, even as young as one year old! "I wonder how that would feel?" "Yeah, I hear that child crying, too. I wonder what they're feeling." Model it as an adult and say it out loud. "I saw her walking with that big stroller, so I held the door for her. If I was her, I'd want someone to help me, too." When you get cut off in traffic, instead of all the curse words you're thinking, try, "I wonder what that person is in such a hurry to get to. I hope everything is okay." The tiny humans will learn from what you actually do, or model, infinitely more than from what you tell them to do. Lead by example.

5. **Read books about emotional development** and highlight the emotions and related social cues of characters in all your books. You can pause on a page and say, "I see that person's tears on their face. How do you think they're feeling?" "I might feel embarrassed if that happened to me. What helps your body feel calm when you feel embarrassed?" Talk about what it might be like to experience that feeling. Discuss how you could support that person if you were there. Train the children's brains to think empathetically. If you want to dive more into empathy, check out Michele Borba's research and resources, including her book, *UnSelfie: Why Empathetic Kids Succeed in Our All-About-Me World.*[1]

6. **Cultivate nonjudgment with mindfulness activities** like breathing and/or yoga with children. *Yoga Pretzels: 50 Fun Yoga Activities for Kids and Grownups,* authored by Tara Guber and Leah

Kalish, is a helpful tool. These cards offer simple drawings of step-by-step moves for getting into each pose, and there are cards with five different types of breath.[2] Another option is Crystal McCreary's *Little Yogi Deck: Simple Yoga Practices to Help Kids Move Through Big Emotions*.[3] The adult can read each card for instructions so they're a good fit for children who are able to follow verbal instructions. Read the instructions slowly, making sure to pause in between each one. One year the children requested this activity every day after lunch in order to practice. I started making sequences using the cards as they got to know the postures. Moving with intention is one way to let go of the thinking-judging mind and to feel what you're doing as you're doing it. Reading Rashmi Bismark's book *Finding Om* together is also a great way to practice mindfulness with kids.

What if each of us commits to an intention of *entering* each interaction with empathy? Imagine what it would be like to be *received* by others in each interaction with empathy.

Empathy Development Myth Busters

Around the time that I started my business, Engage: feel.think.connect, I started to witness some common misunderstandings about what empathy is and how it's learned. I created these Empathy Development Myth Busters, which I now use in every workshop to clear things up:

Myth 1: Lack of empathy is why children hurt other children.

Instead, it's underdeveloped executive function skills, emotion processing skills, and/or communication skills. Developing these skills will lead to empathy. We cannot relate to a feeling in someone else that we are not able to connect with in ourselves.

Myth 2: Teaching children to say "I'm sorry" will show them that what they did is wrong.

Instead, identify the feeling you think they were having when they demonstrated the antisocial behavior. Did they feel left out? Ashamed? Lonely? Angry? You can help them identify that feeling and, when everyone is calm, let them know it's okay to have those feelings but it's not okay to [*insert undesired behavior*]. Offer suggestions about what to do instead next time—you can even role-play. Revisit Chapter 7 for more on this.

Myth 3: Having the child who made the mistake apologize will help the other child feel better.

Instead, help the other child feel better with *your* help (regardless of where the child who made the mistake is) to identify their emotion and provide validation.

In the real world, people don't always apologize right after they make a mistake. In fact, they may never return to apologize. Let's teach children that their processing and moving on are not dependent on someone else apologizing. They can begin to learn strategies that work for them.

Myth 4: When the child who made the mistake has to face the child who was hurt and apologize, they will learn empathy.

Instead, invite the child who made the mistake to be a part of their peers' experiences with emotions that they did *not* cause to help children begin to understand empathy. And consistently model empathy in your interactions with every child each day.

When shame about making a mistake is a factor, it may be harder for a child to learn empathy. Eventually, it will be appropriate to address the hurt caused to others. But kids who chronically hurt others need to learn about emotions and how one person's behavior affects another's in a less vulnerable way before they can experience empathy. Requiring an apology before a child actually feels regret will teach them to lie rather than to experience empathy.

Teaching empathy starts with practicing empathy, just like the other four components of emotional intelligence. Start by cultivating empathy for your own experience of emotions, and practice self-compassion as you learn to stay in the moment instead of running from it. Then you might find that taking responsibility for your emotions comes more naturally. What are some phrases that you want to try when you're experiencing your own emotions in the presence of children? Write them down and leave them where you'll see them regularly so you can test them out the next time there's an opportunity.

Chapter 12

Changes and Transitions

Transitions can feel overwhelming for the nervous system—things like moving, starting in a new classroom, starting with a new nanny, going through a divorce or separation, introducing a new partner or sibling, or preparing for a long-term separation from a caregiver are all transitions that can be stressful for little ones. When change happens, it's the brain's job to say, "Ahh! Sound the alarm! Things feel different, and different feels unpredictable, unknown, and scary!"

It's normal for your child to experience a wide range of emotions during transitional times, and—just as important—it's normal for *you* to experience a wide range of emotions. Excitement, sadness, relief, grief, enthusiasm, worry, pride are just some of the feelings that come up for people during times like these. Make sure you have your own proactive coping strategies in place so that you can be supportive for your child. This may be one of the first big transitions for you and your child, but it certainly won't be the last. Treat it as an opportunity to practice the art of transition together.

My mantra when I'm moving through transitions is an apt quote from William Bridges: "It is when we are in transition that we are most completely alive."[1] As our brain tries to make sense of the newness, we often operate from our conscious brain more than usual because there isn't an old expectation to fall back on in the subconscious brain yet. We tend to be more alert, our emotions are closer to the surface, and there is an opportunity to be really intentional. During times of transition, things might feel messy as kids are getting to know a new routine, expectations, environment, boundaries, etc.

We are going to walk through what to do with the mess and how to move through it. Transitions and changes can be hard. You aren't failing if things feel out of sorts. Resilience is developed in times of struggle. As children navigate the change or transition, they are strengthening their emotional intelligence muscles. When you're moving through changes and transitions, you can follow these five guidelines:

1. Normalize and welcome the feelings through your words and actions.
2. Use visual aids to talk about the transition/change.
3. Invite curiosity and allow questions, even uncomfortable ones.
4. Plan for everything to take longer than usual.
5. Pre-teach and tell stories and examples prior to the transition/change.

When to Talk About the Transition

We all operate differently. Some of us love a heads-up and want all the info and details as soon as we can get them. For other folx, too much information too soon can lead to anxiety or just be pushed to the side. When my little guy was starting childcare, I reached out to the provider to get all the forms, start date, days they were closed for the next school year, and all that jazz right away. Planning ahead was calming for me. When the forms came for my best friend, she put them in a pile until about a week before, when she filled them out. Neither of us is right or wrong; we just operate differently. In order to best support each individual child, you can ask yourself, who is this child? Do they do best with more of a heads-up and time to ask all the questions, or are they up at 3 a.m. anxious about what's coming if they have *too much* of a heads-up? Will they be anxious with too much unknown and a long lead time, or is having a little bit of information calming for their nervous system? Answering "Who is this child?" and "What works best for *them*?" will be key for what's next.

The transition officially begins when the children's schedule and/or environment *starts* to change. Some children detect the smallest changes in the daily schedule—for example, instead of breakfast being cooked each day, it becomes prepared or packaged foods. They might be conscious of changes like this, but they might also feel uncomfortable without knowing why.

Watch for clues that indicate your child's understanding of time, and rely on these indicators to decide how far in advance to introduce the idea of the transition. Starting earlier doesn't necessarily make the transition easier. Two to three weeks is a good amount of time for many preschool-age children to have for processing news and details of a pending transition; for others one week is best. Depending on their cognition, they may or may not be able to grasp the concept of planning in terms of number of days or understanding sequence. If they're already recounting stories about things that have happened in the past, then they will likely be able to comprehend the idea that life will be different in a few weeks. They'll be interested in the details and may have specific questions. You'll be able to answer more of their questions in the three weeks leading up to a transition than you would three months before the transition. There is one transition that will likely come with questions well before two to three weeks out—the addition of a new sibling, especially if a parent in the household is carrying the baby. We will dive into ways to support this specific transition below.

Infants and toddlers are masters of the present and should not be expected to comprehend what a large-scale transition is until they've experienced one (besides everyone's first major life transition: birth). They are able to understand predictable, daily transitions like going from home to school. You can and should tell them about a big change up to two weeks in advance, but it will not be fair to expect that talking about it will help infants and young toddlers understand the transition or make it easier for any of you while it's happening.

How to Talk About the Transition

All children will benefit from hearing about what will be the same and being made a part of the process when it's possible. There are also some questions that you can answer that children may be asking consciously or unconsciously. Here's what this can look like in various situations:

Moving

What will be the same? What will be different?	**For local moves:** It's helpful if the child can visit the new space in advance of moving. If your route to school or to the grocery store will be different, you could practice taking that route together to "test it out," especially if you'll switch from driving to public transportation or vice versa. **For long-distance moves:** If they can't visit the space in advance, then show them photos. If your child likes to draw, you could print the photos and invite them to help you plan where the furniture will go by drawing it in, especially in the room you think they will spend the most time in. If your main mode of transportation will change, then take some time to explore the new mode. For example, if you're getting a car instead of using public transportation, see if you can borrow someone's car seat so that your child can play with it. Older toddlers and preschoolers will love connecting the buckles while their lovey sits in the car seat. If you'll be switching to public transportation, then check the library for some books about buses and subways that you can read together. If you'll start using FaceTime to hang out with Pop Pop and Grampa, then practice this while you're visiting them in person so your child can see how they'll use their device to talk to you.
Imagine they would like to hear the answers to questions like these:	• Is everyone in our household coming to the new place? • Where will I sleep in the new place? • Where will you sleep in the new place? • Are we bringing my lovey? My toys? • Are we bringing [*insert pet's name(s)*]? If not, who will take care of them? • Will I still see my friends and family?

(box continues)

Involve them in the process.	Cardboard boxes are magical to young children. Big boxes create hiding places that have the benefit of reducing sound and sight stimulation. Dedicate at least one box for the child to play with. You can invite them to help pack a box if they show interest in what you're doing. This will take more time than it would to just pack it yourself, but it will provide the child a sense of control when they might feel out of control. Talking to them about how to carefully wrap or pack something can give more context for how the move will go. Something like "Aunt Kim and Uncle Adhi are going to come help me and Mama move these boxes in a few weeks. We'll carry them to the elevator and then bring them downstairs and into a truck. Let's wrap these cups with towels so they don't jiggle around in the box while it's getting moved."

New Provider and/or Classroom

What will be the same? What will be different?	Homemade books with photos of the new space and/or new people will help them to build a narrative around the transition. Teachers may create these for your child's class to look at throughout the day. If they share one with you electronically, print out a copy to read together at home if possible, or look through the photos together on a device. Visual aids like this are powerful tools for making sense of a transition before, during, and after it happens. They can include information about what will be the same and what will be different. For example, "Mama will still drop you off on Monday and Wednesday, and Papa will still drop you off on the other days—that will be the same. Before vacation when you needed a diaper at school, [*current teachers' names*] helped you, and after vacation when it's time to change your diaper, [*new teachers' names*] will help you—that will be different." Routines that children experience on a daily basis related to basic needs are central to a child's experience no matter who is providing the care in any setting.

Practice going to the new center, school, or provider's house on the weekend, if you're able to. See if you can get permission to play in the outdoor space while it's empty.

If your child will go to a center where food is served family style, then practice that at home a couple of times. Help your child to help themselves from a shared bowl of food or pitcher of milk or water.

Imagine they would like to hear the answers to questions like these:	• Where is my new classroom? (Check with the administrator, childcare provider, and/or teachers to see if you can visit the new classroom with your child in advance, and if your child already gets to visit during their regular day.)
	• How will I say goodbye to you in the morning?
	• Who will take care of me at school?
	• What should I do if I need help with something?
	• Who will I play with?
	• What will I be able to play with?
	• Where will my diaper be changed/I go potty?
	• Where will I sleep?
	• Who will pick me up at the end of the day?
Involve them in the process.	Do you have to drop off paperwork at the new center/school? If you can, bring your child with you so they can take in the new sights, sounds, and smells for a short period of time. Are you ordering nap time bedding, a lunch box, extra diapers, etc.? Show them pictures of the new items, and if it's a good fit culturally, then you might help them choose between options. When you have the new items, you can use them in pretend play or in real life so your child can see and feel how they'll be used.
	If you need to immunize your child in order for them to start the new school/center, refrain from making a connection between getting shots and the new location. Instead, keep the explanations simple and related to staying healthy.

(box continues)

New Sibling

What will be the same? What will be different?	Whether the new sibling is joining the family by birth or adoption, books are a helpful tool for explaining what that will look like. You can let your child know that their new sibling will definitely cry like the baby in the book. Or that their new sibling might be shy like the character in the book, but they might not be. If you have a photo or an ultrasound of the new sibling, then show it to your child and make guesses together about what you think the new sibling will like to do and what they will need. Explain that there will be times when your first child will have to wait while you're helping the new sibling. You can make a book together, if they're interested, with some ideas for what they can do if they have to wait. Emphasize that you'll love them even when you can't help them right away. If the new sibling will be a baby and your child doesn't have a baby doll, then it might be helpful to get one so that they can either practice playing with it now (you'll get to see what they know about caring for babies) or play with it after the baby comes in order to make sense of what they're observing.
Imagine they would like to hear the answers to questions like these:	• Will you still love me? • Will the new sibling play with me? • What do babies need? • Where will they sleep?
Involve them in the process.	As you prepare space for the new sibling, allow but don't force your first child to help. If you're going through your child's old clothing, then ask them if there is a special outfit that they would like to keep for themselves instead of passing it along to the new sibling. They might want to put it on their lovey or baby dolls. As you are putting out equipment like a crib or bed, bottles or other dishes, diapering station or potty seat, etc., talk to your child about the new child's development. Will they be lying down or held most of the time? Will they crawl or walk? How will they eat? You can compare this to your current child's experience joining your family.

Divorce/Separation

What will be the same? What will be different?	Talk about where everyone will live once you have that information. The suggestions for moving will apply here, too, even if the child is exploring a space that they will not live in but that one of their parents will live in. If you are using calendars and visuals as described in Chapter 9, then make the new one(s) ahead of time to compare with the current one to talk about how routines will be different. If the child will live in two places, call both of them the child's house, rather than the parent's house. For example, "Tonight you'll sleep at your Martin Street house. Tomorrow you'll sleep at your Commercial Avenue apartment." This way the child learns that both places are their home.
Imagine they would like to hear the answers to questions like these:	• Will you still love me? • Was I "bad"? Is that why this is happening? • Where will everyone live? • Who will help me with [*insert all the routines that either parent usually does, such as feeding, getting ready for bed, toothbrushing, diapering/toileting*]? • When will I see you after you move to the new place?
Involve them in the process.	When moving is involved, you can use the same suggestions given earlier for Moving. Involving children in the process of separation/divorce is not necessarily helpful outside of environmental and routine changes. Beyond that, we recommend signing up for a class for parents who are experiencing divorce/separation. They're becoming more and more accessible, and are required in some states. A quick Google search will provide many options.

(box continues)

New Partner

What will be the same? What will be different?	New relationships change in level of intimacy over time, and to the child, this can look like: they're joining us for regular routines, we're joining them for new things, they're sleeping over, we're riding in the same vehicle, we're traveling together, they're moving in, or we're moving in. Think of each new level of intimacy as a mini transition. Use visuals and books to proactively talk about what each step will look like before it happens. Then take opportunities for Collaborative Emotion Processing as they arise throughout the transition. Your child may react differently to each new level of intimacy.
Imagine they would like to hear the answers to questions like these:	• Will you still love me? • Is the new person more important to you than I am? • Is this new person my parent? • Whose expectations and boundaries are more important—yours or your new partner's?
Involve them in the process.	The "process" in this context applies to the levels of intimacy that your child experiences, mentioned above, such as: they're joining us for regular routines, we're joining them for new things, they're sleeping over, and so on. Involve your child in the planning process for any or all of these activities. For example, if you're planning an outing with your child and your new partner, consider allowing your child to make some simple decisions about it. You could invite them to choose one of two familiar walking trails to take. If you'll be cooking dinner at your place, you could invite your child to choose which vegetable you'll prepare.

Long-Term Separation (i.e., Military Deployment, Deportation, Incarceration, Rehabilitation)

What will be the same? What will be different?	Long-term separation happens for a variety of reasons, and the ways in which these situations will be the same or different can be approached just like the other transitions are. Stick with tangible changes the child experiences in their environment and routines. Examples are living situations, caregiving routines and providers, and ways to connect with the parent who is leaving/has left.
Imagine they would like to hear the answers to questions like these:	• Do they still love me? • Are they coming back? When will I see them again? • Is my parent a "bad guy"? (If it's relevant, refer back to Chapter 8 for talking about unfairness in punishment-reward systems with children.) • Is my parent safe? • Who will help me with [insert all the routines that this parent usually does/did, such as feeding, getting ready for bed, toothbrushing, diapering/toileting]?
Involve them in the process.	The "process" in this context refers to those tangible changes the child experiences described above. With long-term separation, you may have time to prepare, and you can use many of the strategies mentioned throughout this section regarding all the other categories (except New Partner). However, the transition might happen suddenly and without warning. Then your mindfulness and self-care practice will be essential buffers for you, and we encourage seeking extra support if you often feel overwhelmed. Find someone who you can lean on and fall apart with. During interactions with the child, CEP is your most powerful tool. Consider seeking extra support, such as therapy and/or social services for the child, since unexpected and long-term separation can be traumatic for you both.

When you talk about a transition with children, there's no need to make it seem like everything's going to be perfect, or to pretend it won't be challenging. Allow your feelings, model the use of coping strategies, and anticipate practicing CEP with your child more often than usual. Also, allow your child space from talking about the transition if they are resistant to your strategies. It's okay for them to process on their own timeline.

What to Expect from Your Child During the Transition

Expect things to be different during the transition period. The following are some details:

- Plan for *everything* to take longer than it usually does.
- Plan for big emotions to happen more often than usual.
- Eating, sleeping, and toileting are the three things children can control. Expect that at least one of these routines will be different. It's normal to feel frustrated when this happens—allow and validate that for yourself. And in order to prevent taking frustration out on the child, maintain your proactive self-care strategies, even if you have to modify them. You may feel tempted to let go of a strategy that takes ten minutes because you're even shorter on time. Instead of letting it go, try doing something that takes only five minutes instead. For example, if you usually mindfully moisturize your hands and then paint your nails for self-care, you could at least moisturize with mindfulness and let go of the nail-painting part. A few weeks after the transition is complete (although sometimes it takes longer), the regular sleeping, eating, toileting routine will return or a new one will start to become established.
- Children may test boundaries, wondering if your expectations are still the same, considering something is really different. After you practice CEP as usual and probably more often, maintain your expectations while offering extra support for your child to meet them

(see Chapter 9 for ideas). When life is unpredictable, it's comforting to have help with something even if you've already mastered it—like having someone help you get your shoes on if you're a child or having someone help by running an errand for you if you're an adult. Just because you're helping with it now doesn't mean you'll be helping with it forever.

- There's sometimes a delay in the child's response after the transition is first introduced. There's a brief grace period because of the novelty of the experience. If your child handles the initial transition well, and then a week or weeks later unexpected behavior increases, don't be alarmed or worry that your child isn't happy in the new setting. It's more likely that the integration of the transition is taking place. This is a natural part of the process, and establishing routines that are as predictable as possible during this period will help. Trust the process.

Childcare and School

In this section, we will be using the word "school" for all childcare, day-care, and school experiences.

Drop-Off/Pickup

Plan a drop-off/pickup routine or ritual for you and your child and include your child in this process if feasible. Teachers and providers will have ideas and be happy to plan with you. Include collaboration or cooperation with others if it's possible for you. The following are some tips:

- If possible, spend the first week of school gradually increasing the amount of time the child spends there. A longer drop-off process also allows the child to have time at the school with you, get used to the space in small doses, and build comfort and safety there while you, their safe person, is there, too. This is not essential but can be helpful if it's feasible. During the first week or first few days, if possible, spend about twenty minutes on your drop-off process to allow your child time to get settled before saying goodbye. There are always exceptions to this: children who are really worried about the goodbye might not be able to settle until you go. Shorten your child's first day away from you, if you can, with an early pickup. If it works for the teachers, arrive five to ten minutes early for pickup time so you can ask your child to show you what they played with or where they played before you leave.

- Examples of a drop-off routine are using a sand timer to show how long you will play with your child before saying goodbye, handing your child to a teacher (this sends the message to the child that you trust the teacher to care for them in your absence), or always reading one book together and then saying goodbye. Your teachers will have additional suggestions.

An infant drop-off might sound like . . .	A toddler drop-off might sound like . . .	A preschool/school-age drop-off might sound like . . .
"We've put your bag away! Now it's time for me to leave. I'm bringing you to Ms. Mara. You are safe and loved here! I'll be back after nap. Love you!" Offer kisses or a gentle touch. "Bye bye!"	"Let's say goodbye! I've got three kisses for you. Where would you like the first kiss? [*Pause.*] The second kiss? [*Pause.*] The third? [*Pause.*] I can't wait to see you after school! I'll wave to you from the window. Love you! Bye!"	"It's time for me to go to work. Before I go, let's do our special handshake. I love you so much. Abuela will pick you up after snack."

- *Do not sneak out* instead of saying goodbye—this is very tempting because then you don't have to experience the tears that sometimes accompany the goodbye. But this won't prevent the tears and it often causes the child to develop anxiety about drop-off because they develop a fear that you might leave at any moment. Many teachers and care providers are experienced with coaching children through a tearful drop-off. It is healthy for children to know when their parent is leaving so that they're set up for success in processing their feelings about it. If your child has a tearful goodbye, it's okay to call for an update when you get to your car, work, etc., in order to find out how they are doing. Often children cry the most during the actual drop-off and move on quickly once it's over. The anticipation of goodbye is often much harder than moving on after.

- Tell your child you're going to leave and say goodbye only when you are actually ready to go. If you have doubts about going, then your child will sense it since your nervous systems are talking to each other. Your child may even test to see which strategies are successful in getting you to stay longer than you planned.

What to Expect After School

Coming home from school can be such a doozy. We can see a child's dysregulation from the stimulation of the day, unprocessed emotions, and needing a safe space to let it all out. Children go through a lot during the school day. We often overlook the multitude of sensory experiences that drain their battery all day—interacting with peers, extra transitions, bright lights, learning new concepts, other kids' emotional expressions, etc. Even if children are offered times to recharge their battery throughout the day, they can come home feeling depleted, especially during a transition time to a new school, classroom, or caregiver. Kids will often "let go" of all they are holding on to once they get home, in what's called "restraint collapse." It can feel like you are taking the brunt of their frustration. Although it can be hard, know that it indicates the safe relationship and attachment you share. Follow these four steps to support your child after school:

1. **Check.** Take a quick check of their physiological needs. Are they tired or hungry? Do they need to change clothes? Are they seeking sensory input or deprivation? Head to Chapter 4 (pages 46–47) or www .seedandsew.org/more for a list of ways to recharge their battery.

2. **Connect.** Take a moment to connect without distraction. Each child seeks connection differently and they rarely say, "I'd like to connect." Instead, they might say, "Watch this" or "Play with me." They might throw a ball, climb on your body, ask for a snuggle, hit a sibling, or whine or cry. Children use many behaviors to say, "Will you connect with me?" Some ways you could connect include:

- Read books together. (Add a flashlight in a dark space for extra flair!)
- Ask them to tell you three good things. (Anything goes!)
- Pretend to call them on the way out of a room. ("Ring, ring! Oh hey, I love you.")
- Create a special handshake.
- Ask them to pick an animal and pretend to be that animal.

You can fill your child's cup with phrases when you don't have 1:1 time to give. These might sound like:

- "I love being your parent."
- "I enjoy being around you."
- "You're an important part of our family."
- "I'm proud of who you are."
- "You matter to me."
- "Nothing would ever change my love for you."
- "I appreciate your help."
- "I love laughing with you."
- "I'm thankful for you."
- "I like it when you share your ideas with me."

This helps them feel seen, connected, and loved.

3. **Process.** If you can, take a moment to process with your child. When they are calm, talk about how they were feeling while they were at school. Recognize and acknowledge those feelings. Some

kids benefit from doing this after being at home for a little while—at dinner or bedtime—while others like to process sooner. Journaling, drawing/coloring, or talking are great ways to process.

4. **Play.** Allow them time to unwind through play. Having a routine of uninterrupted time to play helps a child recharge from a busy day and brings them some autonomy. You might also notice them processing experiences from the day through their play. When the evening routine includes a consistent time for them to play, they come to expect that time and relish in it.

How Long Will the Transition Last?

When I was pregnant with my now toddler, even though I knew a lot of humans carry babies past 40 weeks (and my mom had carried four of the five of us for 42–43 weeks), I had this timeline of 40 weeks in my head. Every single day for 12 long days after that 40-week mark, I cried. I was convinced that I'd be the first human never to birth the child and just be pregnant forever. Timelines can be tricky because they can set expectations, and when the timeline goes beyond the expectation, it can leave you sobbing every day like me.

Transitions are a process, not an exact day on the calendar. As kids build attachments with their new teachers and come to understand the routines and rhythms of the school day, their nervous system learns what to expect and can start feeling safer. When the nervous system is not on high alert anymore, their battery isn't being drained as fast throughout the day and the transition period wanes. For children who are in school five days a week, the transition period is generally about two weeks. For children who are in school less frequently, the transition period can be three to four weeks. I've had kids in my class who adjusted and started to get into the flow and feel safe in about a week and some kids who took six weeks. It truly depends on the child, the frequency and duration of school, and the emotional safety in the new environment. During the transition period, if you can, scale back on extracurricular activities and adjust expectations of your child. Trust that those skills they had mastered before—which seem to have disappeared—will come back around when they feel grounded in their new routine.

New Sibling

There is so much that we adults know and expect when it comes to adding a child to the family that the other tiny humans in the family don't have the lived experience and cognitive understanding to grasp yet. There are four helpful approaches to welcoming a new sibling:

1. **Pre-teach to prepare.** In Chapter 9, we introduced the idea of pre-teaching in order to give children an idea of what to expect when experiencing something unfamiliar. Revisit the discussion on page 182 and the New Sibling section "What will be the same? What will be different?" in the box on page 240 for tips.

2. **Remember that grief is okay.** I was driving a four-year-old home from school, chatting about his one-month-old baby sister, whom he adored. I tried to open the conversation by acknowledging that sometimes babies cry, and it can be overwhelming or inconvenient. You might hear them at night when you're trying to sleep, or they might occupy some of your parents' time that used to be spent focused on you. He was only down for acknowledging the easy, "good" parts, saying things like "No, she doesn't wake me up," and "I don't care that Mama feeds her." I said, "Oh, okay, well, it's okay if there are hard parts, too. I'm here if you want to talk about it." About five minutes later in our drive, he said, "I love baby Tiana so much, but when is she leaving?" "What do you mean leaving?" I asked. "When will it just be me and Mama and Mommy again?" he asked. "It's different having her in your family now, huh?" I responded and then paused. In the silence I added, "Before you were born, your family was just Mama and Mommy. Then you came and the family grew bigger to include all three of you." "Yeah, then we got Henry

dog!" "Yep, then you added Henry dog to the family and now your family has Tiana, too. There are four people and one dog in your family now." I don't have to go into "Buckle up, bud. This is forever. Time is a hard concept, even for us as adults." What he was really saying to me was "I'm grieving the loss of my old family routine as I move into this new routine. Grief isn't linear and it doesn't happen all at once."

It's common to see older siblings have periods of grief, just as you may grieve parts of what was—sleeping through the night, traveling without kids, having an adult conversation during a meal, and so on. Grief can be a natural part of the transition process for adults and kids alike. Allow the hard conversations and space to grieve without popping in a silver lining like "But now we get to have so much fun as a family of four." Or for yourself, "But I wanted this for so long and now I have to be grateful for it." Grief and gratitude aren't mutually exclusive.

You can emotion-coach with children using the Phases of Emotion Processing in Chapter 5 (page 111) to help them process their emotions. Letting them know what they can do is crucial: "If the baby is crying and you need a break from it, you can put your headphones on or move your toys into the kitchen to play." Honestly, as adults we could use some of these recommendations, too. It is overwhelming, busy, loud, chaotic, and frustrating sometimes when you're getting to know a new family member. It makes sense to need coping support through the process.

3. **Expect changes in behavior, as these changes are normal.**
Children will be asking what the expectations are now that the family structure is different. Are the boundaries that were there before still the boundaries in place now? They might ask (through their behavior) if you still notice and love them. You have an opportunity to show and tell them that there is nothing they could do to make you love them less or more. They are loved for who they are, even as the family grows. Sometimes these behavior changes come right away and sometimes they show up more when the child realizes that the sibling is here to stay or starts getting

into their space or taking their toys. You aren't failing if you notice
upticks in behavior change with new developments for their sibling.
Acknowledge the changes and hold those boundaries steady.
When everything else changes, knowing that you'll still hold the
boundaries helps the child feel safe and secure. It's also okay to
change your expectations and boundaries if you no longer have the
capacity to see them through. My four-year-old cousin had a specific
bedtime routine before her twin siblings were born. My aunt and
uncle needed to adjust their expectations for her at bedtime because,
with two newborns, there were no guarantees about how present
either of them could be for the regular routine. Letting it go until
they had the capacity to design a new routine worked for their family
during that transition.

4. **Include the older sibling.** When a new sibling joins the family, the
   other child(ren) might wonder what their role is now. You can help
   them feel included and loved by bringing them into the new daily
   routines. Some ways to include an older sibling are reading a book
   to their younger sibling, feeding the baby a bottle, getting a diaper
   and wipes when it's time to change the baby, humming or singing
   to their sibling, and narrating what the younger sibling is doing.
   You can model these behaviors and tell the big kid why you're doing
   them. "Ohhh, your sister is learning how to move her body to try and
   roll to the toy. Look, she's stretching her arms and kicking her legs.
   We can say, 'Wow! Lydia, you're getting so close to rolling over. I see
   you practicing!'" You can also invite the older sibling to wonder with
   you about what the baby is asking for when they cry. Their guesses
   will give you some information about what they understand about
   babies so far. Some kids love hearing about what they did as a baby
   or seeing pictures and videos of themselves at the age their sibling is.
   You can share with them and talk about things they liked and didn't
   like as another way of including them. As you include the big sibling,
   you can set safety boundaries and let them know what the other
   child can/can't do yet. You know a newborn can't walk, but that
   might be news to an older sibling.

Ultimately, we can trust that older siblings want to connect, feel included, and are loving humans. When their surface behavior doesn't reflect that, it's not about who they are, it's about what they're experiencing and what they know or don't know yet, or the skills they have or don't have yet.

Divorce/Separation

Successful relationships are not only those in which humans remain in partnership. Through separation and divorce, children may learn that it's okay for them to advocate for their needs in relationships, collaborate through disagreement, and that families exist in many different forms. It's normal for children to enter into a grieving process as the life they'd known shifts into a new routine. You aren't failing if it's hard. You can do hard things. They can do hard things. And no one has to do it alone. Therapy can be a great resource for children and families going through the transition of divorce and separation. A therapist can give children an outlet for expression as they try to make sense of and understand their changing world.

Death and Dying

If you've had an experience with death, then the mention of the topic is likely to bring up memories and/or emotions. Your nervous system might even be activated right now simply by reading about it. Take a moment to notice if you feel that in your body. If so, where do you feel it? What does it feel like? Or maybe you're flooded with memories. Take a moment to notice what's happening inside. Before reading on, take a deep belly breath in . . . and out.

As adults we have an experienced lens on death and dying. Our experience includes subtle or explicit messages we get through the media and marketing that encourage fear of and/or resistance to aging, death, and dying as natural parts of life. As children encounter death and dying, they're experiencing it for the first time and in the present moment—they aren't familiar with the long-term pain of loss that you might associate with it. Remembering this can help us approach this topic with children in a simpler, more child-centered way.

How to Talk About Death and Dying

Use accurate information and vocabulary when you share information about the reasons someone is dying or has died. You can check the Dougy Center regarding the specific situation (i.e., cancer, accident, suicide) to find suggestions for accurate terminology to use and the kinds of information to share with a child. In any case, in general, avoid saying someone died because they were "sick." This is not specific enough and may cause a child to worry that the next time they are "sick" with a stomach bug, for instance, they will die, too. Same with using the phrase "They went to sleep" to explain death. This may cause the child to worry that the next time they go to sleep, they might die, too.

Sometimes we approach the topic with kids when someone is sick and dying, while other times we are telling a child about someone who died or is dead. If somebody got hurt or sick, you can start by defining the hurt/sick with clear terms. Nana has a disease called cancer. Daddy's body was very hurt in a car accident. Spot has a part inside his body called a kidney that keeps him alive but is not working. Then pause for their questions and only answer the questions asked. Then provide what to expect next. Maybe you don't know, and that's okay. You can say, "We don't know what's going to happen. We're hopeful that Nana will get better, but we also are being told that she might die." If a loved one has already died, help the child understand what happens next; most important for them to hear is who is going to take care of them now and how. If a loved one or a pet is going to die, be honest with the information you have and stick to the facts.

Clinical psychologist and child life specialist Ali Waltien says there isn't one right way to talk about death and dying. It will be clunky, and that's okay! She suggests statements like "I have something hard to tell you and this might be a hard or uncomfortable conversation." Use words like "death," "dead," and "dying," because kids need concrete terms. "When your dad was driving to work today, his car slipped on ice on the road and crashed into a pole and he died." It might sound really abrupt for us as adults. It *is* really abrupt. This helps the child hear the information of what happened without details that can make the information cloudy or confusing. Start with what the child knows—what do they understand about death and dying? "Do you know what happens when somebody dies?" [*Pause.*] Maybe they don't respond or maybe they do. "When someone dies, their body stops working." [*Put your hand on your heart.*] "Their heart is not beating anymore." [*Put your hand by your mouth.*] "They are not breathing anymore. They don't eat or sleep or play or go to the bathroom. The really hard part is that when someone dies, we don't see their body anymore. That's why you might see people crying or feeling sad." Listen more than you talk. We often have the desire to fill the uncomfortable silence and make sure every detail is included, but allowing the child time to take in what you said and following their lead is powerful. They will lead you to what they are trying to understand.

The goal is to create a safe environment in which to have these hard conversations rather than focusing on exactly what to say.

This isn't a one-time conversation; it's multiple conversations and an ongoing process. You will have the chance to go back and try again, to explain it in a new way, and to support them. You don't need to have all the answers to start. The goal is to create a safe environment in which to have these hard conversations rather than focusing on exactly what to say. For more resources on death and dying, head to www.seedandsew.org/more.

When Are They Coming Back?

Even after you explain your beliefs about what happens when someone dies and where they go, a child may ask you when they're coming back, or when they will wake up. This is a good time to practice CEP. Help them identify how they might be feeling: Sad? Lonely? Confused? Grief? As you allow validation, you can offer that you miss this person or pet, too. When you get to coping strategies, be intentional by including your own so that the child does not interpret your grief as their responsibility. In the moving-on phase, assume that this is a mini moving on, meaning that grief is a process and not a box on a checklist. Grief will come and go as memories surface. It's likely they'll need to move through a range of emotions multiple times in relationship to losing someone. During a mini moving-on phase, you can let children know that the person won't be coming back, and you might share what you do in order to feel connected to the person you've lost. Invite the child to participate if it's appropriate. When many of my family members see a red cardinal, they think of my grandfather; it feels like he's visiting them. My family's practice of teaching children to remember their grandfather/great-grandfather when they see a red cardinal is a good example. Other ideas are to visit the loved one's favorite place, hang a special photo on the wall, light a candle, engage in practices associated with your religion, etc.

What Happens When You Die? Where Did They Go?

On my grandfather's last day, a red cardinal sat outside the window for a long time, bringing my family a hint of comfort during an excruciating moment. Our beliefs about what happens when someone dies are powerful ways for us to make meaning of the mysterious transition that we will all go through one day.

When someone in you and your child's life is on the threshold of this transition or has just passed through, you can rely on your beliefs to explain to your child what's happening or what's happened. As a teacher, I didn't share my beliefs because I wanted the children to learn about their family's spirituality. Instead, I would let them know, "Each family has beliefs about what happens when someone dies. I wonder what your family believes?" If you want your child to know that other people's beliefs might be different, you can let them know that, too.

If your family is agnostic about death, then you could invite your child to imagine what happens. When my four-year-old cousin asked me, "Where do people come from?" I started to explain that babies grow inside someone's belly. She interrupted me, "No, like where did the *first* person come from?" I decided to ask her what she thought, and she replied, "I'm thinking they came from the ocean," and she went back to playing. Sometimes you don't have to know the answer. Children are constantly building their own theories, and this can apply to death and dying if it's a good fit for your family. You can find some books on death and dying to read with kids at www.seedandsew.org/more.

The guidance we've shared here applies to any situation where the child is experiencing the death of a loved one. In addition, the death of a child's primary caregiver should be treated with special care and include the guidance and support of a trained professional, such as a therapist or child life specialist.

Transitions are part of life. They're rich times to be practicing CEP. Remember, we're not striving for perfection. Honor every child's humanity—and your own—as you do the best you can. We've provided a lot of strategies here without the expectation that you'll use all of them. Start by choosing one that feels manageable for you as well as helpful for your child.

Chapter 13

The Future Is Emotionally Intelligent

When we start reading to babies, our expectation is not that they will read back to us the next day, week, or even year. We read that same book over and over and over and over (and over and over and over) for years to build a foundation for them to read to us *years* down the road. Similarly, for the tiny humans' emotion processing, this is a long-term game. When we allow children to express their emotions, recognize them, and provide symbols, develop security with a range of emotions, identify coping strategies, and teach them how to regulate their nervous system throughout, we are co-creating a system they will use for the rest of their lives. Right now, at this very moment, it may seem like you're teaching them not to hit or scream in the grocery store. You are—and you're providing a foundation that goes so much deeper than that.

As you notice your desire to foster these skills in your child, remember to meet them where they are. If you walked into a third grade classroom where children were reading chapter books and a child didn't know the alphabet, you wouldn't hand them a chapter book and expect them to read it. You'd meet them where they are and start with the alphabet. If you are looking ahead at a milestone, such as recognizing when their body is dysregulated, you can start with a ministone, such as noticing when someone else is dysregulated. Check out the table opposite for some common milestones and some ministones that lead up to them.

Milestones in Emotional Regulation	Ministones That Come First
Child communicates their boundary, e.g., "I don't like it when you push me."	• Child screams instead of reacting physically. • Child asks for help when in distress. • Child takes a breath before reacting.
Child self-regulates when they're feeling frustrated.	• Child thrashes their body and screams for a while before taking deep breaths. • Child screams, "I HATE YOU," instead of hitting. • Child asks you to sit with them as they regulate.
Child participates in an activity, even though they're feeling anxious.	• Child refuses to participate, but agrees to watch. • Child practices taking deep breaths while sitting with you. • Child participates in the activity for a short period of time.

How Do I Know I've Arrived?

CEP is a practice, an imperfect process. When we prioritize growth over perfection, we accept that failure is part of the process. Failure is often when we grow in the most meaningful ways, because any type of growth involves risk or vulnerability. Sometimes it will feel like you've got it and these are moments to celebrate. You'll release good hormones when you pause to celebrate the small steps. So, if you find yourself thinking, "Wow! I've got it," take the time to celebrate where you've come from and the skills you've cultivated. Then, invite a healthy sense of curiosity about how you will continue on the journey.

About nine months after starting her CEP practice, our friend Angela started talking about her process and how what used to be hard is now easy. She reflected back to the start of the school year, and how she would feel stressed when a child presented a behavior challenge. She worried that because she was struggling on the inside, she likely seemed that way on the outside, but she knew intellectually that she did not want that to affect her response to the children.

Simply put, at the beginning, Angela was in the *launching phase*. Think of it like the first time you try to ride a bike on your own—it can be awkward and wobbly and filled with feelings of apprehension about whether or not the bike will act like you want it to. What if I crash and fall? It can feel like pretending until it gets comfortable.

At the core of the launching phase is a very authentic desire to change one's behavior, and ultimately one's brain. We know that we don't want to just do what we *used* to do. Changing the brain and deep neural pathways is not a quick process, it can feel like launching into the unknown, and it seldom feels natural. But it's real. It is awkward and vulnerable. We say things imperfectly because we are learning.

Once she was further along in the process, Angela found herself in the flow. Her struggle in the face of challenges was reduced drastically after lots of practice, after she first went through the motions and then slowly integrated what she'd learned over time. This is not to say that Angela has arrived—and neither have we. No one can truly arrive, but we can confidently say that we are on the CEP journey, and we've made a commitment to intentionally develop our emotion processing skills.

There is no need to wait until you feel you've achieved something to start working with children on emotion processing. It is only imperative that you have initiated a reflection practice and have made a commitment to your personal process. The fact that you are reading this book is evidence that you have initiated your process!

Who Is in Your Village?

*Somehow, we've come to equate success with not
needing anyone. Many of us are willing to extend a
helping hand, but we're very reluctant to reach out for
help when we need it ourselves. It's as if we've divided
the world into "those who offer help" and "those who
need help." The truth is that we are both.*
—BRENÉ BROWN[1]

My mom is one of eight children, and there are twenty-three of us cousins. When I was growing up in the '80s, I often heard my aunts use the phrase "It takes a village," usually when one of their sisters had just cared for their own children over the weekend.

"It takes a village to raise a child" is an Igbo and Yoruba African proverb. Many African communities have long practiced raising children together. Systemic and social structures in the United States starting with colonialism have interfered with parents' ability to raise children in proverbial villages here. Our history includes the fact that indigenous children were taken from their families to be deculturated in boarding schools by white people. African children were stolen from their families for enslavement. Throughout US history, domestic laborers have been economically forced to leave their own children to work for upper-middle-class and wealthy families. Children continue to be separated from their family members at the border, by deportation, as well as by the prison industrial complex. Some families have resisted the barriers that colonialism has created in order to build their villages and raise children together.

For many families, the closest thing that we have to a village is a patchwork of services, such as paid childcare, afterschool programs, and ordering online and eating on the go. The transactional nature of these paid-for services is what separates them from the village's collectivist mindset. No one has your back in the patchwork of services if you're not paying. That is not to say that using these services is a bad thing. The relationships between early childhood professionals and the children and families that they care for can be beautiful and mutually rewarding! These are helpful solutions for families in which parents are working outside the home. As you build your village, see if you can think of the people who are there for you—regardless of transactions—and who you want to be there for when you can.

If you want to build a village of trust where you can be vulnerable with one another, it can't be a place of judgment and it requires reliability. So many of us are treading water, trying to stay afloat in keeping up with the demands of life. So much of the work of parenthood is unseen—the mental load, the emotional load, the logistical load. Things that nobody notices unless they're not done.

One of my friends calls this "living in a Magic House," where it appears like these things just happen by magic—when in reality, somebody is keeping track and taking care of them. We need more wipes. We don't have enough groceries for lunches this week. What is the dinner plan? If we have swimming lessons this morning, what will baby's nap schedule look like today? It's time to switch clothes for the season or the next size up. He needs more sunblock and diapers at school. When was the last time we had a date? When can I find time to exercise? We should send some of their artwork to Nana.

Do all the things for the kids, take care of yourself, connect with your partner, be all the things to everyone, and do everything on your own. What is this martyrdom message we've created and perpetuated? What would it look like to find our village? To ask for help? To be inconvenienced when others ask for help so that we, as a collective, can lean on each other? A mama reached out feeling like she needed a couple hours to herself to get things in order and get organized. She texted me asking if I was free. My family and I were off to the farmer's market, so we offered to take her little one with us. We didn't have to totally change or cancel our plans to be there for her, and she got some time by herself.

The crucial part of that story was her willingness to ask for help. Raise your hand if you grew up in a cultural context that saw having needs as negative. Perhaps the way you showed love in your family was by not inconveniencing someone. I grew up in a low-income family of five kiddos. My parents both worked multiple jobs to put a roof over our heads and food on the table. In my cultural context, having and expressing needs was seen as a weakness, as being *needy*. Although I am now an adult, those narratives still live within me and surface when I want to ask for help or lean on someone for support. That part of me will say, "Is this really necessary to inconvenience them? Can't you just figure it out?" It takes a lot of work to be aware of that part, to notice its fear of being seen as needy, and to rewrite the narrative into "It's okay to ask for help. It's the other person's job to say no if they don't have the bandwidth." This also means saying no when I don't have the bandwidth to take on more and being in charge of setting my own boundaries.

There are so many things we do by ourselves that we don't have to be doing solo. The following are ten ways you can ask for help:

1. Can we rotate solo parenting on Saturday so we can each have an hour or two of not being on?
2. Would you be able to grab Gia from practice when you get your kids?
3. If you are going by the library this week, can you drop these books off?
4. Hey, Nana, can the kids nap at your house on Saturday?
5. Can you pick up my grocery order?
6. Want to swap date night childcare? I can do bedtime with your kids on Friday if you can do bedtime with ours next weekend.
7. Want to work from my house today and we can tag-team the sick kids and work?
8. Can you grab my kids at the bus stop and hang with them for an hour until I get home from my appointment?
9. Can we carpool for practice? I can drop the kids off if you can pick them up.
10. Can you take June to Abel's birthday party this weekend?

So how do you find these village people? Maybe it is your neighbor or someone you see consistently at the playground. It might be someone who has a child in your kid's class or on their team. It might be someone at work who also has a kid or you just connect with. If you say you want to grab coffee sometime, then you've gotta make it happen; this is where you begin to form trust. It's the grown-up version of the serve-and-return in attachment relationships. Trust building happens in the small moments when we show up for each other, when we keep our word and demonstrate reliability. One of my closest villagers is someone who said, "Hi, we would like to be your friend and parent together." It was perfectly awkward, and honestly, I was yearning for someone to say that.

There is no "supposed to" on this journey.

Some schools have opportunities for parents to connect, or perhaps you can find a yoga class with other parents. There are also so many social media groups that you may fit into. You might even have to organize and start something yourself to build your village—making a connection with one person is a good start. It's important to be your *authentic* self in order to build and maintain your village, not some image of who you think you're supposed to be as a parent. There is no "supposed to" on this journey.

When you can get a break, some time to breathe, and focus on yourself as an individual, children can learn the value of taking space and taking care of oneself. You can also have the head space to be a more regulated version of yourself when you do this. It's never too late or too early to build your village.

Accepting Help and Letting Go of Control

So how do you parent in a village with folx who may respond differently than you would? What will this mean for your tiny humans? Good news: The little ones can differentiate expectations.

Sometimes this comes up when you have family or friends care for your little ones—sometimes it can be your own partner. If you usually handle bedtime and stick to a fairly strict routine, what happens when your partner takes over one night and doesn't handle it the exact same way? If she gave an extra five minutes for bath and read an extra book, will your little one demand that tonight? The good news is that children can differentiate the expectations with different adults, and so long as you hold firm to your bedtime boundaries, tomorrow night won't be a struggle even if you took the night off tonight.

That said, letting go of control can be hard. We often have fear living underneath that control. Recognizing the trigger without judgment is mindfulness. Paying attention to the emotion under your desire to control the approach your partner is taking is self-awareness. Every child needs one person they feel safe to express their hard stuff to and be vulnerable with. You can be that safe space for your child. It's okay if another adult is not, even if that's what you desire and maybe envisioned for your child. What does this look like in action with a partner, co-parent, other family member, or fellow caregiver?

- **Notice** your desire to control your partner's relationship with your child.
- **Allow** them to parent differently from you as long as your child is safe.
- **Regulate** your reaction to their response to your child.
- **Hold space** for your child if they need a safe space to express their emotions, while holding the boundary your partner set.
- **Release** the responsibility for creating a relationship you desire for your child and partner to have.

Sample things to say to them in the moment:

- "They get to have this feeling. I'm supporting them to calm them and will hold your boundary."
- "I know that my validating their feelings might feel uncomfortable for you in this moment."

- "I'm going to hold space for them right now. Can we talk about our views of this situation in a bit when all is calm?"
- "Let me know if you want to tap out. I know it's hard to see her upset."

When You Disagree on the Approach

At childcare pickup, I overheard a teacher say, "It's okay. You're okay. It isn't scary. It's just a shadow." Sage was crying as he noticed a shadow, his newest fear. Is this how I want to respond to his fears? No. It invalidates his experience and, well, never in the history of being scared has "It isn't scary" or "It's okay" made the fear go away. What I really heard was the teacher saying, "I'm uncomfortable with your fear and want it to disappear so I can feel comfortable again." The truth is, that's probably what Sage heard, too. I wish he could live in a world where every teacher and caregiver he encounters could handle his big feelings and help him process experiences.

I believe that the more emotionally intelligent humans we are raising in this movement, the more likely that will be for future generations, but right now, it's okay if his teacher can't hold space for his fear. It's okay if at the end of the day he melts down with me as he releases all the things he has pent up because he didn't feel emotionally safe to release them. The two key factors in relinquishing the desire to control how someone else responds are outlining core values with the people who will interact with the child most frequently and creating a safe space for the child to express and process with you. You can uphold boundaries that other people in your village, like a co-parent, partner, grandparent, or teacher, set while holding space for your child's emotions about the boundary. You don't have to agree with how the boundary was set or use the same approach. You can connect with the adult outside of the moment to let them know you'll uphold their boundaries and that you'll help the child process the emotions and experiences when needed. You aren't choosing sides; you're choosing emotional intelligence. If the other adult is not practicing CEP, they may feel like you're choosing the child over them in that moment. It's not your job to keep the peace. It's your job to provide a safe, secure attachment for the child.

I started doing this work on myself before my husband came on board, and it was hard to be in that space of waiting. As I practiced CEP, I learned how to set boundaries for myself, take care of myself, and be a more regulated human who was ready to respond with intention. CEP transformed how I show up, not just with kids, but in all my relationships because I stopped taking on the discomfort of others as something for me to fix. CEP allows us to tune in to our authentic selves and hear that voice inside us without the cloudiness of other people's opinions.

You might be the only emotionally safe person for your child to break down to, and you are enough. You might find yourself grieving the loss of the relationships you envisioned for your child to have with another parent, grandparents, or caregivers. Perhaps what you're really grieving is the loss of the relationship you yourself hoped to have with parents, grandparents, and caregivers and thus yearned for your child to have. Allow that grief and know that children can do hard things, especially with you in their corner.

Emotional Development in Motion

If you've made it this far, it's safe to assume you want to support your children's emotional development, so what does that look like? Some keys things to look at:

- Do you want to end each day with a sense of hope instead of feeling overwhelmed with stress?
- Do you want to overcome the fear of another meltdown?
- Do you want to free yourself from trying to solve problems while children are still crying or yelling?
- Do you want to start following through on your boundaries?

- Do you want to learn how to help tiny humans when they experience big emotions?

Let's start here. Once all of your answers are yes, then we are cooking with gas. If you are feeling exhausted by the end of each day, dreading those tantrums, what can you do to build in self-care? How can you change your perspective so you know this isn't a personal attack on you, but rather your child's way of communicating a message to you? Working on your mindset is the first step, so you can respond instead of react.

Children crave boundaries because structure helps them know what to expect. It helps them feel safe knowing that they can explore, express, and engage freely because you will make sure they are safe. You won't let them run into the street. You will help them get the sleep they need to keep them healthy. You will set expectations to nurture their growth and development. That is the message they hear when you hold boundaries. It's imperative to emotional development. Create a safe space for them to be and to feel. Let them know you can handle whatever they bring to the table; they'll come to you when they need you most if they know you can handle it.

Thriving Instead of Surviving

These tiny humans are undoubtedly exhausting. You give so much of yourself to them, rearranging your daily life and finances to care for them, waking up each morning to a human alarm clock; your love runs so deep, and it's a thankless job day in and day out. Even if being around them isn't stressful, you are constantly thinking about a million things when they're with you—always trying to stay ahead of their needs. It's constant.

Let's pause and return to the question we started all this with: *What do you want for your child when they grow up?* When you look down the road—to school age, teenage years, existing in the world independently from you—what are your hopes? If we are constantly in survival mode, it'll be hard to keep those long-term goals in mind, making it easier to say "You're in time-out for hitting your brother" than "You seem really disappointed that your brother doesn't want to play with you. I wonder how you could help your body feel calm so we can solve this problem." In the second scenario, we are helping our child build coping strategies, finding their calm, so we can problem-solve other ways to communicate feelings. It's hard to find the ministones to the milestones when we're *in* them—to notice the small changes and growth that lead to self-awareness, self-regulation, empathy, social skills, and motivation. Emotional intelligence develops with practice.

Take a second, close your eyes, and imagine your childhood self. What would life look like if you knew what you were feeling in your body, had tools to navigate the hard stuff, and had a safe place to collaboratively process your emotions? You are creating this for and with your children. Every time you practice these skills in the small moments—when your little one gets the wrong color cup or doesn't get the thing they wanted at the grocery store—you're creating this. Every time you model taking care of yourself and show them that they aren't responsible for your regulation, you're building their emotional intelligence. Every time you stretch their rubber band as they wade into something new and learn that they can do hard things, every time you repair with them, showing them that imperfection is an integral part of vulnerability and growth, every time you show up as your authentic self with the goal of connection, you build their toolbox for living with emotional intelligence.

Acknowledgments

ALYSSA: My deepest gratitude for Lauren being with me on this long, sometimes exciting, and other times exhausting journey of reading research, creating CEP, applying with the IRB, writing, and rewriting, and rewriting this book. You challenge me in ways that help me deepen my understanding of this work and become a better, clearer, more inclusive teacher. Thank you to Angela Garcia for encouraging us to research the CEP method and joining us on that journey. Getting nerdy with you is so much fun.

A million thanks to our Seed team—to Beki for helping us bring our words into visuals, to Rachel and Erika for answering every call with stories to include real-life examples to pull from, and a shoulder to lean on every single step of the way. To everyone else behind the scenes who has made it possible for me to step back from other Seed work to focus on the book, thank you, thank you, thank you.

To Sally, our agent from the Ekus Group, thank you for DMing me (and to Cara for holding Sage in that IG photo, which brought Sally into my DMs). You have been such an incredible gift on this journey. To Sarah, our editor, and the entire Harvest and HarperCollins crew for being fantastic partners on this journey. Sarah, I'm so grateful for your commitment to the integrity of the work, while helping us make our nerdiness accessible.

To my parents, Mike and Margaret, who have always helped me swim no matter how deep the waters. Your trust in me has led me here. Thank you for allowing me to make mistakes, loving me even when I said "I hate you" every single day as a fourteen-year-old. (I didn't mean it. I was still learning, but you knew that.) Thank you to my in-laws for being in my village, for helping me parent, and for your willingness to implement this work with Sage. And to Ellen, thank you for providing such intentional care for our little guy. Writing this book was possible because he was in great hands while I stepped away to do it. It takes a village and I'm so grateful for mine. Thank you to my husband, Zach, for being in the trenches with me every day. There is no one else I'd rather be on this wild ride of parenting with. And to Sage, may you always know that your messiness, your imperfections, your easy and hard feelings are welcome here. You are so loved exactly as you are.

LAUREN: I would first like to honor my teachers Patty Townsend, Dianne Bondy, Todd Norian, and J Vecchia for sharing your understanding of the eight limbs and for cultivating the sanghas where I've learned how to practice strength and vulnerability. I would also like to acknowledge the ancestral wisdom that is the roots of the practice. Thank you to Professor Sprout, who always said, "Draw what you see, not what you *think* you see," during our 1999 life drawing class. In metaphor, this phrase has shown up as a mindfulness mantra for me again and again.

Alyssa, I'm so grateful that we serendipitously decided to teach at the same school in 2016. CEP was born at that intersection of our paths, our careers, and our passions. I'm so proud of our work and how far we've come since that initial idea emerged—thank you for saying yes to a book! This process has been exciting, tedious, nerve-racking, fun, and educational. I can't think of a better collaborator on this—I appreciate your attentiveness to accuracy, readiness to go deep with concepts, long-term commitment to keeping children at the center, and stick-to-it-iveness. And to the Seed team: You're amazing! Thank you for sharing your nerd alert powers, design skills, and attention to detail. Thank you to Sally, our agent, and the Ekus team for believing in the power of CEP and to Sarah, our editor, for your clear vision and commitment to integrity of the method.

I have a deep well of gratitude for my "sister" and colleague, Angela Garcia, who is a reflective practice nerd like me and always up for researching, thinking out loud, and playing with the ideas in this book (and beyond). We are indebted to you for suggesting action research with CEP. And a warm thanks to our colleague Lori Goodrich, who shared her OT superpowers with us and our students. It's thanks to Lori that I understand the sensory system.

I wouldn't be here if it wasn't for each parent who allowed me to be in their family's life as their child's teacher and/or care provider. I learned something about child development and how to be in the world from each child that I've spent my days with. And a special shout-out to my aunties, who taught me how to change diapers and heat a bottle, and trusted my twelve-year-old self with their littles.

Thank you to Martha Lees, at the beginning of my career, for valuing deep pedagogical practices, advocating tirelessly for professional days, and giving us access to the latest research in our field. Thank you to Maryanne Gallagher for modeling meaningful leadership and seeing my potential. And thank you to Polly and Balbir at CECE for sharing your wisdom about infants and toddlers, and to Kait, Nora, Jen, Thea, Nancy, and Val for your collegiality and friendship. And thank you to the teachers of CEEC for trusting me to practice co-regulation with your students who needed it most when your co-teachers were out. For the assistant teachers and teaching fellows (Kelly!) throughout my sixteen years in the ECE classroom, who asked questions about my teaching practice or for feedback on your own—you gave me the opportunity to articulate my philosophy and knowledge, and your presence motivated me to refine my skills. There will always be a special place in my heart for the teachers and admin at PTCC. You trusted my leadership and taught me what it means to be part of a community of practice. Thank you to my ECE students for choosing to enter this field and asking great questions, including "Is there a book out there with everything you've taught us?"

Thank you to my mom, and number one cheerleader, Bets. Your capacity to listen to me talk about my work (and anything else that's on my mind) is astounding! I'm grateful for the way you taught me to return every serve from the moment I was born. You've always assumed my competence, which was a little nerve-racking as a kid, but as an adult has inspired me to take on challenges without hesitation. Thank you to my dad, Conrad, who wins the prize for most chill dad ever. Your calmness, authenticity, and puns were a grounding force throughout childhood.

My heart and mind are sustained by the authentic presence of my "sisters," Raquel, Gina, Annie, and Fabienne. It is a gift to know that I can be myself, and feel my feelings with any of you at any moment, no matter where we are on this earth. I am motivated to make the world a better place by mi ahijada, Saiya. Your enthusiasm for life and deep thinking are contagious! I've loved you since before you were born.

Finally, I am eternally grateful to my yoga buddy and husband, Kurt. Your unwavering encouragement, enthusiasm, vision, and ability to order takeout during the times when I felt tiredness or doubt propelled me forward. Your commitment to keep showing up in life is inspiring, and your willingness to grow in love rivals my own. I can't imagine a better match.

Additional Tools

The CEP Deck

Humans use symbols like words, gestures, and pictures to communicate. Pictures can help young children make sense of the words adults say, especially for neurodiverse children and multi-language learners. When we started CEPing, we were using some commercial emotion cards that included images and words, but we were missing some key emotion concepts like "frustrated." Plus, the more we learned about what emotions are and how we learn them, the more we realized that the words on the cards might limit someone's ability to use the emotion concepts that match their culture and experience. We decided to design the CEP Deck to provide a pictorial tool that would empower adults to use the words that they associate with emotions when coaching children through the phases. If you're not sure where to begin, or you want everyone in the family or class to use consistent words, then you can use the sticker labels included with each deck.

The research of Claire Brechet suggests that five-year-olds have more success identifying emotion expressions in *drawings* of faces than in *photos* of faces expressing emotion. A 2008 study, "The Causal Effect of Mental Imagery on Emotion Assessed Using Picture-Word Cues," presents strong evidence that images are more powerful than spoken words when it comes to emotions because they get our brain connected to autobiographical memory and personal involvement in events.[1] This is the reason the CEP Deck has drawings (created by artist Viki Stathopolis) rather than photos. Also, when we're asked to analyze an image like an emotion card ("Is this how you're feeling?"), we need to use higher-level thinking, which turns on the prefrontal cortex—what we've been referring to as the rational thinking brain. Remember, it's the rational thinking brain that helps the reactive brain determine whether or not there's a real threat, so we want it online for emotion processing.

Emotion cards can also be used when no one is having big emotions, and everyone's battery is full. These are moments when the rational thinking brain is easy to engage, so reflection and analysis skills are readily available. It's a good time to build emotion concepts consciously. You can pause in the middle of reading a story or watching a show that has a character who is feeling something, so you can practice the four qualities of empathy as identified by Theresa Wiseman: "perspective taking, staying out of judgment, recognizing emotion in other people, and then communicating that."[2] When my tiny human was around six months old, I started using the cards while reading them books. In *Chicka Chicka Boom Boom* when "J and K are about to cry," I'd snag the sad card and say, "I wonder if they're feeling sad." I didn't do it every single time we read the book but would do so when I could. Around eight months old, my tiny human would crawl over and grab the board with cards on it when we got to J and K crying. He would mimic a crying sound as he looked at me with the cards. He didn't correctly locate the sad card every time, but he was starting to connect emotions with the cards. It is never too early or too late to start.

You can also make the cards available for exploration and provide names or stories that you think match an image the child is choosing to look at for longer than the others. Balance that with time for the child to just look at and

feel the cards without interruption (without you saying anything). Sometimes a child is not ready to express their own emotions yet, so they express through their lovey/stuffy. You can use the cards to pretend to coach the lovey/stuffy through the Phases of Emotion Processing, knowing that this is an indirect way for your child to "play" with emotion processing from a distance.

No matter when you're using the cards, think of them as a tool and show reverence for them as such. The way each family or classroom uses them will be unique, and those expectations need to be modeled and explained. For example, in my preschool classroom of twenty children and a different set of teaching assistants each day, the cards might have been destroyed or lost in a matter of hours if they were allowed to be played with in an open-ended way, especially at the beginning of the year. We had a special place on the shelf where everyone could see them but only the adults could reach them. The children knew that we would get the cards anytime they requested, and that we would stay engaged with the child as they were used. They also learned quickly that we would get them on our way to help someone who was having big emotions. There was a symbolic exhale when I would announce that I would bring the cards over.

When you introduce the cards for the first time, choose a limited number of them, between three to six of the ones you think you need the most. I chose four "easy" emotions that we often talk about in my household and four "hard" emotions that my tiny human was most often expressing or struggling with. We kept them available in the living room, our main play space, and he would interact with them during his play. When he grabbed a card and I was nearby, I'd say which one it was and then add another cue. "Excited! Woo!! I feel excited!" as my tone matched that emotion. We later chatted in our household about changing "excited" to "jazzed" because that's the term we most frequently use. Remember, it's about using them in a way that makes sense in your cultural context. It's okay if that's different from someone else's. When I would say "calm" or "safe," I would take a deep breath, something he wound up modeling and practicing well before he brought that skill into a big emotion moment. Using the cards outside of big emotions helps build the child's toolbox for navigating the phases *during* big emotions.

Notes

Introduction

1. Wheatley, M. J., & Kellner-Rogers, M. (1996). *A Simpler Way*. San Francisco: Berrett-Koehler Publishers, 67.

Chapter 1: What Is Emotional Intelligence?

1. Goleman, Daniel. (1998). *Working with Emotional Intelligence*. New York: Bantam Dell, 317.
2. RSA Shorts. *Brené Brown on Empathy*. Voiced by Brené Brown (2013). YouTube. https://www.youtube.com/watch?v=1Evwgu369Jw.
3. Goleman, 258–77.
4. Maguire-Fong, Mary Jane. (2015). *Teaching and Learning with Infants and Toddlers: Where Meaning-Making Begins*. New York: Teachers College Press, 123.
5. Staff, *Harper's Bazaar*. (2017). "21 of Maya Angelou's Best Quotes to Inspire: Remembering the Late Activist and Literary Icon's Most Uplifting Words of Wisdom." harpersbazaar.com.
6. Center on the Developing Child. (n.d.). "What Is Epigenetics and How Does It Relate to Child Development?" https://developingchild.harvard.edu/resources/what-is-epigenetics-and-how-does-it-relate-to-child-development/.

Chapter 2: Your Role in Your Child's Emotions

1. Kolb, B., & Whishaw, I. (2015). *Fundamentals of Neuropsychology*. New York: Worth Publishers, 169–70.
2. Centers for Disease Control and Prevention, Kaiser Permanente. (2016). The ACE Study Survey Data [Unpublished data]. Atlanta, GA: U.S. Department of Health and Human Services, Centers for Disease Control and Prevention.

3. Bretherton, Inge. (1992). "The Origins of Attachment Theory: John Bowlby and Mary Ainsworth." *Developmental Psychology*, 28:759–75.
4. Oleinic, J. (January 24, 2020). "Shelf Awareness." https://shelf-awareness.com/readers-issue.html?issue=887#m15518.
5. Doyle, Glennon. (2020). *Untamed*. New York: Dial Press.

Chapter 3: What's Happening in the Brain and the Body When You Have Big Emotions?

1. Barrett, Lisa Feldman. (2017). *How Emotions Are Made: The Secret Life of the Brain*. New York: Mariner Books.
2. Barrett, 57.
3. Uddin, L. Q., Nomi, J. S., Hébert-Seropian, B., Ghaziri, J., & Boucher, O. (July 2017). "Structure and Function of the Human Insula." *Journal of Clinical Neurophysiology*, 34(4):300–306. doi: 10.1097/WNP.0000000000000377.
4. Barrett, 72.
5. Immordino-Yang, M., Darling-Hammond, L., & Krone, C. (2018). *The Brain Basis for Integrated Social, Emotional, and Academic Development: How Emotions and Relationships Drive Learning*. The Aspen Institute.
6. Chappa, K. (2019). *The Revolutionary Power of Bilingualism*. YouTube. TedX Talks. https://www.youtube.com/watch?v=BMHEygNw6r0.
7. Barrett, 75.
8. Satter, Ellyn. (2023). "Troubleshooting with the Satter Division of Responsibility in Feeding." Ellyn Satter Institute. https://www.ellynsatterinstitute.org/family-meals-focus/81-troubleshooting-with-the-division-of-responsibility/.
9. Allen, R. E., & Myers, A. L. (November 2006). "Nutrition in Toddlers." *American Family Physician*, 1;74(9):1527–32. PMID: 17111891.
10. Shanker, Stuart. (2016). *Self-Reg: How to Help Your Child (and You) Break the Stress Cycle and Successfully Engage with Life*. Toronto: Penguin, 67.

Chapter 4: The Collaborative Emotion Processing Method

1. Konner, Melvin. (2010). *The Evolution of Childhood: Relationships, Emotion, Mind*. Cambridge, MA: Belknap Press of Harvard University Press, 516.
2. Immordino-Yang, M., Darling-Hammond, L., & Krone, C. (2018). *The Brain Basis for Integrated Social, Emotional, and Academic Development: How Emotions and Relationships Drive Learning*. The Aspen Institute.

3. National Symposium on Early Childhood Science and Policy. (2009). INBRIEF: The Science of Early Childhood Development. https://harvardcenter.wpenginepowered.com/wp-content/uploads/2007/03/InBrief-The-Science-of-Early-Childhood-Development2.pdf.

4. INBRIEF: The Science of Early Childhood Development.

5. *Merriam-Webster*. https://www.merriam-webster.com/dictionary/collaborate#:~:text=1%20%3A%20to%20work%20jointly%20with,of%20collaborating%20with%20the%20enemy.

6. Belic, R. (Producer), & Shadyac, T. (Director). (2012). *Happy* [Motion picture]. United States: Wadi Rum Films & Shady Acres.

7. Brach, Tara. (2016). *True Refuge: Finding Peace and Freedom in Your Own Awakened Heart*. Audiobooks.com. https://www.audiobooks.com/audiobook/true-refuge-finding-peace-and-freedom-in-your-own-awakened-heart/177613?refId=38712&gclid=Cj0KCQjw2efrBRD3ARIsAEnt0eiHA5poiq45b9L4LMgXQIHXwhlXkm_wyo9W4-6tlZDG9CG73KFXMBYaAveDEALw_wcB.

8. *The Body Awake* [Podcast]. "Clarification, Patience and the Ocean with Patty Townsend." https://podcasts.apple.com/us/podcast/clarification-patience-and-the-ocean-with-patty-townsend/id1115392724?i=1000434171766.

9. David, Susan. (2016). *Emotional Agility: Get Unstuck, Embrace Change, and Thrive in Work and Life*. New York: Avery Publishing.

10. Bryant, Edwin. (2009). *The Yoga Sutras of Patañjali: A New Edition, Translation, and Commentary*. New York: North Point Press.

11. Nhất Hạnh, Thích. (1976). *The Miracle of Mindfulness: An Introduction to the Practice of Meditation*. Boston: Beacon Press, 11.

12. Brzosko, Marta. (November 21, 2019). "Alternatives to Meditation for Better Self-Awareness." betterhumans.pub. https://betterhumans.pub/how-to-increase-your-self-awareness-without-meditation-47a7ab99594.

13. Hülsheger, U. R., Alberts, H. J., Feinholdt, A., & Lang, J. W. B. (2013). "Benefits of Mindfulness at Work: The Role of Mindfulness in Emotion Regulation, Emotional Exhaustion, and Job Satisfaction." *Journal of Applied Psychology*, 98(2):310–25.

14. Brzosko. "Alternatives to Mediation for Better Self-Awareness."

15. Brown, Brené. (2018). *Leading from Heart versus Hurt*. Brenebrown.com. https://brenebrown.com/articles/2018/12/04/leading-from-hurt-versus-leading-from-heart/#:~:text=Without%20self%2Dawareness%20and%20the,disengagement%2C%20and%20an%20eggshell%20culture.

16. Allyson Dinneen (@notesfromyourtherapist). "Your feelings aren't a problem." Instagram, August 11, 2022. https://www.instagram.com/p/ChHfidPAixn/?igshid=YmMyMTA2M2Y=.

17. Adam Grant (@AdamGrant). "What others say doesn't directly affect your emotions." Twitter, July 23, 2022. https://twitter.com/adamgrant/status /1550834492587315201?s=46&t=f_ovo2K0FRU2mgnQsLgOeg.

18. Wilson, Cristin. (2017). "Study: 'Adultification' Has Black Girls Facing Harsher Punishments." *ABA Journal*, 103(11):20. https://search-ebscohost -com.proxy16.noblenet.org/login.aspx?direct=true&AuthType=cookie,ip,cpi d&custid=bhc&db=buh&AN=125868636&site=ehost-live&scope=site.

19. Gilliam, W. S., Maupin, A. N., Reyes, C. R., Accavitti, M., & Shic, F. (2016). "Do Early Educators' Implicit Biases Regarding Sex and Race Relate to Behavior Expectations and Recommendations of Preschool Expulsions and Suspensions?" [Research study brief]. Yale University Child Study Center. https://medicine.yale.edu/childstudy/zigler/publications/Preschool%20 Implicit%20Bias%20Policy%20Brief_final_9_26_276766_5379_vl.pdf.

20. Halberstadt, A. G., Cooke, A. N., Garner, P. W., Hughes, S. A., Oertwig, D., & Neupert, S. D. (2020). "Racialized Emotion Recognition Accuracy and Anger Bias of Children's Faces." *Emotion*. https://doi-org.proxy16 .noblenet.org/10.1037/emo0000756.supp (Supplemental).

21. Brown, G. L., Craig, A. B., & Halberstadt, A. G. (2015). "Parent Gender Differences in Emotion Socialization Behaviors Vary by Ethnicity and Child Gender." *Parenting: Science & Practice*, 15(3):135–57. https://doi-org .proxy16.noblenet.org/10.1080/15295192.2015.1053312.

22. Deutsch Smith, D., Chowdhuri Tyler, N., & Garner Skow, K. (2018), *Introduction to Contemporary Special Education: New Horizons.* New York: Pearson.

23. Siegel, Daniel J. (2011). *The Neurobiology of "We": How Relationships, the Mind, and the Brain Interact to Shape Who We Are.* Boulder, CO: Sounds True.

24. *PBS NewsHour.* (June 10, 2020). "Making People Aware of the Implicit Biases Doesn't Usually Change Minds. But Here's What Does Work." pbs.org.

25. King, R. (2018). *Mindful of Race.* Boulder, CO: Sounds True, 127.

26. Kolb, B., & Whishaw, I. (2015). *Fundamentals of Neuropsychology.* New York: Worth Publishers.

Chapter 5: What to Do in the Moment

1. Rivero, L. (2012). "Mister Rogers' Emotional Neighborhood." *Psychology Today.* https://www.psychologytoday.com/intl/blog/creative -synthesis/201203/mister-rogers-emotional-neighborhood?amp.

2. Gottman, J., & DeClaire, J. (1997). *Raising an Emotionally Intelligent Child: The Heart of Parenting.* New York: Simon & Schuster.
3. Shanker, S. (2017). *Self-Reg: How to Help Your Child (and You) Break the Stress Cycle and Successfully Engage with Life.* Toronto: Penguin, 93.
4. Senge, P., Ross, R., Smith, B., Roberts, C., & Kleiner, A. (1994). *The Fifth Discipline Fieldbook.* New York: Doubleday, 242–43.
5. Galinsky, Ellen. (2010). *Mind in the Making: The Seven Essential Life Skills Every Child Needs.* New York: HarperStudio.
6. Gold, M. S., Blum, K., Oscar-Berman, M., & Braverman, E. R. (January 2014). "Low Dopamine Function in Attention Deficit/Hyperactivity Disorder: Should Genotyping Signify Early Diagnosis in Children?" *Postgraduate Medicine,* 126(1):153–77. doi: 10.3810/pgm.2014.01.2735. PMID: 24393762.
7. Hathaway, Bill. (March 12, 2019). "New Way to Combat Childhood Anxiety: Treat the Parents." *Yale News.* https://news.yale.edu/2019/03/12/new-way-combat-childhood-anxiety-treat-parents.

Chapter 6: How to Set and Hold Boundaries

1. Tawwab, Nedra Glover (2021). *Set Boundaries, Find Peace: A Guide to Reclaiming Yourself.* New York: Tarcher Perigee.

Chapter 7: When and How to Talk About the Behavior

1. Brown, B. (January 15, 2013). "Shame vs. Guilt." Brenebrown.com. https://brenebrown.com/articles/2013/01/15/shame-v-guilt/.
2. Lumen Learning. (n.d.). "Psych in Real Life: Moral Reasoning." Introduction to Psychology. https://courses.lumenlearning.com/waymaker-psychology/chapter/psych-in-real-life-moral-reasoning/.
3. Yamamoto, K., Kimura, M., & Osaka, M. (August 26, 2021). "Sorry, Not Sorry: Effects of Different Types of Apologies and Self-Monitoring on Non-Verbal Behaviors." *Frontiers in Psychology,* 12:689615. doi: 10.3389/fpsyg.2021.689614.
4. Bronson, P., & Merryman, A. (2009). *NurtureShock: New Thinking About Children.* New York: Hachette Book Group.

Chapter 8: Consequences, Punishments, and Rewards

1. Oxford Languages and Google. https://languages.oup.com/google-dictionary-en/.
2. Oxford Languages and Google. https://languages.oup.com/google-dictionary-en/.
3. Derman-Sparks, L., Olsen Edwards, J., & Goins, K. (2020). *Anti-Bias Education for Ourselves and Our Children*, 2nd ed. Washington, DC: National Association for the Education of Young Children.
4. Hawthorne, Britt. (2022). *Raising Antiracist Children: A Practical Parenting Guide*. New York: Simon Element.
5. Cotton, G. (2013). "Gestures to Avoid in Cross-Cultural Business: In Other Words, 'Keep Your Fingers to Yourself!'" https://www.huffingtonpost.com/gayle-cotton/cross-cultural-gestures_b_3437653.html.
6. Mueller, C. M., & Dweck, C. S. (1998). "Praise for Intelligence Can Undermine Children's Motivation and Performance." *Journal of Personality and Social Psychology*, 75:33–52. doi: 10.1037/0022-3514.75.1.33.

Chapter 10: When There's More Than One Child

1. Munakata, Yuko. (2021). "Why Most Parenting Advice Is Wrong." YouTube. https://www.youtube.com/watch?v=5g8tHEXtCXE.

Chapter 11: Developing Empathy

1. Borba, Michele. (2016). *UnSelfie: Why Empathetic Kids Succeed in Our All-About-Me World*. New York: Touchstone.
2. Gruber, T., & Kalish, L. (2005). *Yoga Pretzels: 50 Fun Yoga Activities for Kids and Grownups*. Concord, MA: Barefoot Books.
3. McCreary, C. (2021). *Little Yogi Deck: Simple Yoga Practices to Help Kids Move Through Big Emotions*. Boulder, CO: Bala Kids.

Chapter 12: Changes and Transitions

1. Bridges, William. (2020). https://wmbridges.com/about/what-is-transition/.

Chapter 13: The Future Is Emotionally Intelligent

1. Brown, Brené. (2014). *The Gifts of Imperfection: Let Go of Who You Think You're Supposed to Be and Embrace Who You Are.* Charleston, SC: Instaread Summaries.

Additional Tools: The CEP Deck

1. Holmes, E. A., Mathews, A., Mackintosh, B., & Dalgleish, T. (2008). "The Causal Effect of Mental Imagery on Emotion Assessed Using Picture-Word Cues." *American Psychological Association*, 8(3):395–409. doi: 10.1037/1528–3542.8.3.395.
2. RSA Shorts. *Brené Brown on Empathy.* Voiced by Brené Brown (2013). YouTube. https://www.youtube.com/watch?v=1Evwgu369Jw.

Index

Note: *Italic* page numbers indicate illustrations.

About the Authors

Alyssa Blask Campbell is the CEO of Seed & Sew, an organization serving parents, teachers, and caregivers with tools for mental wellness and building emotional intelligence. She created the S.E.E.D. Certification, a professional development program and teacher community, to bring these tools into early childhood programs across the United States. Her podcast, *Voices of Your Village*, reaches more than 100 countries around the world, and her social media following of more than 300,000 people connect over the challenges and triumphs throughout the journey of raising children. After co-creating the Collaborative Emotion Processing (CEP) method with Lauren Stauble, she and Lauren researched it across the United States. In 2019, the *Washington Post* named Alyssa an emotional development expert. She is a global presenter on how to raise emotionally intelligent humans. Alyssa grew up in a small farm town in western New York as the only girl in a family with four brothers. She is curious, forever raising her hand to ask "why" and learn more. She believes deeply in cultivating the modern parenting village and proclaims not to be the villager who will make the banana bread, but is the one you can drop your kids off with while you run errands or enjoy a date night. Alyssa lives in Burlington, Vermont, with her husband, Zach, and child, Sage.

Lauren Stauble is a professor of early childhood education as well as consultant for her business, Engage: feel.think.connect, co-owned by Angela Garcia. She taught and cared for children ages birth to eight years in centers as well as in her home-based program for sixteen years, before moving into program administration and higher education. Lauren's work evolves daily and is the result of more than nineteen years of practice, which includes emergent curriculum, anti-bias education, community activism, in-depth study and personal practice of yoga/meditation, psychology coursework, mindfulness-based therapy, healing-centered education training, and being raised by a mother with a healthy sense of agency. She's interested in deepening her understanding and expertise of collaboration as an essential tool for early childhood education and how the presence of emotional intelligence in the group enhances the process. Lauren takes every opportunity to explore the applications of behavioral science, neuropsychology research, and mindfulness within the contexts of emotions and implicit bias, using this information to reimagine systems that are equitable, relationships-based, and sustainable. In between she enjoys spending time with dear ones in the mountains, in the tropics, around the fire, on the mat, and in our kitchens. Lauren lives with her husband, Kurt, and their two cats, in Holyoke, Massachusetts. She would like to acknowledge that this land she is a guest on, where Holyoke now sits—and this land she is benefiting from—is the homeland of the Nipmuc Tribe, People of the Fresh Water.